KNACK
MAKE IT EASY

WEDDING FLOWERS

KNACK

WEDDING FLOWERS

A Complete Illustrated Guide to Ideas for Bouquets, Ceremony Décor, and Reception Centerpieces

SHARON NAYLOR

Principal Photography by Rich Penrose
Photo Research by Anna Adesanya

Guilford, Connecticut
An imprint of Globe Pequot Press

To buy books in quantity for corporate use
or incentives, call **(800) 962-0973**
or e-mail **premiums@GlobePequot.com.**

Editor-in-Chief: Maureen Graney
Editor: Katie Benoit
Cover Design: Paul Beatrice, Bret Kerr
Text Design: Paul Beatrice
Layout: Joanna Beyer
Additional photo research by Anna Adesanya
Cover photos by (left to right) Norman Chan/Shutterstock;
© dreamstime; © Rich Penrose; © Rich Penrose
Backcover photo by Eddie Lepp/Shutterstock
Interior photos by Rich Penrose with the exception of photos listed in credits on p. 239.

Library of Congress Cataloging-in-Publication Data is available on file.

ISBN 978-1-59921-515-0

The following manufacturers/names appearing in *Knack Wedding Flowers* are trademarks:
eBay®, eHow™, Home Depot®, LinkedIn®, Sam's Club®, Scotch® tape, Styrofoam®, Target®

Printed in China

10 9 8 7 6 5 4 3 2

The publishers would like to thank Anna Adesanya, Rich Penrose, and author Sharon Naylor for their hard work and dedication to this project.

CONTENTS

INTRODUCTION

You're about to design one of the most gorgeous aspects of your wedding day! Brides say that choosing their bridal bouquets, centerpieces, and floral décor is one of the things they dreamed about from girlhood through their pre-engagement days. Flowers make the wedding scene, after all! They're a romantic, beautiful part of your Big Day, and now you're in the enviable position of creating your own floral designs.

Before you take your first steps into the wedding floral world, the two most important considerations are developing an overall vision for the visual presentation of flowers in your wedding, and using in-season flowers. Both set the foundation for every detail you'll choose throughout the process, and both will work together to achieve your wedding floral dreams.

Develop Your Floral Vision

At the start of your wedding flowers planning, you might have visions of a sea of white roses on every guest table, a glorious bouquet filled with gardenias and stephanotis, and radiant white calla lilies in your bridesmaids' hands. You've seen plenty of beautiful floral photographs in the bridal magazines, and you're thinking, "I want that!" Before you decide on that all-white bridal bouquet or the pink rose centerpieces, take a moment to think about the bigger picture of your wedding and which style of flowers would work best for your grand Wedding Day scheme. Are you a traditional bride, wanting all-white or pastel flowers, or are you a city-chic, trendy bride with an eye for bright colors and unexpected touches? Are you planning a destination wedding at a tropical locale? Do you want an indoor or outdoor wedding?

Your wedding flowers set the stage for your dream wedding, and they have to work with the flavor of your day. They also have to work with your budget. So don't decide on anything until you have a set style for your wedding.

Popular Wedding Styles

According to TheWeddingReport.com, a national bridal survey Web site, almost half of brides and grooms are moving beyond traditional wedding plans. Here's the breakdown:

- 51 percent of brides and grooms are planning traditional weddings
- 19 percent are planning casual weddings
- 13 percent are planning formal weddings
- 10 percent are planning "unique" weddings
- 2 percent are planning extravagant weddings

- 3 percent are planning theme weddings
- 2 percent are planning other types of weddings.

Where do you fit in? You need to be able to define your wedding style before you can accent your wedding with the most appropriate flowers and floral plans.

The Formality and Setting of Your Wedding

Certain wedding bouquet and centerpiece styles say formal, such as elaborate arrangements with white roses, gardenias, ranunculus, stephanotis, and lily of the valley. Others say informal, which includes anything other than bridal roses and gardenias. An example of informal bridal flowers is a collection of brightly-colored Gerber daisies at a garden wedding. For an informal spring wedding, collections of tulips are a fitting choice for bouquets and for centerpieces. At a casual backyard wedding, you might hold a bouquet of soft wildflowers.

Location plays a big part in your flower choice-—happy white daisies at your garden wedding or birds of paradise at your island wedding, for example. The location will help define the formality of your flowers. For instance, a formal wedding at a lavish estate is going to call for a more elaborate bouquet style filled with upscale roses, orchids, and other blooms befitting your surroundings, not a bunch of wildflowers.

Your Shopping List

Once you decide on vision, style, and location, the next step is deciding what you will need to fulfill your wedding vision. The size of your shopping list, as well as the types of flowers you want, will determine the scope of your floral plans (and also your budget). If you require fifty centerpieces, for instance, that's a lot of work for your floral design team, and it may be too much for you to take on as a DIY project. If, however, you need twenty centerpieces, you might be able to do it yourself. Here is an example of your average floral shopping list:

- Bride's bouquet
- Bride's tossing bouquet
- Maid or Matron of Honor bouquet(s)
- Bridesmaids' bouquets
- Flower Girl flowers
- Mother of the Bride flowers

- Mother of the Groom flowers
- Grandmother and godmother flowers
- Groom's boutonniere
- Best Man's boutonniere
- Groomsmen's boutonnieres
- Father of the Bride boutonniere
- Father of the Groom boutonniere
- Centerpieces
- Altar décor
- Additional ceremony décor
- Additional reception décor
- Rose petals for décor

Do-It-Yourself

The average national wedding floral budget is over $1,200, according to TheWeddingReport.com. You might wish to beat the system by employing a range of DIY methods in order to make your own bouquets and/or centerpieces. Many couples enjoy working with family members and other volunteers who know how to create pretty bouquets on the cheap.

You can buy loose flowers at floral wholesalers and at organic suppliers, such as Whole Foods, which is where many professional floral designers buy their own blooms and supplies. With its budget-priced supplies and floral accents, the craft store will be your second home. In Chapter 19, you'll find out how to make the most common bouquets, centerpieces, and other accents for your day. It's easier (and less expensive) than you might think.

In-Season Wedding Flowers

To save costs and increase efficiency, consider choosing flowers that will be in-season at the time of your wedding. When flowers are in-season, they are plentiful at floral shops and suppliers in your area, and you'll have a wider range of colors and varieties to choose from. In-season flowers also cost less, since they won't have to be shipped in at a high cost. For instance, you could get purple irises for your winter wedding, but they would have to be shipped from overseas where the climate is right for their growth. That can double or triple the price.

Seasonal flowers fit naturally into the month of your wedding, such as tulips for a spring wedding or poinsettias for a winter wedding, so it's not very difficult to consider the most appropriate floral choices for your season. If you have more than a year to plan your wedding, it's a wise idea to visit floral shops one calendar year before your wedding, just to see which kinds of blooms are in stock, how plentiful they are, and perhaps discover a unique type of flower you didn't consider before, such as lisianthus or ranunculus, flowers that add a unique touch to your floral arrangements and bouquets.

Certain flowers are in-season year-round. They are: baby's breath, bachelor's button, calla lily, carnations, delphinium, eucalyptus, gardenia, gladiolus, heather, lily of the valley, orchid, rose, and scabiosa.

Visit your local arboretum or garden club to see different types of flowers in-season in your region of the country. Get on their mailing list for seasonal displays to expose yourself to a world of interesting blooms, greenery, and flower pairings.

Spring

Spring flowers are usually in-season from February through April, to the beginning of May. Here are the most popular choices among spring blooms: anemone, Bells of Ireland, casa blanca lily, daffodil, delphinium, hyacinth, lilac, narcissus, peony, ranunculus, stargazer lily, sweetpea, tulip.

Summer

Summer flowers are usually in bloom from May until August, and sometimes into September. Here are the most popular choices among summer flowers: alstroemeria, bells of Ireland, chrysanthemum, english lavender, forget-me-not, freesia, Gerber daisy, hydrangea, iris, larkspur, lily, lisianthus, Queen Anne's Lace, snapdragon, stephanotis, stock, sunflower, tuberose, yarrow, zinnia.

Autumn

Autumn flowers are usually in season from September through November, often in fiery shades of red, orange, and yellow, as well as bridal whites: aster, chrysanthemum, dahlia, flowering cabbage, marigold, zinnia.

Winter

Winter flowers are usually in season from December until February. You *can* find flowers from other seasons for fitting design use in your winter weddings, but you'd have to order them to be imported from other regions or other countries, at higher prices. In season choices include: amaryllis, anemone, Bells of Ireland, camellia, casa blanca lily, cosmos, daffodil, forget-me-not, holly, jasmine, narcissus, poinsettia, ranunculus, stargazer lily, Star of Bethlehem, sweetpea, tulip.

ROSES

What are your roses saying about you and your wishes for a long and happy marriage?

Although we live in modern times, we still cling to several Old World beliefs—especially in regard to weddings. One of those beliefs comes from the Victorian-era tradition of the language of flowers, which maintains that different types and colors of flowers hold symbolism, conveying sentiments that can add very personal touches to your day.

In bygone days a gentleman courted a lady both openly and secretly (such as when the lady's family either didn't approve of the match or the parents hadn't been approached yet) by sending her a flower or bouquet. The particular flower he chose might have symbolized everlasting love or said to her that she was precious to him. The lady in question might

White Roses

- Perhaps the most popular choice for traditional wedding bouquets, the white rose carries several different meanings including virtue, innocence, and chastity.

- White and red roses together symbolize unity.

- A full bouquet of white roses symbolizes gratitude.

- A garland or crown of white roses symbolizes victory or reward.

Pink Roses

- Pink roses are the most popular of colored bridal flowers, with the delicate hue adding romance and femininity to a bridal bouquet. Pinks may range from barely there blush to vibrant pink.

- Dark pink roses symbolize gratitude.

- Light pink roses symbolize grace, desire, passion, joy, energy, and youth.

- Pink roses given to mothers symbolize the gratitude and joy of the love and support mothers have always provided.

have returned a message to the gentleman by wearing a symbolic flower in her hair, or carrying one in her hand, for his view and a message of her own the next time he saw her. Flowers, then, played a large part in the ritual of courtship, as love letters in bloom. The language of flowers grew from a secret form of communication to our modern practice of sharing that symbolism for all the world (and all the wedding guests) to see.

In this chapter, you'll find out what some of the most popular wedding flowers and colors express. You may wish to give your own bouquet a depth of symbolism, incorporating heartfelt messages, or you might find that your own favorite flower has a traditional meaning that is perfect for your day.

Yellow Roses

- Yellow roses are a favorite for spring and summer weddings, with colors ranging from pale buttercup yellow to bright sunshine yellow.

- Yellow roses symbolize joy, friendship, and devotion.

- As with many symbolic items, there's a flip side. Yellow roses have also been branded with some negative meanings, namely jealousy and—yikes!—infidelity. Such is the nature of traditions that have been handed down over time, subject to translation issues from generation to generation.

Red Roses

- When brightly colored bridal flowers came on the scene in the late 1990s, red was the number one color chosen by brides for their bouquets. After all, a bright red bouquet stands out in contrast to a pristine white wedding gown and photographs well.

- It symbolizes true love, passion, desire, deep love, and respect.

- Red and yellow roses together symbolize excitement.

- A red rosebud symbolizes purity and loveliness.

LILIES
Expressing messages of love with the exotic bloom of lilies

These bright or white flowers, which come in several different varieties, have become a favorite of brides for their fragrance and because the large dramatic flower is a unique addition to any bouquet or arrangement.

Lilies are also a good way to save on your wedding budget, since one big stargazer lily can take the place of several roses or other smaller flowers in a bouquet. Growers have perfected the art of variegating lilies to provide more colors than ever before, and they're also producing enormous blooms that brides often choose to carry in place of a bouquet. You may have seen this effect in the movie *Love Actually*, where Keira Knightley's character totes a single white lily to accent her delicate, romantic gown.

Lilies are not just a spring flower anymore. The lily is now

White Lilies

- In religious lore the white lily is a symbol of sainthood and great virtue, heroism, and faith.

- White lilies symbolize purity and virginity and communicate the sentiment, it's heavenly to be with you.

- The day lily symbolizes

motherhood in Chinese symbolism, so consider this flower for your mothers' pieces.

- The Eucharis lily symbolizes maiden charms, which makes it a popular choice for bridesmaids.

Pink Lilies

- Hues of pink add a touch of color to traditional and unique floral pieces for weddings, and brides often like to add some dimension to their bouquets by mixing the colors and meanings of pink and white flowers.

- Pink lilies symbolize beauty, charm, happiness, fondness, and friendship.

- The pink perfection lily symbolizes a man's appreciation of a woman as perfect in his eyes, and it can also be used to connote the perfection of marriage.

considered a hot summer flower, and the Casa Blanca lily is a top choice for winter weddings. You can also choose from a large variety of lilies: tiger, Asiatic, Turk's cap, Madonna, leopard, Easter, trumpet, Canada, meadow, Carolina, prairie, Sierra tiger, alpine, and Asiatic hybrid. Do an online search or peruse photos from your floral designer to see the beauty and differences of each variety. You'll find solid colors as well as striped or ruffled-edge lilies, and each has its own symbolism.

Those who believe in the language of flowers might also remember an age-old superstition that lilies are the flowers of death. (Pop culture experts say this is the reason behind the naming of Lily in *The Munsters*.) That dark symbolism no longer holds true. Lilies have been depicted as a symbolic flower often associated with images of the Catholic saints, with a meaning of virtue attached. So don't fear using lilies in your wedding day flower plans.

Stargazer Lilies

- The stargazer lily is known for its big, bright, open and sometimes multicolored petals.

- Stargazers are one of the most fragrant lilies, and some people have strong allergic reactions to their scents. So test these flowers against your sensitivities and consider that guests too may have allergic reactions to the stargazers if they are put in the table centerpieces.

- Stargazer lilies symbolize brightness and beauty.

- Stargazers symbolize the love of astronomy.

Lilies with Negative Meanings

- Orange lilies symbolize hatred. You might not like your future mother-in-law, but don't hand her this telltale bloom. Many guests are well-informed of the language of flowers, and they may tell her the symbol within the flowers she is wearing.

- Tiger lilies symbolize pride. As one of the seven deadly sins, it's not a symbol you should bring into your wedding day.

- Yellow lilies can symbolize falseness. On your wedding day you want everything to be truth. A dark-meaning flower like this one has no place at a wedding, where symbols are all about love and faithfulness.

3

TULIPS

There's no tiptoeing around it; tulips have special meaning for your wedding day

Tulips are a traditional spring flower, considered one of the bright blooms that give you the most bang for your buck. They're wonderfully inexpensive when you order them in season and are available in a wide range of colors from barely there blush pastels to vivid brights, primarily in solid colors.

Fashion-forward brides looking to pair a bright bloom with their bridesmaids' gown colors look to the tulip for jewel-toned purples and oranges that pop in wedding day photographs.

Tulips cluster extremely well for both bouquets and low-set centerpiece settings. Because they are not as delicate and fragile as gardenias, they hold up well in arrangements,

White Tulips

- In an all-tulip bouquet, or as a part of a multiflower bouquet, white tulips symbolize fame and a perfect lover.

- The tulip in general is, of course, the symbol of Holland, so wedding couples with Dutch backgrounds often like to include the tulip as homage to their heritage.

- Variegated tulips were once given with a meaning of beautiful eyes, making them an ideal choice for the moms' and men's boutonnieres.

Red Tulips

- Red or pink tulips communicate a declaration of love or express the sentiment, believe me.

- Red tulips are also thought to express a message of irresistible love, bringing the passion of red to this springtime flower.

- Red tulips are often added to clusters of red roses to add some shape dimension to a bouquet or centerpiece, and the meanings of both work together.

- Red tulips are most often mixed with pink tulips, a mix far superior to red and white.

whether you go monochromatic or multihued in a bright grouping such as all red or all pink. As for size, you'll see minitulips and full-size glorious ready for mix-and-match arrangements, as well. Growers have perfected the science of different bell shapes and sizes for mature tulips, as well as ideal narrow bells for flowers just about to bloom.

Tulips work best in large groupings of twelve or more as both bouquets and centerpieces. Smaller, more subtle bouquets may be comprised of three to six tulips.

With regard to symbolism, tulips are a sign of spring's return, new growth, and color after a cold, dark season of dormancy. As such, some couples who have gone through tough times, cold and dark seasons, see the tulip—among other spring flowers—as the perfect symbol of the bright new season beginning with their new marriage. Other couples look to the history of the tulip trade, back to when tulips were a symbol of great wealth in ancient Persia. Presenting a tulip meant a promise of an abundant life.

Yellow Tulips

- Yellow tulips symbolize brightness and warmth, joy, and seasons of sunshine, which in farming eras symbolized a good crop (i.e., abundance).

- Yellow tulips can also communicate the sentiment, there's sunshine in your smile.

- Springtime brides and grooms favor the yellow tulip for its bright visual punch—its electric charge—to a multicolored bouquet.

- Yellow tulips come in a range of colors, from soft buttercup yellow to bright sun yellow, and gold.

Tulips with Negative Meanings

- What is it with yellow flowers? They often have positive and negative meanings.

- Legend has it that while yellow tulips speak of sunshine in your smile, they are also a symbol of hopeless love. This, of course, depends on your interpretation of the word hopeless. It may be that you interpret it along the lines of being a hopeless romantic—which is a good thing—or your meaning of hopeless may be the literal meaning—without hope.

DAISIES
Add a playful touch to informal bouquets and centerpieces

When you think of daisies, you probably think of adorable little girls in a garden, picking white or yellow daisy heads and forming them into garlands. These flowers are symbols of happiness, youth, and natural beauty, and as such they are a light and playful flower that can be added to more informal bouquets and centerpieces.

Of course there are several different kinds of daisies. Standard daisies of the white or yellow varieties are extremely plentiful and inexpensive, while bright Gerber daisies in vivid oranges, pinks, and yellows are among the pricier blooms. Each provides a distinctive effect: Traditional daisies provide a casual, traditional look, while Gerbers pop with modern flair.

Additional daisy varieties include blue, prairie, giant, kingfisher, sunshine, gloriosa, butter, painted, Paris, crown, ox-eye,

White Daisies

- White daisies symbolize innocence, loyalty, loyal love, and purity.

- Brides often choose a white daisy as a way to pop a touch of white into an all-yellow bouquet. This makes for a natural springtime look.

- In keeping with the loyalty symbol, more men wear this type of flower as boutonnieres.

- Also in keeping with loyalty, and also for purity of friendship, white daisies are now used for bridesmaid bouquets, as well as for flowers for the mothers and grandmothers.

Yellow Daisies

- Yellow daisies bring in the meanings of joy, natural beauty, happiness, friendship, innocence, and youth. Yellow daisies symbolize the return of springtime, a new season, new abundance, and cheerfulness.

- They also symbolize a child's innocent play, because Victorian-era children often used them to make bracelets and necklaces.

- While many other flowers have negative meanings from their yellow color, the yellow, springtime daisy is free from this stigma.

and—the most popular varieties—Shasta and African daisies. Even though these types of daisies are quite different in appearance, the same symbolism has been applied to most if not all of them.

Each variety can be clustered to different effect, with dozens of happy yellow daisies creating nearly the same-size bouquet as a half-dozen Gerbers. These sister blooms couldn't be more different in appearance, but they hold a marvelous heritage in the meaning of flowers: Have you ever done the he-loves-me-he-loves-me-not petal-picking game?

Gerber Daisies

- Gerber daisies, also known as Gerbera daisies, are bright and vivid, but they're also fragile beauties of sorts. With such big, beautiful heads comes a degree of weight, so special sleeves need to be attached beneath their heads. As such, they symbolize brightness, joyfulness, play, and a bright future, and they communicate the sentiment, I'm strong when supported by you.

- Since Gerber daisies are among the pricier blooms in the daisy family, modern couples have assigned a symbol of wealth and abundance to these flowers.

YELLOW LIGHT

In the language of flowers, the color yellow often has some dubious meanings. Yellow carnations mean rejection, and they communicate the sentiment, you have disappointed me. Yellow chrysanthemums mean slighted love. Yellow hyacinths mean jealousy. Not all yellow flowers are curses in disguise, but some brides and grooms decide against the bad luck yellow choices, just to be safe.

Daisies with Negative Meanings

It's pretty difficult to find a daisy with a negative meaning, so the true danger is in pairing a white and yellow daisy with one of the negative-meaning yellow flowers.

You might be tempted to do this when you see a yellow hyacinth and believe this to be the perfect springtime blend.

But in fact what you're saying is, jealousy at play!

If you're wary of using flowers with potential negative symbolism, or that might put a curse on your day, daisies are among the safest flowers out there.

TRADITIONAL BRIDAL FLOWERS

Gardenias, lilies of the valley, and orchids are some traditional wedding flowers that express a lot

When you think of bridal flowers, you think of roses, gardenias, lilies of the valley, hyacinths, and orchids. These are considered the traditional flowers of the bridal world, the expected elements of bouquets and centerpieces, often the top choices for men's boutonnieres as well. They are bridal, after all. And since these blooms have a long-standing tradition in the

world of marriage, they have the deepest meanings in the language of flowers. They've been around a long time; your mother probably had them in her wedding pieces, as did your grandmother, as did brides back in the Victorian era.

As bridal flowers, they're often more expensive than other non-bridal flowers, even in off-peak wedding seasons. Floral

Gardenias

- This delicate white flower symbolizes secret love.

- Even though your wedding removes the "secret" aspect of your love for one another, the gardenia is still in demand as a reminder of a couple's earliest dating days, when one may have secretly fallen in love with

the other . . . perhaps from day one.

- Gardenias also communicate the sentiment, you're lovely, which makes this a fantastic choice for the mothers and grandmothers. This is a sweet message to give to your mother-in-law.

Hyacinths

- Yellow hyacinths symbolizing jealousy, but most of the other colors of this delicate spring bloom are quite beautiful in symbolism.

- White hyacinths symbolize loveliness. Blue hyacinths symbolize constancy. Red or pink hyacinths symbolize playfulness. In general,

hyacinths represent a sense of playfulness.

- Avoid the purple hyacinth, as it symbolizes sorrow and the sentiment, please forgive me. This is an apology flower from antiquity, so unless you were a total Bridezilla, steer clear of this bloom.

suppliers and floral designers know that these are the flowers with the most emotional impact, and brides with blank checks will pay more to have the flowers of their dreams. So up goes the pricing. Before you decide to scratch these from your shopping list, though, make sure you don't eliminate their beautiful meanings from your wedding day bouquets and centerpieces.

Build your bouquets and centerpieces to include one to three of these top-priced, dramatic bridal flowers surrounded by lovely flowers in the lower price brackets.

ZOOM

Of the pricier bridal flowers, roses are the most moderately priced, and the most flexible in terms of fitting into different formalities of arrangements and bouquets. Gardenias on the other hand are definitely formal blooms. Roses also encompass the traditional bridal look, so a piece with three to five roses will suit a wider range of floral styles. Orchids, by contrast, are often more expensive.

Lilies of the Valley

- These tiny, white bell-shaped blooms draping on a delicate stem are a longtime favorite of brides, adding a feminine touch to a bridal bouquet. Men may also wear a sprig of lilies of the valley as a boutonniere.

- Be careful: Lilies of the valley hold their shape for just a few hours before their lack of a water source causes them to droop, especially in hot weather.

- Lilies of the valley symbolize sweetness and tell someone, you've made my life complete.

Orchids

- It doesn't get more expensive than this exotic flower, and many floral designers say the cost to import orchids will rise dramatically in the coming years.

- The value of this flower makes it all the more precious to the wearer, which is why many mothers choose orchids as their signature flowers for the day.

- Orchids symbolize love, beauty, and refinement.

- Cattleya orchids symbolize mature charm, another indicator of moms' affinity for this bloom.

FLOWERS SYMBOLIZING ABUNDANCE
Some flowers symbolize good fortune for the bride and groom

Wedding flowers traditionally symbolize love and fidelity, affection, loyalty, and friendship, but many brides and grooms also want some luck and prosperity to come their way as they build a future together. Since so many wedding traditions are built on age-old superstitions, even the most modern bride becomes a believer in good luck charms and positive superstitions. A penny in your shoe? That's for good fortune. Wedding toasts? Most will wish you a long and happy future filled with prosperity and a freedom from want. Even the wedding cake started off as a ritual designed to bring the bride and groom a "mountain" of prosperity.

With so many good luck charms built into your big day, you might wish to add some additional symbols of good fortune and financial gain in the form of the flowers you select.

Bells of Ireland

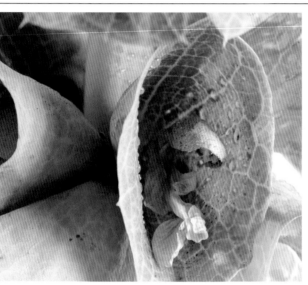

- These little bell-shaped white flowers symbolize good luck—not just with money, but also for a lovely home.

- Bells of Ireland also symbolize abundance in the form of beauty, and their white color symbolizes purity.

- Because this is a grouping of tiny flowers, they also symbolize the abundance of loving and helpful souls in your life.

- Bells of Ireland paired with other flowers that symbolize good fortune and abundance are said to magnify the attraction of wealth.

Buttercups

- The buttercup is another yellow flower that doesn't have a negative meaning! It symbolizes riches.

- In bygone eras, children would hold buttercups under their chins. If the chin turned yellow, the child would be wealthy someday. This tradition evolved into the incorporation of buttercups into springtime weddings.

- Modern-day children perform the same buttercup-under-the-chin game, but the meaning has become, you like butter. This silly game has brought a symbol of playfulness to the bloom.

Keep in mind that some cultures consider the greenery of bouquets and arrangements to carry the symbol of abundance, and great care is taken to make sure that greenery is fresh and healthy for a healthy flow of income. The language of feng shui in Eastern traditions holds that a lucky number of flowers, such as seven or nine, also brings good and increased fortune.

GREEN ● LIGHT

One of the best symbols in all of nature is ivy, which represents loyalty, wedded love, affection, friendship, and fidelity. Many invitation designs incorporate green ivy motifs, bringing this traditional bridal symbol into the grand theme of the day. Ivy can be used in print but is considered most powerful when used in bouquets, as boutonnieres, within centerpieces, and as site décor for the ceremony itself.

Flowering Cabbages

- Flowering cabbage symbolizes profit and many returns. As a good luck charm, this flower was often given to those starting new business ventures.

- Cabbages are fall plants, often bright green (the color of money) tinged with the good luck color of purple at the edges.

- Purple was considered the color of kings, so flowering cabbages now symbolize a king's riches.

Cattails

- The cattail is a tall, imposing plant, adding a sense of height and architecture to centerpieces.

- Cattails symbolize prosperity as well as peace.

- Cattail mixed with ferns sends a combined message of prosperity and good shelter.

- Since cattails grow near water, the feng shui element of earth and water attracts prosperity and, some say, good health.

SMALL ROUND BOUQUETS

They may not be large in size, but traditional round bouquets make a beautiful bridal impression

Many of the gorgeous wedding bouquets you see in magazines are traditional, round bouquets, also known as posy bouquets. The small round, or posy, was the world's introduction to bridal bouquets when Queen Victoria premiered her own small round and set the standard for the bridal design in vogue during her era. The rest of society took her sense of style as the "it design," and we still look at the posy as a classic, traditional choice. Back in Victorian days, the posy was quite simple and petite, with just a small selection of blooms. Over time they grew in size, with larger clusters of flowers and the addition of ribbons, lace, and bows.

Posies went out of style for a few decades, perhaps owing

White

- The ultratraditional bride often chooses this bridal white, petite round as the elegant look for her first appearance at the ceremony. She wants all eyes on her, not a her flowers.

- The small round bouquet is one of the top choices for formal weddings.

- An all-white small bouquet is budget friendly, because you don't need as many flowers to create a visual impact.

- All-white round bouquets are ideal choices for brides wearing gowns with color in them, such as a blush pink dress.

Pink

- Still an elegant bridal look, the addition of pink allows for a gentle contrast against a white or ivory wedding gown.

- If your wedding colors include pinks in any shade from blush to vivid hot pink, choose a softer pink for your bouquet.

- Why is pink a traditional bridal color? You see baby pink rosebuds in most bridal advertisements, and the covers of many wedding books include pink hues. The bridal industry has crowned pink as the color of femininity.

to the decadent styles of the 1980s, when big was in and everyone seemed to carry dramatic cascades. But now the simplicity and elegance of the posy is back. Brides are choosing from small, medium, and large round bouquets, according to the formality of their weddings, the designs of their dresses, and even the locations of their weddings. Here is a primer on what comprises a small round bouquet and how to decide if this style is right for you.

Pastel Colors

- Today's modern brides love their color! Some look at sample photos of bridal bouquets and yawn at the look of all-white bridal bouquets.

- The range of pastel colors that brides wish to carry includes yellow, lavender, baby blue, sage green, light coral, and soft orange.

- For a small round you're better off choosing one color of pastel flowers for a monochromatic look. There's not enough room for a collection of colors in a small round.

The Benefits of a Small Round Bouquet

- A smaller round is lighter to carry. With the inclusion of so many flowers, filler, stems, and ribbon ties, a bouquet can weight up to five pounds!

- A lighter bouquet is less exhausting to hold during long photo-taking sessions.

- A small round allows you and your gown to be the focal point. You're not hidden behind a big mass of flowers.

- A small round is budget friendly, as fewer flowers are needed to create it.

- A small round can double as your tossing bouquet if you wish to enact this tradition.

MEDIUM ROUND BOUQUETS

Not too small, not too large, these "just right" rounds are flattering for most brides

If you love the look of a round bouquet, but the posy style is just too diminutive for you, take a step up to a slightly larger round—anywhere from eight inches to a foot in diameter. This size gives you enough room to include a larger collection of flowers, mix different colors, and add more greenery and accents, yet still keep the elegant, classic, sophisticated look of a round bouquet. What's more, it's still a comfortable weight for you to hold and carry.

Bridal magazine editors say that medium rounds are what you're most often looking at in their photo spreads and online galleries, as the larger size allows room for more creativity, detail, and color.

White

- This typifies the classic, bridal bouquet both in wedding white and in size.

- Create a ballerina bouquet featuring tufts of white tulle or netting with just a few white flowers. This style originated during the World War II-era, when flowers weren't readily available and volume was added with tulle.

- Include one to three different flowers, such as roses, ranunculus, and mini white callas, still keeping the round shape but adding an array of blooms.

Red

- Medium rounds measure six to eight inches across, giving you plenty of room for a larger collection.

- Red works for a summer, winter, or Valentine's Day wedding, but is too powerful a color for springtime.

- Red flowers come in a range of hues, from lipstick red, deeper burgundy, and deep red chocolate cosmos, a mix of which provides greater color dimension than all-red roses.

- Red rounds are best accessorized with a few touches of pink or yellow, rather than white.

The medium round is most often selected by brides who consider themselves conservative. They don't want to make a statement with their bouquets, but they do want them to look pretty and serve as an accent to their entire wedding look. That's the job of any bridal bouquet, but the medium round seems to be the saving grace of brides who worry about going too small or too large with their visual statement. A medium round just is, and that may be your definition of the perfect bridal bouquet.

ZOOM

To figure out the best size round for you, cut out pieces of paper in small, medium, and large circles and place each one in front of a photo of you in your wedding gown or a gown style you like at this moment. You'll be able to see which size best represents the bouquet size that flatters you and then use the template to design your bouquet.

Bright Colors

- Oranges, purples, corals, yellows, and blues are the perfect bright colors for medium round bouquets.

- Mixing bright colors adds new dimension, such as vivid yellows mixed with hot oranges for a stylish summer or seasonal fall bouquet.

- Choosing bright colors allows your photographer to digitally "paint" a burst of color onto black-and-white images from your day.

- A medium round opens the possibility of carrying a cone bouquet, in which the bottom is elongated slightly for a cone effect.

The Benefits of a Medium Round Bouquet

- A medium round bouquet allows you to include more types of flowers, giving you more visual punch with your blend of large and small flowers.

- A medium round can be made lighter to carry by adding more green filler and leaves, instead of packing the round with flower heads.

- A medium round is the perfect size to show off tiny filler flowers like lilies of the valley, which gives a sense of motion and liquidity to a tightly packed bunch of flowers.

15

LARGE ROUND BOUQUETS

Go big, bold, and lush with an oversize round bouquet featuring your favorite blooms

You're all about the drama, so what better way to inject some wow factor into your wedding day look—which may include a dramatic designer wedding gown—than to make your flowers really stand out? You don't want a tiny bouquet that looks like something your flower girl should be carrying. You want your bouquet to be big and eye-catching. You want guests to drop their jaws when they see the floral masterpiece you've designed to carry. A big round bouquet takes the traditional round and supersizes it, giving you room for dozens of beautiful classic and exotic flowers, lots of texture, and gorgeous fragrance. You can just see the photos of you accented by your cluster of perfect Ecuadorian roses.

White

- A big, bright, white bouquet makes a grand statement, especially if you have a higher budget for pricier flowers, including gardenias, lilies, and roses.

- This big arrangement gives you plenty of room to use five to eight different types of flowers in your bouquet.

- A white large round bouquet benefits from a mix of large and small white flowers, such as tiny lilies of the valley accenting roses.

- A popular filler for the white large round bouquet is the softer Queen Anne's lace.

Pastel Colors

- Stick with four or five different types of flowers for a pastel round, since color adds dimension.

- For a more polished look, stick with a range of pastels in one color family, rather than mix several different pastels.

- Soft, small fillers are important for pastel large rounds, because they provide backdrop for larger flowers.

- Don't limit yourself to matching the color of the bridesmaids' dresses; complement them with a different hue.

A large round bouquet is the essence of exorbitance when filled with roses, gardenias, birds of paradise, stargazer lilies, and enormous callas, but you have to be careful not to go too big. You don't want guests to think, "She's carrying around a centerpiece!" In all things wedding, there is such a thing as going too far—especially if your large round is just too large for your frame. The bouquet has to fit. And a large bouquet fits a bride who has a large personality as well as a larger or taller frame.

Keep in mind that large bouquets are going to cost more, due to the sheer number of flowers and fillers needed to make it look lush and full. And if you are hiring a floral designer, that expert and his or her team will spend a greater amount of time perfecting your oversize piece. So make some room in your wedding budget. If you choose pricier blooms—this piece is going to cost you.

Bright Colors

- When you go big and bright, you display the joy of your wedding day in vivid color.

- Many brides like to make a statement with big, bold, bright bouquets when their gowns are simpler and less adorned.

- A bright large round bouquet can take too much attention away from your face. So test the size by holding five or six supermarket floral bouquets up to your face and take one away at a time until you reach the perfect size.

The Benefits of a Large Round Bouquet

- A large round bouquet makes a big bridal statement that perhaps your gown isn't able to make on its own.

- If you've chosen a simpler gown that's on the lower-budget end—and you feel sad about not having that pricy designer dress you saw at the gown shop—your large round can add the wow factor you feel you are missing.

- Large rounds complement taller or larger brides, offering the perfect balance to a body type.

17

HAND-TIED BOUQUETS
While a slightly more relaxed style than rounds, the hand-tied bouquet is a modern classic

Hand-tied bouquets allow the flowers to shine in a round, gathered arrangement, but the stems also participate in the traditional bridal look as ribbon-wrapped handles of beauty. The result is a tightly clustered round of flowers with a little something extra underneath, such as satin ribbon wrapping or a handle that trails lengths of ribbon or lace.

The hand-tied bouquet can be either formal or informal, depending on the types of flowers you choose and the combination you create. The most commonly used flowers in hand-tied bouquets are roses, ranunculus, calla lilies, daylilies, tulips, coneflowers, phlox, cosmos, and peonies. These so-called sturdier flowers with thicker or stronger stems will

Pastel

- Pastel flowers stand out in a hand-tied bouquet when you add plenty of greenery.

- Hand-tied bouquets made of one kind of flower, such as roses, make for a classic, sophisticated look.

- Mixing flower varieties allows you to change the

formality level. Daisies and tulips are less formal, while roses and calla lilies are more formal.

- A pastel color scheme allows you to complement your bridesmaids' dresses or the wedding décor for a more unified look.

Bright Red

- Bright red bouquets are perfectly fine for daytime weddings, so don't eliminate this color choice just because your wedding takes place in the afternoon.

- Passionate, lipstick red roses are the top choice in this style of bright bouquet.

- Select a range of reds and add even more depth by selecting flowers in a cranberry color.

- Reds are almost impossible to match perfectly in hue, so eliminate any clashing tones by purposefully choosing a collection of bright and deep reds.

hold the weight of a flower head and keep the shape of the bouquet.

Smaller flowers such as lilies of the valley, Queen Anne's lace, and Bells of Ireland are often added to give a delicate touch to balance out a collection of big, dramatic blooms.

Hand-tied bouquets are also referred to as clutch bouquets, and you can design them to have the entire stem wrapped in ribbon or just tie the stems with ribbon directly under the flowers, leaving the natural green stems exposed. This effect gives your bouquet a just-picked-from-the-garden look.

Orange

- Orange is a bright, happy color suitable for spring, summer, and fall weddings, which makes it popular for hand-tied bouquets.

- Orange calla lilies are the perfect curl of sophistication in an orange or orange-based bouquet.

- Look at vivid yellows and pale oranges as accent colors for your bouquet.

- Again, greenery brings out the natural look of the hand-tied bouquet's stem and provides the perfect top and bottom color accent to make a tangerine floral cluster pop.

BOUQUETS

The Benefits of Hand-tied Bouquets

- Hand-tied bouquets are often a great choice when you have a small floral budget. If you're working with a floral designer, this type of bouquet is easy to construct, takes less time to put together, and requires less material.

- The effect of a decorated stem treatment gives an appearance of more length to your bouquet.

- A hand-tied bouquet can be as small or as large as you want it to be and as light or as heavy as you wish.

- Hand-tied bouquets are the easiest style to make yourself. You just need to gather and wrap the flowers securely.

BIEDERMEIER BOUQUETS

Add some European influence with these circles of flowers in a tightly clustered bouquet

The Biedermeier bouquet is a tight, round cluster of flowers arranged in circular patterns, each consisting of the same flower. You may have a circle of pink roses at the center and then a ring of white roses along the bottom edges of the round. Swiss floral designers first created this unique arrangement of flowers in the late 1800s, naming it after a German style of interior décor. Back in the 1800s the most common style of Biedermeier bouquet included orange and lemon peels for added scent, as these bouquets were often small with fewer flowers.

Today the Biedermeier is back in bigger and fuller glory, sometimes with three or four rings of flowers making up a

Small Biedermeier Bouquets

- A small bouquet consists of one central flower placed at the top of the bouquet, one circle of the same color and type of flower, and then one ring of flowers of a contrasting color.

- A small Biedermeier might also consist of a central bloom and then two rounds

- of flowers of the same type and color.

- Never use more than two colors in a Biedermeier, as you don't want the effect of a striped bouquet.

- Small bouquets are perfect for monochromatic arrangements.

Medium Biedermeier Bouquets

- A medium-size Biedermeier gives you one extra layer of flowers.

- Again, avoid alternating layers of colors to prevent the striped look.

- A medium bouquet is also ideal for a monochromatic arrangement of flowers.

- Add some contrast with tiny stephanotis or lilies of the valley.

- Since this is a round bouquet, make sure you have the right body type to carry this shape and size of bouquet. If you're short and round, this is not the style for you.

20

dramatic round with intricately placed blooms. On the other hand, some are created as dense balls of one kind of flower, such as baby rosebuds or stephanotis.

Due to the intensive nature of this bouquet's composition, with so many flowers and so much wiring and pinning required to secure each bloom, this is one of the more expensive bouquets to create or order. It also takes a large amount of skill to craft on your own.

ZOOM

If you'd like to remove some of the weight from your Biedermeier bouquet, or make your DIY approach easier, start with a small Styrofoam ball and use long, crystal-studded pins from the craft store to easily attach each flower in concentric circles. Hot glue guns are often ineffective, as the glue might not take to the Styrofoam.

BOUQUETS

Bright Biedermeier Bouquets

- Use two bright colors for smaller bouquets and no more than three for larger ones to avoid the striped look.

- The most common bright Biedermeiers include reds, oranges, and purples.

- If multiple colors are used in a Biedermeier, they are usually close in color family, such as reds and pinks, rather than contrasting colors like reds and yellows. The bouquet's size is enough of a statement. Going too big with bright colors turns this style into a garish display.

Biedermeiers and Formality

- Biedermeier bouquets are ultraformal, ideal for white- or black-tie weddings.

- They may also be used for daytime formal weddings, in white, pastel, or bright colors.

- This style of bouquet is ultra-involved and ultra-expensive to construct, so when a similar, formal look is desired, you might choose a round, tightly-packed, hand-tied bouquet.

- The same round, hand-tied bouquet can be designed for your bridesmaids to match your pricier Biedermeier.

- Tiny round nosegays carried by your flower girls and the mothers coordinate for a lower price.

MATCHING BOUQUET TO GOWN

Make sure your bouquet works with your body size and with your wedding gown style

Your bouquet is such an important part of your wedding day look, so you want to be sure it works for your body, as well as with the style and design of your dress. Floral designers say they won't design a bouquet without seeing a photo of the dress first. After all, it would be a professional embarrassment to them if their creation looked inappropriate, made a super-detailed dress look even busier, lost you behind a bouquet that was too large, or failed to produce a wow factor for a simpler gown.

If you're looking for what's trendy, you may be doing yourself a major disservice. Forget about those online trend reports that say that wedding bouquets are getting larger.

Small

- When we say small, we're talking about the size of the bouquet, not the size of a bridal gown.

- Small bouquets complement simpler, less-adorned wedding gowns such as a column dress, an informal knee-length A-line, or an informal suit dress for a civil wedding.

- Petite brides can carry small bouquets as a good balance to a tiny frame.

- Tall brides can carry a small bouquet to show off an intricate dress bodice.

Medium

- A medium-size bouquet allows room for a wide range of colors and flower varieties that add visual punch to a bride of any height or body size.

- Medium bouquets work well with simpler A-line, column, sheath, and other formal dress styles.

- Mermaid-style dresses with fabric attraction at the bottom of the dress call for a balanced, medium-size bouquet.

- Floor-length dresses often call for a medium bouquet to accent the long line of fabric in the front of your dress.

National surveys don't take into account the major bridal rule that you need to choose a bouquet that fits your body size and the style of your dress. You wouldn't go out and buy big shoes if you have size five feet just because an article told you size elevens are all the rage, right?

Read on to discover how to choose the bouquet size that flatters your dress style. And, again, you can use the cut-out template trick of placing paper circles of different sizes in front of a photo of you in your gown to see how a bouquet silhouette will add to or detract from your wedding look.

Large

- Larger, more detailed bridal bouquets are ideal for taller brides, as they create a balancing circle at the center of the body.

- Plus-size brides should consider a larger bouquet, which provides balance with a wider bouquet at the center of your body.

- An apple body shape benefits from a round bouquet, which makes the waist appear smaller.

- A simpler gown style, such as a long satin column dress or sheath, looks beautiful with a larger, more detailed bouquet.

Bouquets and Destination Weddings

- You can design bouquets that flatter your dress style and wedding formality.

- If you'll be wearing a full ball gown, a cascade bouquet allows you that waterfall effect that plays into your surroundings.

- Incorporate the colors native to the locale, such as sandy tans, turquoise blues, corals, and the oranges and pinks of a sunset.

- Bouquet accents can include starfish, seashells, and coral.

- Incorporate indigenous island flowers such as hibiscus and bird of paradise.

SMALL CASCADE BOUQUETS
Give a little bit of length to your bouquet with a cascade effect

Cascade bouquets provide a waterfall effect, in which the blooms seem to spill down in front of you in an arrangement with length. Also called a shower bouquet, this design provides a draping display of flowers and greenery from a wider top to a narrower bottom.

Cascades have returned from a short hiatus, with many brides again favoring the flowing natural look, especially since this style allows a greater degree of greenery and a variety of flower sizes—bigger on top and smaller on the bottom.

Certain flowers work best in cascades because of their size and sturdiness. Larger flowers to use include roses, Dendrobium orchids, calla lilies, and daylilies. The best small flowers are baby rosebuds, lisianthus, stephanotis, and mini daisies for an informal cascade

White

- A petite bride may wish to hold a small white cascade bouquet, as its size is a good balance to a smaller frame.

- With a white bouquet you have the option of using one to three different types of flowers for optimal effect.

- Using a single size of the same type of flower creates a sophisticated, classic look.

- Even with a small cascade, you can start with larger flowers on top and trail down with smaller flowers at the bottom.

Pastel Colors

- You have your choice in color range, from barely there blush pastels to more vibrant pastels.

- Mix blush and vibrant pastels for a lovely "color fading" effect from top to bottom.

- The most popular pastel cascade bouquets are pink, lavender, yellow, and baby blue.

- Small white flowers complement the pastel cascade—either as tiny dots of stephanotis or trailing lengths of lily of the valley—to create a bridal look.

The best cascades have a proper balance of length, with the piece ending at the top of your thigh. True, yesteryear's cascades practically reached the floor, but you don't want to look like a Kentucky Derby winner with a blanket of flowers.

Small cascade bouquets are also known as teardrop bouquets or trail bouquets. Keep in mind your body size, knowing that the correct cascade design will play up your features, flatter your shape, and show off your gown perfectly.

····· GREEN ● LIGHT ·····

Floral sprays contain multiple small flowers per stem. For the draping part of your cascade bouquet sprays, insert a good curtain of blooms in a matching color scheme and in the natural bunches in which they grow. Sprays are a great way to save money, often priced at 40 percent less than single-bloom flower stems. You'll find sprays as small as three inches long and as large as two feet long.

Bright Colors

- Be careful with a small bright cascade, as a too-vibrant piece can look like a costume in this size. You don't want to look like you're carrying a toy bouquet.

- Fewer bright flowers work best in small cascades, with just a half dozen or so bright flowers at the top and smaller flowers or sprays at the bottom.

- Complement a small bright cascade with plenty of greenery to make your colors pop.

The Benefits of a Small Cascade Bouquet

- A small cascade bouquet gives a gentle flowing effect with its elongated tail, which many petite brides love for its slight elongating of the body.

- A small cascade has motion when you walk—but not to a pendulum degree.

- A small cascade is a formal look, adding classic detail to even the simplest dress.

- A small cascade looks larger than it is, so you may include fewer flowers and still produce a lovely bridal effect.

- A bouquet of this size is surprisingly light to carry.

FLOWING BOUQUETS

MEDIUM CASCADE BOUQUETS

Give a bit more length to your bouquet with a cascading effect

Cascade bouquets came into vogue in the beginning of the 1900s, adding an extra streak of floral length to the previously popular posy bouquet. Brides of that era increased the size of their cascade to show that their families had wealth and elevated standing in society. The trend caught on, and cascade bouquets grew, often formed into not one but two or three different floral "tails" in the front of the bouquet for a wider waterfall effect without the "blanket" look.

The medium cascade is among the most formal of the traditional bouquet styles, good for both indoor and outdoor formal weddings. This style doesn't work for informal weddings, because the draping effect isn't complemented by informal flowers such as daisies and tulips. Roses, ranunculus, lilies, gardenias, orchids, and calla lilies work best with a

White

- The medium cascade holds one dozen large flowers or two dozen small flowers, with plenty of greenery trailing as the foundation for smaller flowers in the waterfall front.

- White cascades fulfill the bridal look, and the cascade gives the bride's bouquet movement and direction.

- A white medium cascade bouquet accented with tiny white flowers and lots of greenery is the most popular cascade design.

- For the most formal look, white cascades usually hold roses, callas, and gardenias.

Pastel Colors

- Given the larger size of this cascade, a pastel arrangement can be lush with over three dozen light-hued flowers.

- Pastel cascades achieve more balance by mixing pastels with white flowers.

- Pastels should be mixed evenly throughout the cascade. Given the larger size, going from dark on the top to light on the bottom can look unbalanced and come across as a cheesy 1970s look.

- Use three to four different types of flowers to create depth and dimension.

medium cascade, which might also have more height at the top of the bouquet (such as with standing callas or lilies).

A sister style of the cascade bouquet, the crescent bouquet holds true to its name as a softly arched arrangement. Strong, sturdy flowers such as roses or orchids—blooms that hold their shape on a strong stem—are wired into a half-moon shape, and this medium-size cascade has only one trailing length in front. This shape adds a bit more modernity to a cascade.

Bright Colors

- Because there is so much area to cover, the top colors for bright cascades are red and orange.

- The medium cascade is the perfect size for flowers of all one shade.

- For destination weddings coral and turquoise are the top shades for cascade bouquets.

- Bright colors also encompass dark flowers such as cabernet calla lilies, deep burgundy roses, and deep terra cotta roses either as the sole color or slightly accented with small white or lighter-shade flowers.

The Benefits of a Medium Cascade Bouquet

- Sturdier blooms have a place to shine with this constructed form of bouquet. Thick stems hold the flower heads upright, adding some architecture to a bouquet that would otherwise point too downward.

- Medium cascades work with the largest range of body types and heights, elongating the body as they accent (not hide) the dress behind them.

- Even though this is a more sizeable bouquet, an angled handle will allow you to carry its weight quite comfortably.

OVERSIZE CASCADE BOUQUETS

A supersize, dramatic cascade bouquet is right for you

KNACK WEDDING FLOWERS

During the World War II era, cascade bouquets grew in popularity, and in size, almost to excessive levels. Tiny, delicate brides carried walls of flowers in their cascade bouquets, almost hiding behind them. You may have seen this bouquet style in your grandmother's or great-grandmother's black-and-white wedding photos. The gown was enormous; the train was huge; the veil stretched for yards and yards, pooled

behind the bride; and the bouquet was a blanket of flowers that you wonder how she held upright.

Cascade bouquets began to shrink over time, until a legendary bride brought them back into vogue. The late Princess Diana carried a large cascade bouquet at her royal wedding, and the trend was back again. Media types renamed this style of bouquet the princess bouquet in Diana's honor, and

White

- Choose large white flowers such as Ecuadorian roses, gardenias, calla lilies, and daylilies for a large cascade.

- Larger flowers mean fewer individual flowers will need to be purchased.

- Two to three dozen white flowers will fill a large

cascade well if accented by several dozen smaller flowers in between the blooms.

- A white large cascade with large flowers benefits from more delicate greenery and filler such as fern.

Pastel Colors

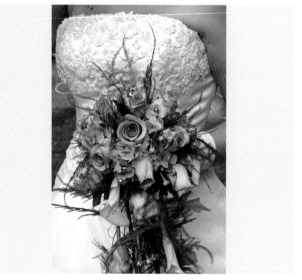

- A light-colored bouquet creates a romantic yet modern look to this traditional style.

- The most popular colors for pastel cascades in this magnitude are pink, tangerine, and sage green, composed of white flowers with green-tinged edges.

- A mix of pastel colors in the same color family, such as tangerine, works far better than multihued pastels, which can look too busy.

- Pastel flowers can be added to a primarily white cascade for just a hint of color to unify this large bouquet style.

brides of the 1980s and 1990s flocked to it.

Today the large cascade is chosen more for its balance to the bride's height and body size in an effort to find that the perfect complement to the bride's silhouette—not too large nor too small. A tall bride may want a large cascade to bring the eye downward and thus give the illusion of being shorter, and a plus-size bride may utilize the cascade's pointing- downward effect to distract from her body width.

ZOOM

Remove some of the heft of a large cascade bouquet by choosing individual flowers that are lighter in weight. A lovely, formal cascade might be composed of gardenias and stephanotis, for instance. Attach a thick, sturdy handle wrapped in ribbon at a forty-five degree angle from the base of the bouquet for the easiest carrying position.

Bright Colors

- The bride who wants to make a statement by matching her big, bold dramatic wedding dress with a big, bold dramatic bouquet chooses vibrant reds en masse.

- Taller brides are best suited to a bold, brightly colored oversize cascade.

- An oversize cascade doesn't have to be all flowers! You can have a dozen or so bright flowers with a mass of greenery for a cascade effect.

- Don't use too many flowers, or your oversize cascade will look too overdone.

The Benefits of an Oversize Cascade Bouquet

- When you carry an oversize cascade, you make a grand statement when you first appear at the ceremony.

- A lush, oversize cascade symbolizes opulence at your formal wedding.

- A big, dramatic cascade presents fabulous photo opportunities, especially solo shots of you holding your once-in-a-lifetime bouquet.

- If you choose a larger bridal bouquet, you can balance the look by going much smaller with your bridesmaids' bouquets and also even out your floral budget.

- Again, large cascades are the best friend of the larger bride, who may be self-conscious about how she looks in her gown.

GREENERY

Add a touch of greenery as both a filler and textured focal point

Green leaves, ferns, ivy, and grasses have long been touted as bridal budget savers, costing far, far less than hundreds of roses. Money savings aside, greenery adds a bountiful, natural look to cascade bouquets, where the leaves and ferns may be the stars of the arrangement.

With silken flowers and beautiful blooms in your cascade bouquet, the lacy bodies of ferns, the deep green ivy leaves,

and the curl of grasses bring additional textures and dimension to your bouquet, as well as to your centerpieces, so be sure to turn back to this chapter when you're designing your table accents.

Some brides decide they love the abundant look of greenery so much that they choose to skip the flowers entirely and build a cascade bouquet entirely of greens, ferns, or ivy—or

Ivy

- The most common ivy used in bridal bouquets is English ivy.

- For a larger leaf to the traditional bridal ivy, choose the six-inch-leaf Algerian ivy.

- For heart-shaped ivy leaves, choose the ivy with the variety name scutifolia.

- For curled ivy leaves, check out the Goldilocks variety.

- For tiny ivy leaves, choose itsy bitsy ivy.

- For ivy with colored leaves and veins, look at California gold ivy, which blends gold, yellow, and green.

Ferns

- Ferns come in many different frond shapes and sizes, so balance size and style with your bouquet.

- Maidenhair fern is the most popular for bouquets due to its delicate, tiny leaves. Southern maidenhair fern has the smallest and most delicate fronds.

- Boston fern stems can reach up to three feet long, making them a good choice for oversize cascade bouquets.

- Verona fern features fronds with a lacy appearance. For ruffled-edged ferns, consider crispum fern, fluffy duffy, fluffy ruffles, and childsil ferns.

a mixture of all three. Greenery is also used as décor, such as cascading garlands draping across a mantel or tucked into chandeliers, and as buffet table fillers, set around food platters to make the table seem more lush and full.

Garden weddings are an ideal setting for an all-green cascade bouquet, as it fits in with the natural aspect and still measures up as a formal bouquet. Can't decide on flowers? Can't afford flowers? Perhaps these greenery options are best for you.

Lilies of the Valley

- You'll most often see lilies of the valley as tiny, white, bell-shaped cascading flowers with twenty to twenty-five individual blooms per stem.

- Lily of the valley is also known as May lily, May bells, our lady's tears, and lily constancy.

- There are Chinese and Japanese versions of lily of the valley, which have larger bells, as well as a Montana-style version, which has a slightly green tint.

- Lily of the valley is a poisonous flower, so never use it as cake décor.

Additional Accents in Cascade Bouquets

- Besides lily of the valley, you can add tiny flowers in different colors. Look at brightly colored snapdragons and feathery astilbe for hue and texture variations.

- For modern, artsy cascades, include feathers, which you can find at craft stores in shades of pastel to bright colors as well as bridal white.

- Use tiny crystal pushpins inside the flowers of your cascade to bejewel your blooms and add a bit of sparkle.

- Use regional flowers such as magnolias to pay homage to your beloved home state or town.

FLOWING BOUQUETS

31

CASCADE HANDLE DETAILS

Add some balance to your cascading bouquet with beautiful handle treatments and trailing accents

A cascade bouquet features beautiful florals and greenery on the front, but you have plenty of room for additional features because you will be viewed from all angles as you make your way down the aisle. This means flowing ribbon cascades can add a delicate extra length of visual punch to your bouquet and even a bit of sparkle within your bouquet.

Appropriate accents on the front, sides, and underside of your bouquet add a finishing touch, give you a chance to get creative, and are often an easy and inexpensive way to dress up a simpler cascade bouquet. For instance, your floral designer can make you a roses and greenery cascade bouquet, and then you can add additional blooms and stick-in

Wrapped Handle

Trailing Lace

- The handle of your bouquet should be fully wrapped from top to bottom.

- Given the size and weight of a cascade, a three-inch wrap will not hold all of the stems together.

- Common wrapping materials include ribbons made of silk, satin, and velvet, as well as lace.

- You can also wrap the handle of your bouquet with material left over from altering the bottom of your gown or trains.

- Lace trails can range from two feet long to floor-length.

- They can be attached to the underside of the bouquet so as not to obscure your flowers.

- They can also be attached to pearl- or crystal-head

- pushpins so that they seem to stream right out from the middle or sides of the bouquet.

- Find Chantilly, Alençon, Battenberg, Venice, organza, chiffon, and beaded or rhinestone-trim laces at craft or fabic stores.

accents you've found at a wholesaler. This accessorizing of cascade bouquets is a new trend, with brides even pinning a saint medallion or charm to the underside as a way to add extra meaning to the floral piece—as a remembrance of a departed relative or friends or just a token of good luck.

The most important thing to remember when adding accents to your cascade bouquet is that less is more. With such a bountiful arrangement, too much additional ribbon or too much adornment to the front or handle of the bouquet makes it look garish and overdone. So plan for a modest amount of accents, and don't be afraid to cut out any accents or flowers that seem extraneous.

Function is key for a cascade bouquet handle. Since this is a heavier floral piece, you'll need a sturdy handle that won't break off. Many floral designers use heavy-duty duct tape to add extra strength to an angled plastic handle and base, and then they wrap it with ribbon, fabric, or another adornment.

Trailing Ribbon

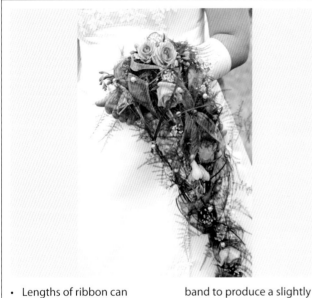

- Lengths of ribbon can extend from the bottom or sides of the bouquet, as well as from the handle itself.

- For a more romantic look, roll the ribbon up into a spiral coil and attach it with a small rubber band. Let it sit for a while, then remove the band to produce a slightly curled effect.

- Different types of ribbons to consider are satin, silk, velvet, brocade (for fall or winter weddings), and those fashioned from the cut alterations of your bridesmaids' dresses.

Pushpins and Inserts

- The most common push-pin accents to a cascade bouquet, as well as to all bouquet styles, are pearl-headed pins and crystal-headed pins.

- These pins may be inserted between the flowers or directly into the flower heads.

- Accent pushpins should be evenly spaced throughout the bouquet.

- Check with your floral wholesaler to see the range of seasonal and decorative stick-ins available, including seashells, butterflies, ladybugs, crystal stars, and faux gemstones.

ALTERNATIVE CASCADE BOUQUETS

They're long and dramatic, but they're not traditional styles of cascade bouquets

With personalized styles adding a tweak of modernity to traditional bridal bouquets, you might love the look of the full, flowing cascade bouquet but still want to make it more modern, artsy, or unexpected.

Basically any type of flower, green filler, or other decorative material can be used as the basis for a cascade bouquet, and those brides who describe their weddings as "classic with a kick" find eye-catching ways to turn a cascade bouquet into a work of art with stock and add-ins, color, and texture.

As with all bouquets, you want to make sure you don't add too much weight to your bouquet, nor that you over-accessorize. Here are the top designs in alternative cascade

Flower Fan

- Attach flowers to the top of an open fan, which you will carry in front of you as you walk.

- Smaller flowers make for a delicate effect across the top of the fan.

- Attach a ribbon trail to the fan, with tiny flowers in a bunch at the end of the ribbon.

- Less is more with a flower fan, as the weight of the flowers can bend the fan.

The Flower-Accented Book

- Carry your family Bible with a single white rose placed in the inside cover.

- Carry your family Bible with a ribbon or lace trail extending from it.

- Carry a favorite book of love poems, again with

the flower or ribbon trail extending from it.

- Insert in your chosen book a bookmark adorned with a tuft of flowers or greenery or a charm or saint medallion at the top.

bouquets, including add-ins you never would have expected to work with a wedding look.

What does this mean for your wedding budget? It could save you a fortune. A flower-free design costs 60 percent less than a flower-filled style, up to 80 percent less if you were planning on the priciest of blooms. An all-greenery cascade may cost just $30 to $40 to make, and then with $20 in add-in materials, you have a stunning creation.

Theme Item

- For a beach wedding, carry a single oversize starfish attached to a handle for a delicate look, especially if you have starfish in your décor theme.

- For an autumn wedding, carry a basket of colorful autumn leaves.

- For a winter wedding, carry a basket of colorful ornaments.

- For a Halloween wedding, get playful with a plastic or ceramic trick-or-treat pumpkin basket filled with candies in your theme color or a tuft of color-coordinated flowers.

Candles

- Go for a lighted effect by carrying a single white or pastel taper candle.

- If you are having an evening wedding, the light effect may coordinate with your site's candle décor, so match your candle to the site's décor size and shape.

- Explore different shapes of glass votives, such as an elongated trumpet, in which your candle can safely glow.

- Do not attempt to carry sparklers, which can ignite your veil or burn you or others.

SINGLE-STEM BOUQUETS

Less is more with a single-flower bouquet wrapped with a pretty ribbon

Sometimes a single flower is all that's needed to make the bridal statement you have in mind. A bride who loves simple elegance might choose to carry one perfect white rose as she makes her approach down the aisle, finding that a single bloom says it all. A single flower symbolizes the unity ritual taking place—with that one flower denoting the one, shared

life about to begin—and it also satisfies the bride who wants herself and her gown to be the focal point during that big moment.

Obviously, carrying one single flower is going to save you a lot of money, since you're purchasing one-thirtieth of the materials that would be needed for a round bouquet. And

Single-Stem Rose

- A single-stem white rose symbolizes purity, an apt symbol for a bouquet symbolizing a pure love.

- The most popular colors for single-stem rose bouquets are white, red, light pink, and bright pink.

- A peace rose comes in hues of pink, ivory, and light orange.

- Use a one- to two-inch-thick ribbon to tie a bow halfway down the stem, rather than wrap the whole stem.

Single-Stem Calla Lily

- Calla lilies are heralded as regal flowers and are best suited for formal weddings.

- Calla lilies are ideal for outdoor weddings, both formal and less formal.

- Calla lilies come in shades of white, pink, light green,

orange, and cranberry or merlot.

- If you carry a single calla lily as your accent flower, your bridesmaids can carry smaller calla lilies as single flowers or as bunches to offset your dramatic, larger flower.

there are almost no labor costs involved. If you're going the DIY route, you couldn't ask for a simpler project to take on, to lovely effect.

Since this single bloom is the entirety of your floral accent, you'll need to make sure that the flower itself is in spectacular condition, smooth and blemish free with healthy petals and in just slightly bud formation so that it has room to open up a bit throughout the day. A fully bloomed flower at the end of its bloom cycle may begin to drop petals during your big day.

ZOOM

Ideally you'll acquire four or five single flowers, store the cut stems in a water-filled vase, and then choose the one best and prettiest bloom to carry during your ceremony. Make your selection two to three hours before the wedding and have the stem wrapped according to your wishes-for design. The leftover flowers can be wrapped for the bridesmaids or mothers to carry.

Single-Stem Gerber Daisy

Be careful of nerves! A single-flower will show if your hand is shaking, so if you do have some anxiety with a shaking hand, just lean the top of the single-stem flower back a little bit so that the bloom is resting on your bodice. This will take the quiver out of the carry.

- A Gerber daisy head is large enough to make a visual impact.

- Gerber daisy heads are extremely heavy for their relatively delicate stems, so many suppliers attach a plastic support cone to the base of each flower head.

- Keep that support cone on the flower until just before you walk down the aisle.

- The most popular Gerber daisy single-stem colors are bright pinks, oranges, yellows, and reds.

FLOWER BUNCHES AS BOUQUETS

Get that just-picked look by choosing a floral bunch for your bouquet

If a single flower is too small, and a round is too formal and expected, consider a floral bunch for your bouquet. This grouping is not as organized and symmetrical as a round or Biederemeier bouquet. Flowers are not organized in circles or definite patterns. Instead, the bouquet has that just-picked look and as such is far more appropriate for a less-formal wedding.

One of the trends in bunches is the presentation bouquet. Think about the long-stemmed bouquet presented to the newly crowned Miss America. She holds the lush collection of flowers across her lower arm as she takes her first walk down the aisle with her new title. That's the same look you're afforded with the presentation, or arm, bouquet.

Bunch of Roses

- Long-stemmed roses are the most popular choice for presentation bouquets and for smaller-stemmed bunch bouquets.

- Roses make this type of bouquet more formal and may be mixed with other formal flowers such as gardenias and calla lilies.

- The most popular colors for rose bunch bouquets are white, red, and pink.

- A simpler bunch might contain a dozen roses, while a larger, more dramatic bunch might contain three dozen roses.

Bunch of Calla Lilies

- A grouping of six to twenty-four calla lilies creates an elegant, formal effect for your bouquet.

- Calla lilies may be used for both daytime and evening formal weddings, both indoors and outdoors.

- The most popular color for the calla lily bunch bouquet is, of course, white. Monochromatic calla bunches are the most formal; mixed-color callas work for less-formal weddings.

- Sage green calla lily bunches are a top choice for outdoor and green or organic weddings.

Many brides love the arm bouquet design, as it allows the bride to comfortably take her father's arm as he escorts her down the aisle, and then the arm of her husband as he escorts her back up the aisle.

Because you will use this bouquet for your wedding and not a pageant, you will want to fill the bunch bouquet—in a long style or as an eight-inch-stemmed, less dramatic bunch that's not so Miss America—with flowers and greenery according to your wedding's formality, location, and theme.

ZOOM

Presentation, or arm, bouquets first became popular in the 1900s as the style often presented to the iconic actress Sarah Bernhardt. Back then they were called Bernhardt bouquets, and brides requested them to share in a bit of Miss Bernhardt's glamour and fame.

Bunch of Gerber Daisies

- Brightly colored Gerbers look best in a bunch of twelve flowers or more.

- A bunch containing fewer than six daisies can look wimpy, especially if a hot day causes them to droop.

- The most popular colors for Gerber bunch bouquets are bright pink, bright red, bright orange, and bright yellow.

- Add a few stems of greenery to a bunch of Gerber daisies because their relatively flat heads and thick green stems need some accenting in a bunch.

Bunch of Wildflowers

- Smaller is better for a bunch of wildflowers, as the mix of different colors and shapes of wildflowers offers more than enough dimension without looking overpowering.

- Always get wildflowers from a floral center or wholesaler; flowers picked from a field or the side of the road may be poisonous.

- For a different wildflower effect, try bunches of heather or lavender.

- Wildflowers work best with a partially wrapped stem rather than a fully wrapped stem.

STEM TREATMENTS

Choose the perfect stem treatment for your small or large floral bunch

While cascade bouquets most often call for fully wrapped stems as a functional aspect of a heftier bouquet that has to keep its shape and be easy to carry, you have far more design options for the stems of floral bunches. You can have a fully wrapped six inches of stem, or you can tie a length of ribbon in a neat bow at the center mark of the stems, allowing the

clean-cut green ends to poke out of the bottom.

A thicker width of ribbon, such as one to two inches, looks best for a taller bunch of wildflowers, while a half-inch ribbon is perfectly balanced on a shorter stem-cut bunch.

Your decision about stem treatment for a bunch bouquet has much to do with balance and color, as you want a pretty

Partial Ribbon Wrap

- The most common partial ribbon wrap is created from two- to three-inch-wide ribbon wrapped one-third to halfway down the stem and then fastened with a bow.

- Use a length of floral tape to spiral wrap an inch of the stems, then cover that

  tape wrapping with fabric ribbon.

- A one- to two-inch-wide ribbon wrap is ideal for a cluster of six to twelve individual flowers.

- Match the color of the ribbon to one of the flower hues in your bouquet.

Full Ribbon Wrap

- For a full ribbon wrap, start wrapping at the base of your flower heads and wrap all the way down to the bottom of the stems.

- Leave the very bottoms of the stems exposed, or wrap them with ribbon to cover the entire stem.

- The most popular types of ribbon for a full stem wrap are satin, silk, and lace.

- A full ribbon wrap looks best when you match the fabric to a color in your flowers.

ribbon bow to serve as an accent and not overpower smaller, more delicate flowers.

Your chosen stem treatment will decide the length of stem you'll leave at the base of your bunch flowers, as some wrap designs look best with shorter stems and others benefit from longer, more eye-catching lengths of stem. Once you discover the proper stem treatment for this less-formal bouquet style, you can then think about how to dress it up with decorative fasteners, pins, and other devices.

The key to finding your stem-length balance is trial and error. Take some inexpensive tulips, daisies, or other flowers you find in the grocery store floral department and bunch them. Then beginning at their original length (perhaps nine inches), cut them down a few inches at a time and wrap and rewrap the stems to find the style and length that suits you best.

Lace Wrap

- The delicate nature of floral bunches lends itself well to the lace-wrapped handle.

- The top types of lace for stem wrap are Battenberg, Chantilly, and Alençon.

- Consider laces embedded with silver thread for a bit of shimmer.

- Look at laces that feature tiny hand-sewn bugle beading for an authentic Victorian look.

- Antique lace is a lovely way to insert "something old" into your day. Antiques stores are a terrific source for a range of lace styles.

Stem Adornments

- Use pearl-headed floral pushpins spaced two to three inches apart along one side of the wrapped stem.

- Use crystal-headed push-pins as an alternative to give your bouquet body some extra sparkle.

- As a new trend, attach tiny silver charms to your wrapped stem handle. You can find charms in craft or card stores.

- Find a circular charm or silver monogram plate to hot glue to the flat bottom of the ribbon-wrapped stems.

ALTERNATIVE BOUQUETS

Take a tiny step away from traditional rounds, singles, and bunches with these alternative bouquets

Everything old is new again in the world of wedding flowers, with styles once popular back in the 1920s and 1940s making a resurgence in the twenty-first century. We call back to the bouquets of our grandmothers and great-grandmothers as a way to carry on a small touch of family lineage and connect with the matriarchs of our family trees. And yet we still seek

individuality and personalization in bouquet styles. In short, we want the best of the past, present, and future.

The bouquets shown in this section are similar to round and hand-tied bouquets, but they have names, identities, and rules all their own. They also tell guests a lot about the bride's personality. What kind of bride departs from a

Nosegay Bouquets

- A nosegay is a densely packed bouquet very similar to a traditional round but smaller in size.

- A small nosegay (called a posy) is ideal for a petite bride, while a larger nosegay flatters a taller or larger bride.

- Use tighter round flowers such as roses, ranunculus, and peonies to best fill a nosegay.

- Nosegay bouquets were originally quite small, just under four inches in diameter, but they have grown in modern times to a width of six inches or so.

Pomanders

- A pomander is a small cluster of flowers formed in a ball shape and suspended by a length of ribbon.

- Pomanders are most often four to six inches in diameter.

- The most common flowers included in pomanders

are the smaller blooms of roses, dendrobium orchids, delphiniums, ranunculus, lisianthus, pansies, and grape hyacinths, with stephanotis pinned in.

- Pomanders are a top choice for junior bridesmaids, flower girls, mothers, and grandmothers.

traditional round and carries, for instance, a tussy mussy? One who romanticizes past days of decorum, or perhaps a Jane Austen fan.

Perhaps you'd like to depart from the usual shape of a bridal bouquet, and you'd like to extend that Biedermeier shape into a completely round bouquet? Thus, a pomander is for you. It's your ornament of floral beauty.

There are no rules about alternative bouquets, and the etiquette of first, second, or destination weddings do not apply. The choice is truly yours to make.

Tussy Mussies

- A tussy mussy bouquet is a small nosegay bouquet inserted into a small metal vase.

- The tussy mussy design allows you to carry a smaller cluster of flowers yet still make an elegant, formal statement.

- Tussy mussies, an import from France, originated in the eighteenth century.

- The tussy mussy cone or holder may be made from silver, gold, pewter, porcelain, or cobalt glass and adorned with beaded designs stamped into silver metals.

Additional Alternative Bouquets

- For a city-chic wedding, flowers might be hot-glued or pinned onto a chic satin purse that you carry down the aisle.

- Fashion a pomander into a circle or hoop using a circle of Styrofoam, and then cover it with pinned-on flowers. Your pomander thus becomes a small eternity sign that dangles from your wrist.

- Pomanders are ideal if you have a biological father and a stepfather—or both parents—walking you down the aisle. Your bouquet hangs on your wrist, and you can take two people's arms.

SINGLES & BUNCHES

PRE-WEDDING CARE

Singles, bunches, rounds, and nosegays may need water sources and cold right before your big moment

Now's a good time to remind you that many floral varieties require a water source to keep them from wilting quickly if their stems are not sitting comfortably in water. Timing is everything with all aspects of weddings, so you want to be sure that your bouquets are stored in the perfect conditions before the wedding so that they're fresh, quenched, and beautiful for the three to five hours of your wedding celebration.

The details of any flower's or bouquet's wellness could very well determine the style of bouquet you want and the types of flowers you will include in it. Perhaps you can easily supply a good water source for notoriously thirsty flowers,

Singles and Bunches Waiting in Water

- Before the wedding, as you dress and pose for photos, your single flowers and ribbon-tied bunches should be placed into vases with an inch or two of water.

- A low-set amount of water will keep handle wraps from getting soaked.

- Don't shock flowers with ultracold water. Make sure the vase water is just on the cool side.

- No need to add flower food to vases that hold your wedding day bouquets. These powdery chemicals shouldn't get on your hands.

Singles and Bunches Waiting in a Cooler

- Take any measure to keep bouquets, boutonnieres, and corsages cool and fresh during transport to the ceremony site and during waiting time.

- An air-conditioned car or van is ideal for transporting flowers, but keep the blooms out of direct sunlight.

- Use an oasis, which is a spongy water source used by florists, to keep the stems immersed in a portable water source during transport and waiting time.

- Oversize thermal coolers are ideal for transporting and storing bouquets.

such as hydrangeas, which should be kept in water until the moment they're attached into a bouquet and the stems given a small water capsule attachment as an all-day water source. Or maybe you'd rather not deal with water issues, so you'll choose hardier flowers that can go a few hours without water.

The heat on your wedding day is also a factor in the types of blooms you'll choose, and how you'll keep your singles, bunches, rounds, or other bouquets cool and comfortable until the moment they're needed.

ZOOM

Your plan for water sources has two steps. For the most delicate flowers, consider a wet wrap around the stem inside the bouquet and then a watery home for the piece, such as a vase, before the wedding and at the reception. Don't mist the leaves and flower heads, however, or they may evaporate and brown.

Singles and Bunches in a Refrigerator

- Arrange for your site manager to clear out a shelf in a walk-in refrigerator for the pre-wedding storage of your bouquets and corsages.

- Be sure that bouquets are well spaced on the refrigerator shelves so that they do not bump into and break each other.

- Do not store your flowers in a mini-size or travel refrigerator, as they are simply not large enough.

- Bouquets fit better in a refrigerator when standing upright in individual, secure vases. This elevation protects a round.

Singles and Bunches Set Out as Décor

- Singles and bunches can do double duty as table centerpieces, so set out vases to hold your and your bridesmaids' bouquets on guest tables.

- Preserve the round shape of a bunch by propping it up in a tall, wide-mouthed vase.

- A grouping of three to five singles or bunches can serve as décor for the cake, gift, or guest book tables.

- Singles, bunches, nosegays, and pomanders can be set on mantles and windowsills as (free) extra décor for the site.

WILDFLOWER BOUQUETS

Choose low-maintenance wildflowers to create lovely, natural informal bouquets

Bouquets of wildflowers add a lovely, natural look to an outdoor wedding in a garden, backyard, rustic setting, state park, or other informal setting that's all about natural beauty. The Mother Nature element of the wildflower bouquet creates a gathering of coordinating blooms and stems, instead of a mass of nearly identical, round, silky roses. The wildflower bouquet has texture and individuality, as well as that often-desired just–picked look.

A wildflower bouquet is not for every bride. Some brides feel the non-rose design looks too "old" or too much like dried flowers, "something my grandmother would have on her kitchen table." And other brides have longtime fond

Flowers in a Wildflower Bouquet

- Wildflower bouquets based on herbs include rosemary, sage, and thyme, which have some scent but not the overpowering aromas from plants like chives.

- Wildflower bouquets based on flowers include lavenders, delphiniums, veronicas, larkspurs, cornflowers, poppies, asters, bellflowers, and forget-me-nots, among others.

- For smaller filler flowers, use lilies of the valley, Queen Anne's lace, columbines, sweet peas, and any small star- or bell-shaped flower.

Size and Proportion

- The average wildflower bouquet is twelve inches long.

- A wildflower bouquet longer than fourteen inches looks too much like a presentation-bouquet and would look like a messy bunch of weeds in your arm.

- Hand tying is the best format for wildflowers.

- A longer, thinner bouquet complements a wider silhouette of gown, while a thicker (eight- to ten-inch) wildflower bouquet looks better with a sleeker silhouette.

memories of picking wildflowers during family vacations to the mountains, scent memories about fields of lavender, or a tradition of creating wildflower bouquets with a younger sister and now with a niece. The inclusion of wildflowers takes on a very personal meaning when you have a history with wildflowers. Including them in your floral design pays homage to a very important part of your background and upbringing.

Or perhaps you just love the natural look, the less-constructed effect, the mix of flower types and soft colors.

Stem Treatments

- Stems should be wrapped either three-quarters of the way or all the way to add strength to the stems and provide a uniform look.

- For more informal bouquets, use a wheat- or pastel-color raffia to either wrap the stems or provide an accent bow.

- For slightly more formal bouquets, use satin ribbon to wrap the stems.

- Lace stem wrap may be used if you have chosen all one type of wildflower, such as lavender.

······· YELLOW ● LIGHT ·······

Many wildflowers don't have long stems, so prepare for a slightly shorter bouquet. Wildflower stems may be more delicate than thick rosebush stems or wide and reedy tulip stems, so if you choose to wrap the length of your stems, choose simpler, solid-color fabric rather than lace, which can look too "busy" with the different textures of wildflowers. For multihued bouquets, solid-color ribbon is a better choice.

Be Careful with DIY Wildflower Plans

- Wildflowers offer the opportunity for you to pick or grow your own flowers, but be careful not to choose poisonous flowers.

- Watch out for wildflower allergies! Test bunches before your big day.

- Bugs, mites, bees, and worms tend to live in wildflower patches, so be sure you don't have a stowaway on your just-picked wedding flowers.

- Acquaint yourself with local poison ivies and oaks so you don't mistakenly pick a troublesome, dangerous plant. Your state parks department Web site should have a list of plants to be wary of.

ALL-WHITE BOUQUETS
Some brides dream of the traditional all-white wedding bouquet

Many brides know the color of their bouquets before they even decide on a shape, style, size, or the flowers that will be included. They have always had the dream of an all-white bridal bouquet, just bursting with silky white flower petals, round white rose heads, tiny dots of lily of the valley, and exotic stars of stephanotis. Just the thought of it takes their breath away.

If you're locked on the idea of the all-white bridal bouquet, you might consider yourself a traditional bride, but you can also be a very modern bride, filling that all-white palette with some unexpected flowers—going beyond the classic bridal flowers of roses and gardenias.

Many brides say they started off with an all-white bouquet as a way to pay homage to mothers and grandmothers

Roses

- The all-white bouquet made only of roses is the number one bouquet style today.

- For the most uniform and traditional look, choose roses that are all the same size.

- Roses may be tightly packed with little else

showing between each rose head placement, or they may be spread out within the round.

- Shades of white vary, with some flowers appearing crisp white and others looking more beige. Specify to your designer that all whites be monochromatic.

Stephanotis

- Stephanotis is a traditional bridal flower, imported and thus a bit more expensive than other traditional wedding blooms.

- The all-stephanotis bouquet is tightly packed with dozens and dozens of tiny star-shaped flowers.

- If money is an object, you're best off using stephanotis as an accent flower, perhaps as a textural accent to a rose bouquet.

- Stephanotis is known as a fragile flower. Oils from your fingers will brown the petals more quickly, so handle them with care.

who also carried all-white bouquets on their wedding days, but then being a modern bride, they took that palette and elevated it to a new level with some quirky or creative style decisions.

It is not true that an all-white bouquet will automatically cost you more money. The price you pay depends on many factors: the types of flowers you select, whether or not they're in-season or imported, the design and style of your bouquet, and the size of your bouquet. True, you may need more white flowers to make a visual impact in any floral piece, but that doesn't always add up to a bigger drain on your wallet.

Another aspect of the all-white bouquet is that it might allow you to use the white version of your birth-month flower, or the birth-month flower of your wedding day, in order to convey a particular message from the language of flowers through your bouquet.

Large and Small Flowers

- Mixing large and small flowers is a top way to build a more lush and impressive bouquet on a budget.

- The differences in flower sizes give the impression of more variety and a greater number of flowers than are actually there.

- Include among your choices calla lilies, dendrobium orchids, roses, ranunculus, peonies, tulips, and then smaller "dot" flowers such as Bells of Ireland, lilies of the valley, and other tiny blooms.

Pros and Cons of All-White Bouquets

- It's a very traditional look.
- White flowers work in every season and with every formality.
- A range of white flowers allows you to get creative and still have a bouquet that looks bridal.
- A wide variety of flowers come in white.
- There often is not enough contrast between the white of your wedding gown and the white of your bouquet flowers. The blooms don't show up dramatically in front-angle photos.
- Smaller white flowers such as lilies of the valley tend to wilt a few hours into the day.

49

SOFT, PASTEL BOUQUETS

Add a gentle blush hue to your bridal bouquet for just a touch of color

Adding pastels to a bridal bouquet, or building a bridal bouquet out of all pastels, allows you to bring color and personality into the flowers you'll carry on your wedding day. As trends continue to evolve, different shades of pastels are "in" during different seasons, often following the fashion trends set by the apparel industry. When sage green gowns are the

new hot color, pastel bouquets serve as accessories by bringing that hot color to the forefront.

Pastel bouquets are also a top way for a bride to coordinate her look with her bridesmaids' dresses and also with the floral décor she'll use throughout her wedding site. Always with a mind toward what will look best in styled photographs, a

Pinks

- Pink bouquets range from barely there blush pinks to deeper pinks with slightly darker pink edges.

- You can have a bouquet of monochromatic pinks or blend different hues.

- The top choices in pink bridal bouquets are

roses, tulips, pink calla lilies, ranunculus, mums, impatiens, violets, clematis, and other big, round pink blooms.

- Pink accent flowers include lisianthus, larkspur, dogwoods, geraniums, and small variety pink violets.

Corals

- Coral-color flowers are best suited for spring and summer weddings because coral is one of the most popular shades for beach or destination weddings.

- Check out the new varieties of roses in coral- to persimmon-color hues, as well as new varieties of

tulips, begonias, peonies, and carnations to fill in centerpieces with a soft coral hue.

- Check out the coral to orange hues in the blossoms of the flower varieties nertera and erythrina.

bride wants color contrast in her floral pieces that will allow them to fit into the surroundings of her dream wedding day. An all-white bouquet denotes the absence of color, while a blush pastel bouquet provides a signature look.

Consider the bride whose favorite color is lavender. She may dress in lavender, own a favorite purple sweater, wear purple earrings, and now gets to carry her signature hue on her wedding day.

Lavenders

- Lavender-color bouquets are very popular for outdoor weddings, both formal and informal, but are also lovely for indoor weddings.

- When you mix light and darker lavenders together, you get the impression of a much fuller bouquet.

- The most popular light purple flowers are tulips, crocuses, asters, candytufts, geraniums, pansies, sweet peas, primulas, morning glories, lilacs, and lavenders.

- Ask about the unique imported hibiscus "Blue Bird," which adds an exotic touch to pastel bouquets.

Mixes

- Blend an array of pastel flowers to create a bouquet that encompasses two to four different shades from your wedding palette.

- A popular mix is pinks, corals, oranges, and yellows for a pastel springtime or summertime mix.

- In the lavender family, mix lilacs with light blues and yellows.

- Combine one shade of pastel with whites for a bridal bouquet that is both traditional and styled with a blue color.

51

BRIGHT, VIBRANT BOUQUETS

Create a burst of color with these eye-catching jewel-toned bouquets

A bright bouquet creates a dramatic effect when you appear for the ceremony and everyone sees you for the first time. It also adds an element of "wow" to your photographs. Imagine the beauty of an elegant black-and-white wedding portrait, with only your bouquet in full, glorious color. As the experts say, the color pops, and professional photographers love to get creative in spotlighting the bride's symbolic bouquet. The color contrast between a pristine white wedding gown and a fiery orange or lipstick red bouquet turns photos into art.

The hue you choose depends on your personality—the bride who chooses bright colors loves to make a statement and wants to depart from bridal white or baby pink roses to be

Reds

- Bright red bouquets range in color from lipstick red to deep burgundies, for a look that floral designers term juicy.

- If you would like to dot your bright bouquet with a slight contrasting color, lime green pops reds to a much greater degree than any other color.

- The most popular flowers to choose from include roses, calla lilies, Gerber daisies, ranunculus, and berries.

- An all-red bouquet conveys passion for your partner.

Oranges

- Bright orange bouquets range in color from tangerine to deep persimmon.

- To make an orange bouquet pop, the top complementary tone is gold.

- The most popular flowers to choose from include roses, ranunculus, tulips, freesia, burnt orange berries, zinnias, and Gerber daisies.

- Oranges work best in spring's brighter shades, as well as in autumn's persimmon or pumpkin tones.

- An orange bouquet photographs beautifully against a dazzling sunset.

modern and original—as well as the season and location of your wedding. Bright oranges, for instance, are ideal for both spring and autumn, while greens may work for any season. Jewel-toned, bright bouquets appear at outdoor, daytime weddings, at beach weddings, and in lavishly decorated ballrooms as a testament to this color palette's popularity in any locale. Worried about a bright bouquet being "too much" as the color indicator for the entire wedding setting? You don't have to have matching, bright, jewel-toned centerpieces, altar and pew décor, and bridesmaids' bouquets. Those can be softened with a mix of brights in complementary shades, pastels, and whites, while yours is the only bouquet to pop with monochromatic or mixed bright color. You'll get the best of both worlds.

Blues

- Bright blue bouquets range in color from amethyst to sapphire.

- Blue-toned flowers are a bit more limited in variety than other brights, so professional florists expand the hue to include purple-toned flowers in the blue family.

- The most popular flowers to choose from include dark blue hybrid delphiniums, monkshoods, larkspurs, and lisianthus.

- Blue is the top color choice for brides marrying by an ocean, coordinating their blooms to the sea.

Greens

- Bright green bouquets range in color from chartreuse to lime green.

- Avoid the St. Patrick's Day look by choosing brighter, deeper greens instead of pale greens.

- Bright green bouquets are a top choice for garden and eco-friendly "green" weddings.

- The top flowers include Bells of Ireland, viburnums, hydrangeas, ladies mantles, spidermums, and callas.

SINGLE-COLOR SENSATIONS

Choosing unity of color with all one shade in your bridal bouquet

A monochromatic flower depends on the uniformity of the blooms in the piece, and special care needs to be taken—especially with round bouquets—to evenly space the flowers when the bouquet is packed with roses, for instance. With a singular color scheme, there's no room for error, and balance is achieved with the perfect choices in matching hues, flower size, and spacing.

Texture is achieved with greenery and filler, and some flowers with ruffled edges may provide all the accent needed in a bouquet of this design.

Monochromatic bouquets are ideal for both formal and informal weddings, both indoor and outdoor, and the personalization comes in the color chosen for this floral spotlight.

Many different flowers are ideal for the monochromatic

Monochromatic White Bouquets

- For a small bouquet, two dozen white flowers are ideal. In a smaller-size bouquet, a single type of flower, such as roses, is ideal.

- For a medium-size bouquet, choose three dozen white flowers.

- A medium to large mono-

chromatic bouquet has room for multiple varieties of flowers such as roses, callas, lilies, gardenias, and stephanotis.

- Add a touch of color to an all-white bouquet with a pastel or bright ribbon. This adds a pretty color contrast in person and in photos.

Monochromatic Pink Bouquets

- For a formal bouquet, choose several dozen pink roses in a tightly clustered gathering of identical blooms.

- For an informal bouquet, consider a hand-wrapped bunch of pink tulips or an array of pink tulips and wildflowers.

- Another informal monochromatic bouquet is one made with a dozen hot pink Gerber daisies or bright pink zinnias.

- Even if shades of pink range from pale to brighter, this still counts as a monochromatic bouquet.

bouquet, including roses, ranunculus, gardenias, and stephanotis on the formal end, and Gerber daisies, tulips, hydrangeas, and peonies on the lighter, less-formal end.

Single-color bouquets may be white, pastel, or bright. Red and pink are the top choices after classic bridal white, and bright orange and cranberry top the list for fall weddings. In spring, lavender and light orange are the front-runners. For destination or beach weddings, bright corals lead the way.

Monochromatic bouquets often need a greater number of flowers, as the uniformity of hue doesn't give the depth and illusion of lushness afforded by a bouquet of multicolored blooms. So expect to order up to two dozen more flowers to pack your bouquet well.

The colors don't have to match exactly. Mixing shades that are close, such as red and cranberry, still creates a monochromatic look.

Monochromatic Red Bouquets

- With vivid red shades, just a dozen blooms is sufficient to make a visual impact.

- Choose your shade of red based on the season. Brights are perfect for summer, and crimsons or burgundies are perfect for fall and winter.

- Your skin tone determines the tone of red that works for you. Paler brides are complemented by lipstick red, and darker or olive-skinned brides carry cranberry red best.

- Add dimension with smaller and larger red flowers.

Monochromatic Purple Bouquets

- Pale lilac bouquets are ideal for spring and summer.

- Darker jewel-toned purple bouquets come to us from the hot colors of fashion runways. So when *Vogue* says purple is in, it's also in for weddings.

- Paler lilac bouquets benefit from the placement of a contrast color, such as tiny darker purple flowers or tiny white flowers.

- In larger monochromatic purple bouquets, add dimension with subtle color contrasts of ruffled-edge flowers for texture, petals with a thin petal edge hue.

COLOR-MIXED BOUQUETS
Choose the perfect blend of light and dark for modern, romantic bouquets

For some brides, one color is not enough. Nor is one color family. Why limit yourself to pink, when there are so many glorious colors of the season that mix together so well?

If you were torn over your selection of the one color for the bridesmaids' dresses—not able to choose between reds, pinks, oranges, and yellows—you can bring in all of your favorite colors in your bridal bouquet. No cuts necessary!

The key is to choose the right mix of colors for a bouquet that looks formal and professional. After all, you don't want it to look like a mass of mix-and-match primary colors, similar to those bouquets sold at gas stations on the Fourth of July.

White and Pastel

- A primarily white bouquet can be "punched up" with the addition of a dozen pastel flowers.

- White and pink are the traditional and most popular bridal-mix flowers.

- White and lavender provide the perfect bridal bouquet

accents to all-lavender bridesmaids' bouquets, while white and sage green allow you to coordinate with your bridesmaids' all-sage bouquets.

- Mix white with a variety of pastel colors for a one-to-three ratio of whites to pastels.

White and Brights

- Avoid equal numbers of white and bright flowers, or the bouquet will look too contrasted.

- Keep the ratio at one to three, with either one-third whites to two-thirds brights, or vice versa.

- For a dramatic mix, choose

white flowers and up to three different bright flowers, such as reds, oranges, and hot pinks.

- Fill your bouquet with brights and use the white flowers as pinpoint accents, either as the color theme for just your bouquet or for all the ladies' bouquets.

As a rule, primary colors of red, yellow, and blue should work alone, with their own complementary colors bringing out their beauty.

You'll find several different "classes" of color-mixed bouquets, from a white and pastel pairing to a husbandry of brights and deeper jewel tones. The palette is up to you to design.

Go to your local home-improvement store and head right for the paint department. Grab a bunch of paint color strips in your chosen shades of colors and hold them against each other so you can see how well that hunter green works with persimmon orange, or the white with the pale blue or the aqua with chocolate brown. When you find the color mixes you love, you can use these shades to guide your shopping spree or inform your floral designer or wholesale assistant.

Pastels work in any season, with any formality, and in any setting and have become a top choice for brides who want a traditional bridal look without everything being pure white.

Pastel and Brights

- Leave the white to your wedding dress and fill your bouquet with a mix of pastel tones and brights in the same color family.

- Pastels and brights allow you to capture a wide range of hues in the same color family, such as pinks and oranges.

- For a less-formal mix, blend pastel and bright tulips or Gerber daisies, with wildflowers as filler.

- For a beach or destination wedding, copy the colors of the ocean—baby blues, aquas, and more vivid blues with sand-color tans or light corals.

Brights and Deeper Colors

- For fall or winter weddings, mix bright reds with deeper burgundy or cranberry colors; add chocolate cosmos for a richer bouquet.

- Bright purple irises will pop against deeper purple geraniums, asters, and tulips.

- Brights electrify a deeper-colored bouquet, whereas pastels soften the arrangement.

- Bright yellows mixed with gold-toned flowers and fillers lend an air of opulence to an evening wedding, or a sense of brightness to a daytime wedding.

57

GREENERY & FILLER

It's what's all around the flowers that can make a bouquet extra lovely

In this age of "green" weddings, you may want to fill or simply accent your bouquet with a unique, eye-catching collection of greenery and filler. Baby's breath may be too pedestrian for you, and lily of the valley appears in over 90 percent of bridal bouquets these days. Since interior designers now decorate homes with ferns and frond plants both live and in the form of artwork,

it's no wonder the all-green look has come to bridal design.

Think outside the box with a veritable world of gorgeous greens and fabulous fillers that can make even the most modest flowers look amazing by virtue of being surrounded by unexpected leaf textures, glossy ferns, and tiny filler flowers in unexpected shapes.

Ferns

- The most common bouquet ferns are leatherleaf and maidenhair, which you'll recognize from the bouquets you see in floral shops and supermarket garden centers.

- For a softer, wispier look, try silk fern.

- Also called ladder fern, *Nephrolepis* is a unique fern to build into a bouquet.

- For softer, larger quarter-size leaves, use roundleaf fern or button fern as a visual effect in your bouquet or centerpieces.

Grasses

- Cut long lengths of ornamental grasses to add to your bouquet as a green, natural replacement for trailing ribbons.

- Ornamental grasses provide movement to your bouquet as you walk and can provide a waterfall effect without the heft and texture of a cascade bouquet.

- Some of the most unique grasses that give a cascading effect to a bouquet are Bermuda grass, wild grass, flax grass, pampas, tropical sedum, hanging grass vine, and kiwi fruit grass.

Today's greens come in feathery textures, curled leaves, and veined striping for added effect. Floral designers say they love to experiment with new varieties of locally grown and imported greenery, and they often visit floral shows and wholesalers to explore the new arrivals. You too can seek out these resources.

The benefit of greenery and filler is that they most often are very inexpensive, which allows you to include more expensive flowers (such as gardenias and orchids) in your bouquet and still save up to 40 percent on each bouquet. Greenery might be available for just a few dollars a bunch, and it's easy to incorporate into DIY projects as well. Plus, if you're not an experienced DIYer, you'll have plenty of greenery available to you on the cheap should you need to scrap a bouquet and start over.

Beyond the lush green color, wispy leaves and grasses can give a waterfall effect to your bouquet without the shaping of a cascade. Just half a dozen fronds of long fern or ivy, or the movement of decorative grass lengths, and you have created a signature bouquet.

Unique Leaves

- Some popular flowers, such as birds of paradise, feature such gorgeous leaves that they're often cut from the flower stems and used as filler.

- Check out the following leaf varieties: bird of paradise leaves, calla lily leaves, magnolia leaves, orchid leaves, and grape leaves (with a marbled or pink center).

- For an autumn wedding blend colorful maple and oak tree leaves into your bouquet.

- For summer weddings, palm leaves provide a fun tropical look for your bouquet base.

Filler Flowers

- Besides lilies of the valley, consider other small flowers with unique shapes.

- Astilbe has a feathery appearance and comes in white, light pink, bright pink, red, yellow, and orange, all of which work well for summer and fall weddings.

- Allium looks like a puffball and adds a playful dimension to a bouquet, especially for winter weddings when you want a snowball effect.

- Chestnut pods are also like puffballs and add fun and round dimension to taller, trumpet-shaped flowers.

TRADITIONAL BOUQUETS

Choose bouquets for your maid of honor and bridesmaids that are almost as pretty as yours

When choosing your bridesmaids' bouquets, you have a choice: They can look exactly like yours, or you can design a little something different for them to carry. In this section you'll explore the traditional choice of having your bridesmaids' bouquets look similar to yours as a way to tie your wedding look together, remain bridal in the effect, and create a unified look in person and in pictures.

Except in rare occasions when a bride wants her bridesmaids to have exactly the same style and size bouquet as her own, the overwhelming trend is to go a little bit smaller in size yet still include the exact same flowers as those in her bouquet.

Traditional Romantic Bouquets

- Traditional, romantic bouquets include soft-petal flowers such as roses, calla lilies, gardenias, and other classic bridal flowers.

- A softer bouquet is designed with plenty of curl to floral petals, such as with callas and lilies.

- To add romance to a traditional bouquet, include flowers with ruffled edges, such as peonies.

- The most common traditional bouquets for bridesmaids are rounds and hand-tied clusters just a little bit smaller than the bride's bouquet.

Traditional Dramatic Bouquets

- A dramatic bridesmaid bouquet almost always includes a bright burst of color.

- The most common bright colors for dramatic bridesmaid bouquets are red, orange, vivid pink, and purple.

- Size does not equal drama, so even a smaller bouquet (four to six inches across) can pack a punch when the colors pop.

- If your bouquet is all pastel, add a few brightly colored blooms to your bridesmaids' bouquets to add that burst of energy.

Another way to set apart your bridesmaids' bouquets is to choose one of the flowers from your bouquet, such as roses, and build the bridesmaids' bouquet with only that type of bloom, while yours includes an array of different, lovely blooms as well.

You could achieve this by simply designing identical rose, calla lily, and gardenia bouquets for you and your bridesmaids, but adding lilies of the valley to yours. Just a small detail like this can set yours apart without making the bouquets look too different.

YELLOW LIGHT

A top trend is for the bride to carry a colored bouquet in contrast with her white gown, while her bridesmaids carry white bouquets in contrast with their colored gowns. There's no rule that says the bride is the only one who can carry a white bouquet. Bridesmaids also consider the white bouquet to be a sign of luck, the equivalent of catching the bride's bouquet as the next to marry.

Traditional Artsy Bouquets

- If your wedding style is partly romantic and classic, but you still want an artsy pop to your bridesmaids' bouquets, add crystal or gemstone push-ins to blooms.

- Decorate with feathers, which give a soft yet artistic texture to the bridesmaid bouquet when used in smaller quantities (fewer than ten feathers per bouquet).

- Bright, colorful ribbon within the bouquet or trailing from the handle gives an artsy effect.

Traditional Copycat Bouquets

- The copycat bouquet is identical to the bride's bouquet in size, shape, and color.

- Many brides find that since their dresses differ, especially when bridesmaids choose their own styles of gowns, the unified look can be achieved through flowers.

- If you're carrying a smaller, hand-tied bouquet, it's often easier and less expensive if your bridesmaids' bouquets are identical.

- A copycat bouquet may still include a slightly softer shade of color from the brighter one in your own bouquet.

CASCADE BOUQUETS

Give your bridesmaids a waterfall of floral beauty for their bouquets

The flowing look of a cascade bouquet is a top choice for outdoor weddings, as it adds another dimension of greenery and the same flowing direction as many trees and flowering plants found in nature. For bridesmaids, this bouquet style can tie them into the scenery, and it can also be a gorgeous way to dress up simpler, unadorned bridesmaid dresses. With the absence of a lot of bodice beadwork or the sleek

silhouette of a silky A-line dress, a cascade gives shape and design to the front of the dress.

For the most part, bridesmaids' cascade bouquets are smaller in size, reaching perhaps just a foot in length, and usually have fewer flowers than the bride's bouquet. They might require up to two dozen flowers rather than the three dozen found in the bride's collection. The size, of course,

Small Cascade Bouquet

- A small cascade bouquet for a bridesmaid can be half the size of the bride's cascade bouquet and still look perfect.

- A small cascade might have six to twelve small to medium-size flowers, or twelve to sixteen small flowers.

- A small cascade can feature flowers at the top in an arch shape and then greenery reaching downward.

- A small cascade looks lovely as mostly greenery, with tiny white flowers added to the cascade.

Medium Cascade Bouquet

- A medium cascade bouquet for a bridesmaid can be three to six inches smaller than the bride's.

- A medium cascade might have twelve to eighteen flowers.

- This bouquet looks best with flowers clustered at the top and smaller flowers placed evenly in the bottom trail of the cascade.

- A medium cascade offers the opportunity for not just one trailing length, but two made from greenery and spots of flowers.

depends on the bridesmaids' heights and body shapes, as a floral piece needs to accent the woman's appearance, not overshadow nor overwhelm her.

When a bride carries a cascade in keeping with the shape that works best with her figure, it's a mistake to give the same size bouquet to all the bridesmaids in an effort to have a matching set. This is the number one mistake made by brides who favor cascades: They hide their bridesmaids because they believe the bouquets need to match. Not so. Smaller is often better, and you can add an extra few inches to a taller bridesmaid's bouquet to balance out her frame.

And don't forget that bridesmaids' cascade bouquets can consist of all greenery, such as ivy, fern, and grasses, while only yours contains flowers in addition to the same mix of greenery.

Cascades with a Twist

- For informal weddings, bridesmaids' cascades might be placed with bright Gerber daisy heads, while the bride's bouquet is bridal white.

- For informal or outdoor weddings, cascades can be filled with wildflowers.

- A cascade can be created from 100 percent Queen Anne's lace, for an ultraromantic and ultrainexpensive look.

- A cascade can be created from ivy, with tiny white or colored flowers, while the bride's bouquet has just touches of ivy throughout.

Cascades and Body Type

- Taller bridesmaids benefit from longer cascades that reach to the top of the thigh.

- Shorter bridesmaids benefit from shorter cascades that reach to the top of the thigh.

- Heavier bridesmaids benefit from wider, rounder cascade tops with longer trails at the bottom.

- Thin bridesmaids look lovely when their cascades match the width of heavier bridesmaids, as you don't want to call attention to the differing body shapes by having bouquets of varying widths.

SINGLE-STEM & BUNCH BOUQUETS

Design a smaller, simpler style of bouquets for your bridesmaids to carry

Giving bridesmaids single-stem flowers or less-formal bunches is a top budget-saving strategy. At the same time, it provides a lovely, delicate look. Because fewer blooms are needed, supply costs go way down and labor efforts are also reduced. This can turn into a savings of 60 to 80 percent on your bridesmaid bouquet expenses!

Some brides decide that they will be the only one to carry a full bouquet, as a way to stand out in person and in pictures. They coordinate their bridesmaids' single or bunch flowers by choosing one to three of the flower types included in their own bouquet, which ties together the look of their entire group.

Single-Stem Roses

- A single-stem rose is the number one choice for the simple elegance bouquet.

- The maid or matron of honor might be given two or three single-stem roses, while the rest of the brides-maids carry one apiece.

- For a coordinated look, match the color of the ribbon tie to the color of the rose, such as white satin for a white rose.

- Single-stem roses look best when you wrap them to include their green leaves as color contrast.

Single-Stem Calla Lilies

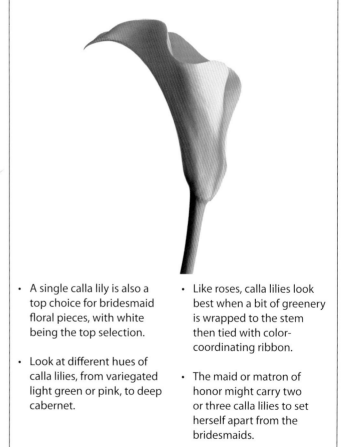

- A single calla lily is also a top choice for bridesmaid floral pieces, with white being the top selection.

- Look at different hues of calla lilies, from variegated light green or pink, to deep cabernet.

- Like roses, calla lilies look best when a bit of greenery is wrapped to the stem then tied with color-coordinating ribbon.

- The maid or matron of honor might carry two or three calla lilies to set herself apart from the bridesmaids.

When it comes to formality, a single-stem bouquet can be every bit as formal as a round bouquet when you choose a "formal" flower such as a rose or graceful calla lily and tie it with a thick satin bow. Single-stem bouquets work for both formal and informal weddings, as do hand-tied bunches. It's all about the composition you choose for these elegant but simple flower pieces.

Single-stem flowers look best with longer stems, no less than six inches, with ribbon ties at the midsection. It is this ribbon accent that can bring gorgeous effect to the bouquet.

········· RED ● LIGHT ·········

As with all single-stem bouquets or groupings of less than six flowers, you run the risk of having a nervous bridesmaid's quivering hand shake the bouquet. Advise your ladies to hold the single or bunch against the front of the body to give it some grounding and support. The upright carrying method also looks more uniform than the arm's natural propensity to hold the flower pointing outward.

Single-Stem Daisies

- Daisies embody a less formal, playful look, and are perfect for outdoor or afternoon weddings.

- Since it's just one daisy in the hand, choose a big, bloomed Gerber daisy in a bright color such as pink, red, orange, or yellow.

- White or light yellow daisies look best in bunches, not as a single-stem bouquet.

- Match the ribbon tie to the color of the daisy, and add a more playful look by wrapping the stem in a wide spiral the green of the stem length.

Bunch Bouquets

- A hand-tied cluster of flowers creates a slightly larger look for your bridesmaid to carry, yet still remains smaller in size and budget than a full bouquet.

- Bunches may be created with formal flowers or informal flowers such as wildflowers.

- Consider giving each bridesmaid a bunch that contains different flowers, such as the roses, callas, and day lilies that comprise your own bouquet.

- Coordinate the ribbon wrap to the color of one flower in the bunch.

COLOR SCHEMES
Choose the best color palette for your bridesmaids' beautiful bouquets

If you've chosen your bridesmaids' dresses, you already have the color from which to base your floral decisions. If you don't have the dresses chosen yet, then you should wait until you do decide on a color before you order any bridesmaid bouquets. The hues need to coordinate, not clash, since the bouquet really is an accessory to your bridesmaids' outfits.

You have several options when it comes to the color or colors of the bridesmaids' bouquets, and one of the most important factors to consider is the season of your wedding. Certain colors, such as pink and yellow, work better in spring and summer, and certain colors, such as cranberry and brighter purples, are perfect for fall and winter. The season of

Pastels

- Pastels work with both light-and dark-colored bridesmaids' dresses.

- When your bridesmaids' dresses are a dark color, the most popular flower color choice is a lighter shade of that same color.

- Pastels look best in color

mixes, rather than in monochromatic clusters.

- Punch up pastel bouquets with a few darker flowers in darker shades, or pastel flowers with darker petal edges.

- Pink and orange pastels are most popular.

Brights

- Bright-color bouquets work best with pastel-color bridesmaids' dresses, such as a light pink dress with a vibrant pink bouquet.

- The most popular bright bouquet colors for bridesmaids are red and orange.

- In fall and winter, brights

take on more jewel tones, such as deeper purples, navy blues, or emerald greens.

- Many brides choose the color of their bright birthstones as the foundation color for their bridesmaids' dresses and bouquets.

your wedding is going to dictate your overall wedding floral design, so the bridesmaids' bouquets will need to coordinate with the overall theme. Many brides choose the colors of the bridesmaids' bouquets first and then choose the dress design and hue.

Your bridesmaids' bouquets don't have to match the color of the dress exactly. A complementary color makes the bouquet stand out, and a vivid color will really make it pop in person and in photos.

Mixes

- Rather than choose one color to complement your bridesmaids' dresses, you get to choose five or six colors for a lush bouquet.

- Mix light and darker shades to give a bouquet more dimension.

- A common cost-cutting tac-tic is to include four or five pricier flowers and then fill in the rest of the bouquet with filler such as stock or larkspur for inexpensive color "dotting."

- When mixing vibrant colors such as red, be sure to add several different lighter shades for dimension.

Matching Bouquets to Dress Colors

- For a pink dress, consider light to darker pinks, or light to darker greens. Avoid peach tones.

- For a red dress, consider pinks and reds.

- For a lavender dress, consider purples, pinks, blues, light greens, and yellows.

- For a black dress, consider richer reds, deeper purples, and jewel-toned greens as well as all white.

- For a coral dress, consider deeper corals, whites, and yellows. Avoid peach and pink. You also can bring in an ocean theme of blue.

BOUQUETS SIMILAR TO YOURS
You can build unity in your bridesmaids' bouquets by coordinating their style with yours

Perhaps you want all of the bouquets to match. You figure you'll be set apart by the fact that you're wearing a wedding gown and that it would unify the look of your group if you all carried matching or similar bouquets. Some brides don't need or want an all-white bouquet for themselves and colorful bouquets for their bridesmaids—they feel it's just too pedestrian.

Brides who choose identical bridesmaids bouquets to their own style say, "We are a group that's so close, we should carry equally gorgeous bouquets," and "It may be my day, but I belong to this group of equals, so it will be identical flowers in our bouquets." Others simply love the look of all-matching bouquets they've seen in photos.. By contrast, they think the

Size

- Choose an identical style, but design it as two thirds the size of your bouquet.

- The bridesmaids' bouquets might match the design of your bouquet but be a much smaller posy bouquet.

- Brides who carry a dozen

single-stem flowers as a bouquet can give their bridesmaids one to three identical flowers to carry.

- In cascades, your bouquet might be longer and more dramatic, while your bridesmaids' bouquet might be a small-scale arch or one-third-size cascade.

Flower Choice

- Choose a similar shape of flower to make your bridesmaids' bouquets like yours, such as tight ranunculus to coordinate with your roses.

- If your bouquet has a large collection of calla lilies, choose mid- to large-size single-stem callas for your bridesmaids.

- Build your bridesmaids' bouquets from one variety of flower in your bouquet.

- To keep your budget in mind, use pricier, more exotic flowers such as gardenias in your bouquet and more inexpensive flowers such as peonies in your bridesmaids' bouquets.

one white bouquet surrounded by little pink bouquets looks too cliché. Identical bouquets also make it easier for DIY bouquet making, because you don't have to keep track of which flowers to set aside for your bouquet or which bouquet needs to be made larger than the others. When you're creating one bouquet style and size, the task may go much faster and easier. Brides who choose similar bouquets prefer a slight bit of difference between themselves and their bridesmaids (even with the wedding gown!), but they too dream about a more uniform look.

ZOOM

Your maid of honor can carry a bouquet identical to yours, just a bit smaller so that yours is still evident as The Bride's Bouquet and hers is slightly different from the other bridesmaids' bouquets.

Colors

- If your bouquet is all white, allow your bridesmaids to carry colored bouquets in pastels or brights, or a mix of colors and white.

- If your bouquet is pastels, have your bridesmaids carry all-white bouquets for a unique twist.

- If your bouquet contains a mix of pastels and brights, build your bridesmaids' bouquets out of all pastels.

- If your bouquet is all brights, mix one shade of pastels into your bridesmaids' matching bouquets.

Accents

- Eliminate the trailing ribbons found in your bouquet so that the bridesmaids' bouquets are less adorned.

- Add pearl stickpins to give your bridesmaids' bouquets a matte effect to pair with the crystal stickpins in your bouquet.

- If you'll have crystals pushed into your flower heads, eliminate that accent for your bridesmaids' bouquets.

- Consider greenery as an accent; give your bridesmaids' bouquets more greenery than flowers for a lush, natural, organic look.

MAID/MATRON OF HONOR BOUQUETS

Honor your most special bridal attendant with a pretty bouquet of her own

Your maid or matron of honor is the VIP of your bridal party, and after all she will do to help you prepare for the wedding, after throwing you a shower, and after organizing the bridesmaids' dress order—just being your support system—you may want to set her apart from the bridesmaids with a little something special in her bouquet design.

Most brides design slightly larger, more lush bouquets for their maids and matrons of honor, or they create a focal point through their choices of flowers. Some brides design a bouquet that's nearly identical to their own and then reduce the size or content of the bridesmaids' bouquets as a way to elevate the maid or matron of honor's piece.

Some brides have their maids or matrons of honor carry bouquets in a different color than the rest of the bridesmaids

Coordinating with Yours

- Some brides have more than one maid or matron of honor, resulting in two or three specialty bouquets.

- If you have two maids of honor and one bridesmaid, make all of their bouquets of equal size and composition for a unified look.

- A maid or matron of honor's bouquet can match your bouquet with an accent of different-colored ribbon on the handle or as trails.

- The most common scenario is designing a maid of honor bouquet that's slightly smaller than your bouquet.

Monochromatic vs. Mixed

- The decision on color for a maid or matron of honor's bouquet is purely a matter of personal style.

- A monochromatic bouquet may be the perfect accent when bridesmaids have two-color or mixed bouquets.

- A maid or matron of honor may carry a monochromatic bouquet, while the rest of the bridesmaids carry mixed bouquets.

- Set the maid or matron of honor apart with three or four colors in her bouquet, while bridesmaids only have one or two colors.

as a way to set them apart or as a color complement to the different dress style or color they will wear.

Regardless of your design choices, you can flex your creative muscles and perhaps use some floral elements you thought about using in your own bouquet. Or, you can get a few exotic and expensive flowers for your maid or matron of honor, while your bridesmaids' bouquets are made of more moderate yet pretty blooms.

Size

- The maid or matron of honor's bouquet might be two thirds the size of your bouquet.

- For a dramatic size difference, choose a smaller posy style for the maid of honor, as well as for the bridesmaids, while your bouquet is grand and lush.

- If your bouquet will be small, honor attendants' bouquets need to be even smaller.

- If bridesmaids will carry single-stem bouquets, the maid or matron of honor can carry either three blooms or a bunch of six to nine.

Accents

- Different-colored flowers— such as bright orange lilies—can be the accent in the honor attendant's bouquet, while the bridesmaids carry paler orange bouquets.

- If crystal or pearl stick-ins will accent your bouquet, add half a dozen of the same stick-in design to your honor attendant's bouquet.

- Your honor attendant can be the only one carrying a bouquet with a stick-in accent.

- For an informal wedding, consider adding a tiny silk butterfly stick-in.

TOSSING BOUQUETS
Enacting the bridal tradition of tossing the wedding bouquet to the ladies

Many traditional brides still uphold the ritual of tossing a bouquet to a group of single ladies. The woman who catches it is said to be the next to marry. Modern interpretations of this age-old ritual say that the woman who catches the bouquet will have good luck all year or that the woman who catches it will soon meet the man of her dreams.

Over time, this ritual took on an aggressive element, with some women practically knocking other women over (fueled by alcohol in some cases) to catch the good-luck bouquet. And that's why the tradition has fallen out of favor; brides don't want their female guests injured! Nor do they want any expenses when a chandelier or table has to be replaced due

Like Yours, but Smaller

- If you don't want to throw your actual bouquet—because you want it preserved— design a smaller version of your bouquet design as a separate bouquet for tossing.

- This tossing bouquet duplicate might be one half to one third the size of your bouquet.

- Design a posy version of your round bouquet at a fraction of the size and price.

- Do not throw a silk bouquet if your bouquet is made of real flowers; guests frown on "fakes."

A Totally New Design

- If you couldn't decide between types of flowers for your own bouquet, this separate piece is the place to use your second-choice flowers.

- If you're carrying a cascade bouquet, you can design a small round bouquet for easier tossing and catching.

- If you're carrying a single-stem bouquet, you can design and toss a posy or round bouquet.

- Use the language of flowers to add more meaning to this bouquet, such as blooms symbolizing luck.

to bouquet-toss mishaps. Here you'll learn all about designing the tossing bouquet, if you do wish to include the bouquet toss in your wedding. You'll also find some alternative bouquet-presentation rituals that take the danger out of what should be a beautiful and sentimental custom.

The tossing bouquet does not have to match your bouquet exactly, and as such can become a great way to use any creative design ideas you may have originally wanted for your bridesmaids' bouquets.

The tradition of the bouquet toss is believed to have originated in fourteenth-century France, when wedding guests believed it to be good luck to "take" a piece of the bride's wedding gown. When guests got too aggressive, brides began tossing the bouquet to the crowd as a means of distraction, giving them the luck token they desired.

Bouquets Not to Be Tossed

- Some bouquets are not designed for tossing.

- Bouquets that should not be tossed incude oversize round bouquets , medium to large cascades with large trailing leaves and stems, single-stem and triple-stem flowers, wildflower bunches with a thin ribbon tie at the stem, and bouquets with rougher filler, including flowering branches.

- If you love these designs, choose to present this bouquet to a special friend or relative instead of tossing it.

Safely Tossing a Bouquet

- Larger bouquets can injure the crowd you're throwing them to, so make sure the tossing bouquet is on the smaller side.

- Any stick-ins in the bouquet can become dislodged midflight and pierce the catcher or an onlooker, so be sure to design the tossing bouquet to exclude them.

- Trailing leaves or stems can whip the recipient.

- Always avoid the section of the dance floor where a chandelier or other ceiling décor element is situated so that the bouquet doesn't send crystal pieces crashing to the ground or knock down the whole lighting fixture.

NOSEGAY TOSSING BOUQUETS
A smaller nosegay tossing bouquet has special form and meaning

A small round bouquet is often the top choice for a tossing bouquet, regardless of which bouquet design the bride carries during her ceremony. Its small size and densely packed flowers give this "floral missile" a sturdy construction to survive both the throwing and the catching.

Be sure to choose a lightweight design with fewer flowers, perhaps just a dozen small blooms, and avoid adding a weighty water source within the middle of the nosegay. Since this tossing bouquet will be stored away in cool comfort, you won't need the kind of water source required by a bouquet that's out in the elements.

You can design this nosegay with your choice of flowers and colors, going all white or matching the color theme of your wedding. You can also infuse this bouquet with

White Nosegay Bouquets

- A small nosegay bouquet can contain a dozen larger flowers or two dozen smaller white flowers.

- An all-white color palette keeps the symbolism of purity and innocence in the age-old tradition of the bouquet toss.

- Use a white nosegay if you designed a colorful bouquet of your own, bringing the classic bridal look into your celebration in this piece.

- If you're on a budget, use up to six white flowers and fill the rest of the nosegay with filler and greenery.

Coordinating Colors

- Choose one to three colors from your bouquet as the color palette for your tossing bouquet.

- Choose the same colors of flowers from your bridesmaids' bouquets, in effect naming the woman who catches it an honorary bridesmaid.

- Choose the same flower color as your invitation design as a way to tie-in the color scheme of your wedding.

- If you are wearing a white gown, be sure your tossing bouquet isn't ivory.

meaningful, symbolic flowers according to the language of flowers (see Chapter 1), announcing to your guests the exact meanings contained within the bouquet, such as love, luck, and everlasting friendship. It's become a trend for the MC to announce the bouquet ritual, and he or she might share your prepared statement about what the bouquet represents.

When you toss this smaller, lighter bouquet to your awaiting single-lady guests, you can do so with more confidence that the toss will be graceful on your part and the reception safe from harm.

Bright Bouquets

- A bright tossing bouquet provides a burst of color against a white gown.

- Choose one to three bright colors from your bouquet design to create a coordinated tossing bouquet.

- The most popular bright color for a nosegay bou-

quet is pink, the color of friendship and fondness.

- A bright nosegay may be softened with the addition of pastel or white flowers, regardless of whether or not you have this color palette in your own or bridesmaids' bouquets.

The nosegay tossing bouquet is a top choice for DIY wedding crafters. Since it is not on full display as part of the ceremony, but only in view for a very short ritual at the end of the reception, it doesn't have to be picture-perfect. A hand-tied construction with secure wiring beneath the ribbon-wrapped stem is an easy creative task for you or a volunteer.

Benefits of Nosegay Tossing Bouquets

- The smaller size is easier to throw.

- A nosegay's round shape makes it more aerodynamic, allowing it to fly farther.

- A smaller nosegay bouquet reduces the risk of two women getting a hold of it and starting a tug-of-war (a big risk with a larger or cascade bouquet).

- Being small in size, a separate tossing nosegay is inexpensive to buy or make.

- Nosegay tossing bouquets do not have to make the same, dramatic impression as a bridal bouquet, so you can use common, inexpensive flowers.

BREAKAWAY BOUQUETS

Bring luck to more than one recipient with a tossing bouquet that separates into pieces

Why limit the luck to just one person? Now you can design a breakaway bouquet that separates in midflight into four to eight smaller, hand-wrapped mini-bouquets or bunches, allowing more of your guests to grab a piece of your good luck. Using this kind of bouquet gives the appearance of your throwing one bouquet, with the added element of surprise

when guests see the bouquet separate into multiple pieces in mid-air.

One way to add even more meaning to the breakaway bouquet, and thus send different kinds of luck out to your awaiting ladies, is to attach tiny silver charms to the handles of each bouquet—a horseshoe for luck, a heart for love, a star

Tying the Breakaway Bouquet

- Gather two to four flowers with a branch or two of filler and cut the stems to a length of six inches.

- Wrap the stems in a spiral design using floral tape, the end of which just affixes to the surface or can be tucked into the collection of stems.

- Starting at the base of the flowers, spiral wrap a length of ribbon down to an inch above the end of the stems, cut the ribbon, fold the edge under, and pin the end securely in place.

- Do not use a hot glue gun to affix ribbon, since it can damage the stems and show through thin ribbon.

- Repeat for each bunch, then gather the bunches together and wrap securely with ribbon.

Size

- A breakaway bouquet includes up to eight hand-tied mini-bunches of flowers.

- A breakaway bouquet may be made larger, including up to twelve dual-stem hand-tied bunches, as a faux-duplicate of your bouquet.

- A six-inch bouquet will split well into four hand-tied bunches, with each section tied with a ribbon bow.

- A nosegay can split into eight or so individual blooms hand tied at the stems.

for a wish come true, a house for a happy home, an apple for good health.

Or, add even more meaning to each section of the breakaway bouquet by inserting a tiny scroll of paper on which you've handwritten a message of luck and love, a poem, or a notable quote. The recipient then finds out that the mini-bouquet she's caught contains a further message or positive symbol. This step adds a modern and personalized twist to an old tradition, bringing it into the twenty-first century.

· · · · · · · · · · · GREEN ● LIGHT · · · · · · · · · · ·
Have the ladies stand slightly farther away from you so that the breakaway bouquet has more airtime to separate into sections. A closer position could defeat the effect, with one recipient catching a group of three mini-bouquets. When the bouquet has more airtime, the sections separate to a greater degree, reaching women to the far left, far right, and center of the group.

Creating a Full Appearance

- Create height by placing longer-stemmed (one inch) in the center of the gathering. Then add shorter-stemmed bunches all around that one longer-stemmed bunch.

- Use flowers that have natural volume per stem, such as peonies or large roses.

- Use plenty of filler or stock in each bunch to fill out the appearance of the grouped bouquet if you like the look of lush greenery.

- Without green filler, achieve a full effect with twelve large-bloom flowers, plus twelve to fifteen medium-head flowers.

Untying a Breakaway Bouquet

- Untie the outside bow to release the individual tied clusters into your hand.

- Be subtle about unwrapping the clusters—for example, turn your back to the waiting ladies.

- Hold the breakaway clusters in one hand while you use the other hand to hide that ribbon tie.

- Holding the cluster of bouquets in both hands, use your thumbs to slightly separate the individually wrapped stems, untangling them for an easier flight.

INCLUDING YOUR BLOOMS
Add your bridal blooms to the tossing bouquet for a more traditional effect

Let's look more in-depth at the practice of incorporating the same types and colors of flowers from your own bridal bouquet into the tossing bouquet. For many brides, the tossing bouquet is a miniature version of their own bouquet, as they may not want to part with their bouquet.

If you chose the flowers of your bouquet because they are of great significance to you—they are the same color and type your fiancé brought you on your first date or that he presented to you when he proposed—you can imbue the tossing bouquet with wishes for the same grand romantic gesture.

Guests want very much to capture a part of the bride's luck,

Your Roses

- Include roses of the exact same variety and size as contained in your bouquet.

- Use smaller-size versions of your roses, for a decreased scale of your bouquet.

- Look for baby rosebuds, which symbolize beauty and youth, as a coordinating look to your full-bloomed roses, which mean I love you.

- Use your choice of rose shade, from an exact match in hue, to a lighter or darker rose in the tossing bouquet.

Your Daisies

- The daisy symbolizes innocence, loyal love, a promise to keep secrets, and purity, which are very appropriate messages for a tossing bouquet.

- If your bouquet is a bunch of white or yellow daisies, create a matching small posy bouquet.

- If you'll carry a bouquet of bright Gerber daisy stems wrapped in ribbon, create a Gerber daisy nosegay as the tossing bouquet.

- Instead of throwing a daisy round or posy, create a small hand-tied bunch of daisies perfect for throwing.

so it means more to them to grab a lookalike tossing bouquet rather than a tuft of bright purple flowers that look nothing like the original. Anything bridal means more to guests— just like anything labeled "bridal" costs more in the wedding world, as you may have already discovered. The wedding image alone adds more meaning and thus value. This is why so many brides choose to create tossing bouquets that are strikingly similar to their own carrying bouquet, right down to the smallest detail.

ZOOM

See Chapter 20 for a list of birth-month flowers so that you can perhaps design your tossing bouquet to include the luck of your own birth month, your groom's birth month, or the month of your wedding date. Using birth-month flowers has quickly become one of the top ways to add personal meaning to weddings, and the tossing bouquet is popular, too.

Your Stephanotises

- You can design a small posy of star-shaped stephanotises for an elegant tossing bouquet.

- Since stephanotises don't have long stems, cluster them with additional greenery or flowers to comprise a bouquet.

- Save money by attaching just a dozen of these small flowers to a round made of greenery, stock, and filler.

- Use stephanotises to form the shape of your new married-name last initial in the center of a nosegay packed with greenery.

Flowers for Finding Love

According to the language of love, the following blooms are considered to bring good luck in the search for one's true love and future mate:

- Amaranth: immortal love
- Apple blossom: reference
- Arbor vitae: everlasting friendship
- Bells of Ireland: luck
- Purple lilac: first love
- Celandine: joy is on the way
- Red rose: true love
- Forget-me-not: true love
- Coral rose: passion
- Violet: love at first sight
- Daisy: loyal love
- Honeysuckle: bonds of love
- Jonquil: love returned
- Orange blossom: marriage
- Peony: happy marriage

STEM WRAPS & TREATMENTS

Create decorative and functional stem treatments and wraps for your tossing bouquet

Because a tossing bouquet becomes airborne, it's visible from all angles, including underneath. This makes it a creation that requires attention to detail in the choice of flowers, the construction, and especially the stem wrap and handle treatment. Those pretty pink flowers on the top of the nosegay must be balanced by an equally pretty underside, with

coordinating color and a finished look. It's simply unacceptable to have a finished front and an unfinished back or bottom. You should never have exposed floral wire twisted around stems and gatherings, which is why floral tape is used in place of floral wire by designers.

The stem or stems of a tossing bouquet become a lovely

Full-Stem Wrap

- Gather the stems in-hand, selecting and placing individual blooms to achieve your desired floral effect.

- Use floral tape in green or black to spiral wrap the stems in one-half-inch circles from top to bottom, securing the tape at the bottom.

- Use a floral knife to cut the stems evenly across the bottom.

- Spiral wrap your chosen satin, silk, or other fabric ribbon all the way down the stem, overlapping half of each layer of ribbon, and secure at the bottom.

Partial-Stem Wrap

- Use one-half- to one-inch-wide ribbon in white or a coordinating color to secure the tossing bouquet at the middle of the stem.

- Wrap the ribbon three times around the center point of the stem and secure it with a pin.

- Cut a twelve- to eighteen-inch length of the same ribbon and use it to tie a pretty bow over the center ribbon wrap.

- Use the ribbon to spiral wrap the stem, leaving one-half inch of stem and greenery exposed between spirals.

focal point when great care is taken to design and create a pretty wrap, a bow accent, a fabric or lace trail, or another accent. Don't forget: The tossing bouquet will not only be thrown to awaiting femaie guests, your photographer will photograph it in great detail. Photo pros love to capture the smallest details of a wedding day, so the tossing bouquet might be laid on a surface, readied for its close-up, and captured for immortality as another beautifully and perfectly designed floral piece from your wedding day. So make sure this bouquet looks fantastic from top to bottom.

Ribbons and Lace

A fun trend for securing the stems of a tossing bouquet—with an eye toward pretty and playful accents—is to use decorative hair bands from an accessory or beauty supply store. Half a dozen pink, red, or purple elasticized ponytail holders with little silk flowers on them can be arranged one-inch apart along the gathered stems for under $5.

- The ribbon wrap should match the fabric of either your wedding gown or your bridesmaids' dresses.

- Ask seamstresses to save lengths of satin, silk, or other fabrics from alterations for you to use for the handle.

- Peruse craft stores for pretty ribbon or corded silk braid alternative materials to coordinate with your or your bridesmaids' gowns.

- Look for pretty lace to use as the bouquet handle wrap and extend the ends for trailing lengths.

Safety in Stem Wraps

- Use pins to secure ribbon wrap around stems, angling the pins into the collection of stems so that they do not poke through the other side.

- Pearl- or crystal-headed stickpins inserted along the length of the bouquet stems or handle need to be securely attached. Bend the pins so they "hook" to the inside wrap of the ribbon.

- Avoid add-in accents for this bouquet and just use securely wrapped ribbon ties along the length of the stems.

- Do not use boutonniere pins to secure handle décor; any kind of straight pin is likely to pierce a recipient.

STORING YOUR TOSSING BOUQUET

Keep your tossing bouquet safe, cool, and protected from the elements for its big moment

For any flowers to look their best, they need to be kept out of heat and too-dry conditions. These same rules apply to the tossing bouquet, which might not get its moment in the spotlight until eight or nine hours after it was created! The other bouquets are seen almost immediately upon completion, and no one can blame them for wilting a bit at a hot outdoor wedding. After all, they've been on display and out of water for most of the day. The tossing bouquet, by contrast, needs to look as fresh as if it was just made. After all, the spotlight will be on this pretty floral piece during the tossing ritual, and it will be in the hands of your wedding guests. So it has to look and feel its best.

In the Refrigerator

- Ideally the tossing bouquet should be stored in a refrigerator set to normal food storage temperatures of forty degrees Fahrenheit or below.

- Remove a shelf, if you must, to allow for the tossing bouquet to be stored standing up in a vase.

- Do not store the tossing bouquet on its side, or you'll flatten one edge of the bouquet.

- Place the bouquet on the bottom shelf of the refrigerator to keep it safely away from the coolest upper area of the refrigerator.

In a Cooler

- At an outdoor wedding a cooler might be your only source to protect the tossing bouquet.

- The tossing bouquet should not share space with anything else in the cooler.

- Don't fill the cooler with ice cubes, which could freeze the tossing bouquet or create a pool of water into which the bouquet could fall.

- Invest in flat chemical cool packs to keep the cooler cold, and lay tissue paper on top of them to protect the bouquet.

Your goals when storing your tossing bouquet are to achieve a comfortable, cool environment, get the flowers plenty to drink, and keep it safe from damage.

You'd be wise to plan for your tossing bouquet's storage by prearranging with the site manager to clear some room in the site's refrigerator for safekeeping of this all-important bouquet. It's important to make this request months in advance so that the manager can reserve some room in the jam-packed cooler or fridge.

On Display

- Rather than store the tossing bouquet, make it part of your décor by standing it in a glass or silver vase set on top of an ice tray within the buffet setup.

- Attach plastic water capsules to the ends of flower stems in the bouquet. Set the bouquet in a vase to hide the water capsules.

- Place the tossing bouquet on the guest book table.

- Display the tossing bouquet on your family photos table.

Storing the Caught Bouquet

- When the lucky recipient snags the tossing bouquet, she will certainly want to keep it safe from harm while she enjoys the rest of the celebration.

- Provide her with a bridal-themed photo storage box from a craft store.

- Provide her with a plastic bouquet protector sleeve.

- Allow her to use the cooler in which you transported and stored the tossing bouquet.

- If she wishes to have the bouquet refrigerated in the site's kitchen, label it with her name and phone number in case she forgets it and the site wishes to get it to her.

IS THE BOUQUET TOSS OUTDATED?

Do you even want to throw your bouquet in today's modern and proper times?

The bouquet toss has been labeled out-of-date now, out, passe, and even dangerous in this litigious society. Indeed, the dangers posed by flying bodies and aggressive maneuvers to grab the bouquet in midflight do open up the potential for injuries and lawsuits, and it's not surprising that some reception halls don't allow the bouquet toss tradition

anymore. They've had enough damage to their chandeliers and tables over the years that the tradition is not allowed on their property.

We've all seen enough YouTube videos of drunk bridesmaids and female guests slamming into the sides of tables, or falling backward over chairs, steamrolling Grandma, and

KNACK WEDDING FLOWERS

Been There, Done That

- Many brides see the bouquet toss as simply cliché, done at every other wedding they've attended.

- If this is your second wedding, you may wish to make this reception different by skipping this ritual.

- Some brides say they personally don't enjoy the anxiety of waiting to catch (or avoid) the bouquet, so they wish to spare their guests the same experience.

- Some brides don't like the cheesy songs played to accompany the bouquet toss—for example, "Girls Just Want to Have Fun."

Too Few Single Women

- It may be that you only have one or two single friends who would be mortified to be called out onto the dance floor as the only single women at the wedding.

- If you have fewer than ten single friends, avoid the ritual.

- If your single females are mostly under age eighteen, be appropriate and avoid this tradition.

- Children under age thirteen should never be allowed on the dance floor for the bouquet toss; they could get trampled.

knocking over a waiter in a frenzied effort to catch the bouquet. Your hesitancy to include the bouquet toss may come from worries about your friends not behaving decently. You might wish to avoid the entire scene, even if single guests boo you for your choice.

Another factor in the disappearance of the bride's bouquet toss is that many single female guests don't want to participate in this ritual. They don't enjoy being led out on the dance floor, looking desperate to be the next to marry. It's not a fun ritual for them, since marriage is not their ultimate goal. They also might dislike the aggressive nature of some of the younger, more inebriated female guests, not wanting to be knocked over by a flailing drunk girl. This ritual is one that many single female guests began to dread, until it faded from the wedding scene. Including it in your wedding now could be considered retro, and many guests may decline to participate, leaving you with a few preteens and Grandma on the dance floor waiting to catch the bouquet.

Let's explore the reasons why the bouquet toss is considered by many to be outdated.

Injury and Chaos

- Aggressive women can knock each other over to grab the bouquet, so judge your guest list. Do you have brutish women on your list?

- Ask your site manager if the bouquet toss is even allowed in the establishment.

- Move tables, chairs, and pedestals out of the way.

- If you wish to avoid injury and chaos, arrange to throw your bouquet much earlier in the reception so that guests don't have too many hours of drinking under their belts.

Formality and Style

Jane Smith

- Perhaps the wild dash for the bouquet doesn't match your vision of propriety, and the ritual doesn't fit with the formality of the wedding.

- Perhaps you know that your friends can get a bit wild when they're drinking, and you don't want the same behavior at your wedding.

- Perhaps you don't want your parents, grandparents, and bosses to see aggressive behavior by your friends.

- You might prefer unscheduled mingling time with no tossing rituals.

PRESENT THE BOUQUET: RELATIVES

You need to decide which of your most adored relatives will be the recipient of your bouquet

If you do decide to forego the bouquet toss, leaving your guests to make their own luck in the love department, there are some alternative traditions to answer the question, "What do I do with my wedding bouquet?" You can share the symbolism without the competition (or bodily harm) by gifting your bouquet to one very important guest.

When you choose to skip the bouquet toss, you open up an opportunity for a classy, elegant, and meaningful spotlight moment at your wedding reception. "Now," says the MC, "the bride would like to present her bouquet to a very special guest."

It's a sign of deep respect and love when you choose a

Presenting to Parents

- In this age of parents being silent partners or playing smaller roles in wedding planning, the bouquet presentation can take the place of a mom being hostess of the wedding.

- A mom can receive a bouquet that includes her favorite flowers or the same types of flowers from her wedding bouquet.

- A breakaway bouquet can be used to present smaller bunches to both mother and mother-in-law.

- A breakaway bouquet can be presented to both mom and stepmom.

Grandparents or Great-Aunts

- It's a priceless moment when you honor the matriarch of the family by handing her your bouquet.

- If your grandmother has passed away, present the bouquet to one of her sisters.

- Don't make elderly guests

- walk to the center of the dance floor or to a dais for this ceremony; walk to their table.

- Let elderly guests know about your plan ahead of time, giving them the option of turning down the public spotlight and accepting the bouquet in private.

spotlight recipient for your bouquet, and all eyes will be on that person when you—the glorious bride on her own special day—walk over to make a special presentation to the person you have chosen for this heartfelt moment. This is not a game of luck or chance or brute force . . . it's a decision you made, a gesture you wanted to include in your day, and the person you choose to honor has been selected for a very big symbolic gesture.

Don't forget that breakaway bouquets may be separated and presented to several people.

Presenting to a Child

- Present the bouquet to your own daughter, using her favorite flowers and colors in this new tossing bouquet design.

- If you have more than one daughter, design separate bouquets for them or design a breakaway that suits their styles.

- If your groom has daughters, include them in the presentation of a posy bouquet or their own separate breakaway bunches.

- Children love charms, so attach a good-luck silver or enamel charm to the wrapped stem or handle of each bouquet.

··············· RED ● LIGHT ···············

Don't talk ahead of time about your decision to present the bouquet to a special guest. Parents especially tend to chime in and either make suggestions or shoot down your idea, saying, "What would Aunt Ida think if you gave the bouquet to Aunt Esther?!" Avoid potential problems by making this presentation a surprise and therefore exactly what you want to do.

Sharing the Significance of the Recipient

- You can choose to say a few words, letting everyone in the room know who the recipient is, such as, "This is my great-aunt Millie, who has been like a grandmother to me for over twenty years."

- For a more private message, write the recipient a letter or get a great greeting card for them to read privately, expressing your gratitude for their presence in your life.

- Get great pictures of the bouquet exchange. These photos only become more valuable over time.

PRESENT THE BOUQUET: FRIENDS
Bouquet presentation ideas for loved ones outside your family circle

Friends can be the most precious people in our lives, so why not plan to present your bouquet to a very special friend rather than a relative? If moms and grandmothers already have their corsages or nosegay bouquets, they have received their honor gift, and now you get to share a little bit of the floral glory with a much-loved friend who means the world to you.

Brides often ask, "How can I involve a friend who is unable to serve in my bridal party due to pregnancy or money issues?" This is how. Honor that great friend with a special presentation of her own good-luck bouquet that also says, "Thank you for being so special to me."

In this global society we live in, you might not see your most special friends very often, and in this hectic world we

The People Who Introduced You

- Create a bouquet for the family friend who first spoke the words, "I have the perfect guy for you!"

- If a group of friends dreamed up your pairing and orchestrated your first meeting, they can all get mini hand-tied bunches as thank-you bouquets.

- If a couple introduced the two of you, they may share one larger bouquet.

- Attach a scrolled thank-you note to the handle of this bouquet, with messages of thanks from both of you.

The Longest-Married Couple

- Ask your mom or grand-mother who on your side of the family has been married the longest amount of time.

- Ask your fiancé's mother or in-the-know aunt for the names of the couple who have been married the longest on that side of the family.

- Present your bouquet to the couple who has been married the longest, thanking them for the example of their inspiring relationship.

- Choose one long-married couple from each side of the family, and give out two bouquets.

live in, you might not get the chance to talk on the phone very often, either. Friendships can drift slightly, just enough to prevent friends from being bridal party choices, but never enough to erase their value as friends during your formative years. What a great surprise to shine the spotlight on your college roommates who steered you toward your current career or perhaps even your spouse!

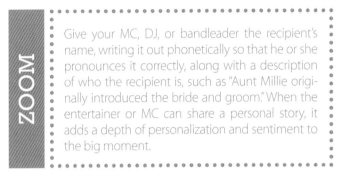

Give your MC, DJ, or bandleader the recipient's name, writing it out phonetically so that he or she pronounces it correctly, along with a description of who the recipient is, such as "Aunt Millie originally introduced the bride and groom." When the entertainer or MC can share a personal story, it adds a depth of personalization and sentiment to the big moment.

BOUQUET TOSS TRENDS

A Couple Who Inspires You

- You needn't choose the couple who has been married the longest, but rather the couple whose love story inspires you.

- If one partner supported the other through a long illness, discuss your plans beforehand to ask permission to share their story.

- The couple doesn't have to be married; consider longtime-engaged or longtime-dating couples.

- If you choose a widow or widower from a couple who inspired you, make sure enough grieving time has passed before you make this gesture.

Above-and-Beyond Friends

- Honor a friend who allowed you use of her vacation home for a beautiful destination wedding at no cost.

- Honor a friend who shared her wedding industry contacts with you.

- Honor a friend who made elements for your wedding day, such as the chuppah, the wedding cake, the table linens, the runner, the food.

- Share your reason for honoring this friend with subtlety so that you don't offend all of the other people who helped plan your wedding.

PRESENT THE BOUQUET: BRIDAL PARTY

Keep the bouquet presentation within your wedding's inner circle of friends and sisters

Even though they have their own bouquets to carry and keep, your bridesmaids would still love to receive a part of your bouquet, since it is such a symbol of hope and good luck. As you consider presenting your bouquet to one special person or breakaway sections to several of your closest female friends and relatives, including junior bridesmaids

and flower girls, think about how you can make the gift even more special.

When you keep the bouquet presentation within the bridal party you hold true to the "keep a piece of the bride's luck" origins, as you're not only thanking your bridesmaids for their support and assistance, you're sharing a symbol of your

Maid or Matron of Honor

- Presenting your bouquet to your maid or matron of honor can be a spotlight moment in the reception, taking place right before the cake cutting.

- The presentation can also be made during a private moment between the two of you in a separate room.

- Be sure to have the photographer capture this special moment.

- Before you present the bouquet, pin to the handle a scrolled handwritten note that expresses your gratitude for such a wonderful friend or sister.

Bridesmaids

- A breakaway bouquet is the best and most efficient arrangement for handing out portions of your bouquet to several special recipients.

- Each breakaway can contain two or three flowers and some pretty filler, wrapped with matching ribbon.

- Attach little silver initial charms to each breakaway, surprising your bridesmaids with the fact that you carried them with you during the ceremony.

- Each bridesmaid can get her own handwritten, scrolled personal note of your thanks for her love and support.

great love and marriage. This allows you to harken back to Old World days, when women wanted to keep a piece of the bride's dress or veil as a good-luck symbol, without the threat of damage to your dress and headpiece.

You may want to present your bouquet to your maid or matron of honor if she has gone above and beyond her call of duty, or honor your entire circle of women with a big, lush breakaway bouquet so that every female member of your bridal party gets her own mini-bouquet. This practice establishes a great level of equality in your bridal party.

Junior Bridesmaid

- Teens and tweens love getting special recognition for doing a good job in an important role.

- Since teens and tweens can sometimes be shy about being the center of attention, ask her if she would like a public presentation before you spring it on her.

- Be sure to tell guests about her delightful nature and how helpful she was in the planning.

- Write her a special note of thanks and attach it to the handle of the bouquet before presenting it to her.

The Wedding Coordinator

- Giving your bouquet to your wedding coordinator is a wonderful way to publicly thank her for her hard work.

- Wedding experts say they love getting positive feedback from cherished clients, especially in a public way.

- This bouquet presentation also serves to promote her and her services to your many wedding guests, which is quite a referral to provide.

- Keep this presentation a secret until the big moment.

KEEPING THE BOUQUET
Avoid bouquet toss or presentation issues by keeping your bouquet

Brides who love the bouquet they've designed can add another dimension to their distaste for the tossing ritual: They can keep their bouquet for themselves. It might serve double-duty during the reception, adding an extra element of beauty to a spotlight site in the room, or it might be safely stowed away in a cooler or refrigerator to keep it fresh for end-of-wedding photos and in better condition for preservation.

Does this mean the bride doesn't want to send love and luck to her guests? Not at all! She may devise a separate ritual for that, such as giving friends and bridal party members little pouches of rose petals as personal tokens of luck (a far more budget-friendly option). She may choose to give out single roses to her sisters, relatives, and friends as part of the wedding ceremony itself, thereby sharing love and luck earlier

Say Nothing

- You don't have to make an announcement that you will not be throwing your bouquet.

- Guests are aware that the bouquet toss no longer happens at every wedding.

- If you have an opinionated, tradition-hungry mother or mother-in-law, keep your plans to skip the bouquet toss to yourself, rather than get pressured into a ritual you don't favor.

- If guests ask when you're going to throw the bouquet, simply say, "We've decided not to do the bouquet or garter tosses, sorry!"

A Tribute Bouquet

- Create a visual honor for departed loved ones by displaying your bouquet with several white votive candles.

- Set the bouquet in a vase.

- Lay the bouquet flat on a memorial table, along with photos of your departed relatives. Place several folded linen napkins under the top third of the stems to elevate the bouquet, which prevents crushing the side of the bouquet.

- Print and frame a statement saying that your bouquet stands in memory of departed loved ones.

in the day. With these handouts, the bride gets to keep her meaningful and beautiful bouquet in hand, and she has still brought the luck ritual into her wedding celebration.

If you have kept all of the flowers your groom has given you over the years, drying them carefully and keeping them as treasured mementoes, then keeping your bouquet will be the natural decision for you.

ZOOM

Again refer to the language of love symbolism to find the perfect type and color of flowers to distribute. You can give all one type and color of flower to female guests, or you can provide a selection with a printed list of meanings so guests can personalize their own choices for luck, abundance, health, and the arrival of their own true love.

Photos

- Don't present your bouquet to a guest until your photographer has taken all shots of the two of you.

- If you do toss or present your bouquet and then realize more photos will be taken, it is okay to ask for the recipient to lend it back to you for a short while.

- It's important for your departure photos that you have your own bouquet in hand.

- Ask your photographer to take plenty of close-up photos of your bouquet.

Your Wedding Night

- When the two of you retire to the honeymoon suite and peel off your wedding gown to reveal your wedding-night lingerie, it's a great image if you're also holding your bouquet.

- Set your bouquet on the bedside table as part of a photo of the marriage bed covered in rose petals, with champagne and candles nearby.

- Use it as your impromptu centerpiece for your post-wedding room service order, since you may be famished after not eating much at the reception.

BOUQUET PRESERVATION

Make that beautiful bouquet last forever with simple preservation steps

Bouquet preservation is a technical art, as flowers are made up of organic material that requires careful handling to capture the flowers' original shape and color. Many brides choose to use the services of a professional bouquet preservation company (see Chapter 20 for a list of professionals) for optimal results achieved with a veritable scientific process.

Bouquet preservation allows you to keep a tangible element of your day, one of the few actual keepsakes of the wedding itself. With your gown preserved and stored in a box, the bouquet might become a spotlight display item in your home of the future. Some brides commission or buy special display cases or glass boxes in which to store them.

Bouquet Preservation Method

- Place your bouquet in a trash bag and blow air into the bag. Carbon dioxide keeps flowers fresher.

- Seal the bag and place it in the refrigerator, not the freezer.

- Send the bouquet to a preservation company that will separate the flowers, freeze-dry each stem, and then allow them to thaw.

- The flowers are then dipped in chemicals that return them to a soft, pliable form. Some flowers preserve better than others. Lilacs and chrysanthemums are poor preservers.

Re-creating Your Bouquet

- If your bouquet wilted or was damaged during hugs at the wedding, or if it laid on its side for a length of time, you can create a new bouquet to preserve.

- Some brides design a second bouquet just for preservation.

- Silk flower artists can recreate your bouquet with faux flowers in identical styles and colors and greenery.

- You can recreate your own bouquet using silk flowers from a craft store, which works well if you crafted your own bouquet from real flowers.

There are two different types of bouquet preservation—air-dry and freeze-dry. With the air-dry technique, you can set your bouquet on its side and allow it to dry naturally. Petals will of course brown and curl in their drying progression, resulting in an old-fashioned look and a fragile bouquet. On a budget, this might be your choice..

If preserving your entire bouquet seems too great a task, simply cut a few flowers and allow them to air-dry naturally as perfect keepsakes. You can also gently pull petals from one or more of your bouquet roses and allow them to dry naturally on paper towels for a few days, then keep them in an extra centerpiece vase or bowl for display in your home.

The Bouquet Scrapbook

- Another way to immortalize your bouquet is to create a bouquet scrapbook containing the original inspiration photos you found in magazines.

- Include any sketches or notes you made about your bouquet.

- Include photos taken at your meeting with a floral designer or as you shopped at a floral wholesaler.

- Include photos of your bouquet at the end of the scrapbook with your own handwritten notes and memories about the bouquet toss or presentation.

Storage

- If you preserved your bouquet, store it in an airtight shadowbox you can find at a craft store.

- For a smaller bouquet, an unexpected source is a Lucite or glass storage box designed for autographed footballs, which you can find at sports memorabilia stores and Web sites.

- You can make a special, custom-designed shadowbox for your bouquet and display it in your home.

- Ask a talented crafty friend to make a bouquet storage box as a wedding gift to you.

PERSONAL FLOWERS TO WEAR

Design beautiful floral accents to wear in your hair, as jewelry, and as gown embellishments

You might decide to include flowers not just in your bouquet but also as beautiful bridal accents to your whole wedding day look. A few fresh flowers pinned into your up-do become a beautiful reveal when you remove your veil for the reception, or flowers in your hair can take the place of a traditional headpiece and veil. This is a lovely bridal look and can save you huge amounts of money, with veils and headpieces sometimes costing more than the gowns themselves.

Brides whose floral dreams include something different for their look often incorporate tiny flowers as jewelry pieces such as bracelets, necklaces, and even floral pendants that hang down to showcase a plunging backline showing off

Flowers in Your Hair: Back

- Ask your hairstylist to pin tiny flowers in natural spots throughout the back of your sophisticated updo.

- Single flowers may be equally spaced along the length of your French braid or twist.

- If you'll wear your hair loose and flowing, tiny flowers may be clipped to various spots on the curls of your hair.

- Choose smaller, lightweight flowers such as stephanotises so your hairdo isn't weighed down.

Flowers in Your Hair: Side

- For an informal look, attach a pin of multiple flowers to a side-swept hairdo.

- With a full updo, a pin of tiny flowers paired with rhinestone accents can be the perfect one-side hair embellishment.

- With a low-set ponytail, your floral hairclip can hold back longer-length bangs that don't reach the pony-tail or top hairclip.

- Hair flowers should match the flowers in your bouquet, or should be the same types of flowers as the men's boutonnieres.

the brides' best assets. The advent of florals in pendants now means you can create a fresh accessory for the front or back of your wedding gown.

Flowers are the new accessories for brides, and they work for both formal and informal weddings, indoor and outdoor celebrations, and at-home and destination weddings. Especially if you have a very simple, classic, elegant gown with a minimum of embellishments, a few well-placed flowers can turn your classic bridal look into an ethereal, floral wonder, all for just a few dollars rather than expensive jewelry.

Flowers in Your Hair: Single

- At an informal wedding, tuck a single Gerber daisy behind your ear.

- Attach a single rosebud to the back clip or ponytail holder as a simple, elegant look.

- When affixing a single flower behind your ear, pin it with a bobby pin that matches your hair color.

- Find bobby pins that match your hair color at beauty supply stores, and get three sizes : small, medium, and long to suit the different lengths of your hair.

Additional Ways to Wear Flowers in Your Hair

- Weave a chain of flowers in cascading, trailing lengths into the braid of your hair.

- Set a net, with flowers attached to a lace or crocheted oval or rectangle, on your head as a veil replacement.

- Attach flowers to a unique headpiece, such as a Juliet cap, either singly or as a cascading veil effect.

- Pin single tiny blooms across the crown of your head in a headband-style arrangement.

- Create a round floral ring around your low-set ponytail by attaching a ring of flowers to a hairclip or ponytail holder.

FLORAL NECKLACES
Replace diamond or pearl jewelry with fabulous, fresh floral accessories

Not every bride wants to be dripping in diamonds on her wedding day. Perhaps you're the nonflashy type as well, and you'd rather create a unique floral necklace to wear rather than expect your groom to give you an expensive diamond or pearl necklace as his wedding gift to you (the wedding band can serve that purpose).

The floral necklace has its place in both formal and informal wedding looks. Its formality all depends on the type of flower you choose, as well as the size of flower you choose. For instance, a delicate single stephanotis as a pendant necklace is the essence of formality, while a circle of bright, happy white daisies can be the perfect accent for your informal

Single Bloom

- Attach a single small flower to a real silver chain for the best pendant effect.

- Single-bloom flowers look best without added greenery or filler.

- The most common single flowers to use are baby roses, mini–calla lilies,

stephanotises, and Gerber daisies for a pop of color.

- The ideal chain length allows the flower to sit flush on your chest just below your collarbones.

- Don't allow floral pendants to hang into your cleavage.

Choker

- Devise a floral choker that sits close to the throat as an accent to a V-neck, square-neck, sweetheart, or princess neckline dress.

- A choker may be made up of all flowers sitting closely together with no greenery or filler.

- A choker may be made up of six to nine individual flowers strung one to two inches apart on clear wire.

- Allow at least two fingers' width between the choker and your throat so that you don't feel constricted.

sundress at your outdoor wedding, with your hair loose and flowing and a matching white daisy tucked behind your ear.

A single flower worn as jewelry can be seen as ultraformal when paired with a formal dress, or ultracasual when paired with a casual dress. The setting is what's important.

And the pricetag? Under $5 for some floral jewelry pieces. Compare that to the $5,000 or more that some grooms spend on their brides' diamond wedding day necklaces. If you're on a budget, but you still want a unique and beautiful jewelry piece to make a statement, consider a floral necklace.

························· GREEN ● LIGHT ·················

A floral designer is often your best resource for creating floral jewelry that's of the perfect size and for expertly designing a clasp that keeps your bloom secure. DIY brides sometimes find that their handiwork falls apart with such a tiny and intricate project. If you have a friend who regularly makes jewelry, perhaps she can teach you how to make clasps and design jewelry pieces.

Daisies

- For an informal look, create a necklace pendant or choker made of small white, yellow, or colored daisies.

- A single bright daisy may be the basis for your pendant necklace, or the center of a greenery choker.

- Take a cue from fashion and string daisies on a long chain so that it hangs down over your bodice to accent the flat panel of your waist.

- Larger daisies are not functional for choker necklaces; use these for chest-accent pendants.

Dos and Don'ts for Floral Necklaces

- Don't use oversize flowers, which can overpower the bodice of your dress and your face.

- Floral necklaces work best on strapless dresses, sweetheart and princess necklines, and square-neck bodices, presenting just enough chest and cleavage for a floral accent.

- Floral necklaces do not work well for keyhole or halter-top dresses that offer little to no space for a floral accent.

- If you choose a white flower, be sure it matches the white of your dress.

PERSONAL FLOWERS

99

ADDITIONAL FLORAL JEWELRY

Take a step beyond necklaces to design pretty floral bracelets, earrings, and other accessories

Flowers have become more of a fashion statement now that floral jewelry is on the scene. From small and dainty earrings to big, splashy bracelets, floral designs encompass whites, pastels, and brights in unexpected ways —again eliminating the need for that ultraexpensive trip to the jewelry boutique.

As with all floral accents, it's your individual flower style and color choices that determine the formality, and you can infuse these pieces with your own wedding personality: classic, romantic, artsy, unique, or "out there." Bring in the colors of your wedding season as a match to your bridal bouquet, and you've captured a one-of-a-kind bridal look. Ideally the

Bracelets

- Create a bracelet from a soft, short garland of greenery and attach tiny white, pastel, or bright flowers for contrast.

- Attach grand flowers such as Majolica roses, hydrangeas, and viburnums to a silver cuff bracelet for a large, impressive piece.

- Attach a phalaenopsis orchid to a silver cuff bracelet for a big, colorful look.

- Design your own version of the diamond tennis bracelet by interspersing rhinestones with baby rosebuds or stephanotises.

Ankle Bracelets

- Create a simple floral ankle bracelet by taking an existing silver ankle bracelet and attaching small flowers such as viburnums or orange blossoms to it.

- For informal, garden, or beach weddings, create ankle bracelets out of cord rather than silver chain and

attach island flowers such as hibiscuses.

- A ring of daisies is ideal for an informal garden wedding.

- Since ankle bracelets will spin, choose a design with flowers all the way around, not a single bloom.

flowers for your jewelry will match the colors of the flowers in your bouquet for a coordinated look.

Floral jewelry needs to be created immediately before the wedding ceremony for its freshest appearance and strength of bloom, so don't even think about taking on the task of making floral bracelets for all of your bridesmaids as well as the moms on the morning of the big day. If you'll be the artist of your floral jewelry, it's ideal to make only one piece for yourself or two tops for the mothers to wear.

⋯⋯⋯⋯⋯⋯⋯⋯⋯ YELLOW ● LIGHT ⋯⋯⋯⋯⋯⋯⋯⋯⋯

If you'll create these floral pieces yourself, be sure to purchase enough flowers and jewelry materials to allow for a dozen mistakes. Having extra materials on hand removes the stress of needing to get it perfect the first time or the risk of not having any extra flowers to work with. Since you're performing intricate work, expect that some blooms will get smashed and others will tear and fall off the wire.

Earrings

- Attach tiny blooms to existing circular metal earrings.

- Attach elongated flower petals, such as an orchid, to the metal clasps of ball-and-hook earrings.

- Dangle earrings may be made with one single small bloom, or a length of two to three flowers.

- The three-flower earring calls to mind the past, present, and future style in diamond pendants, so you copy a classic jewelry style with blooms.

Keeping Floral Jewelry Fresh

- Do not spray flowers with water at the beginning of the wedding. The moisture will evaporate in the sun, thus drying the flower more quickly.

- If your flowers have been sitting in bleach water, be sure to rinse your craft flowers well before using them so that residual bleach doesn't dry into a powder while you're wearing them.

- Store floral jewelry in a refrigerator until just before you put it on.

- If you notice tiny outer-edge petals starting to brown or get damaged, just pluck them off to reveal the next layer of fresh petals.

PERSONAL FLOWERS

FLOWERS ON YOUR DRESS

Add life to your wedding gown with the embellishment of fresh flower bunches

An adorned gown covered with hand-sewn crystals, seed pearls, and silver-thread embroidery can cost thousands, but the bride who wants added visual impact on her dress will spend this small fortune for that extra design. Some brides spend thousands for intricate silk flowers to be sewn in patterns on their gowns and trains. You, however, can achieve

a haute-couture look, indeed the impression that you spent thousands, by adding fresh flowers as accents to your gown . . . for under $30.

As an extension to the "green" wedding trend that is here to stay, adding flowers and greenery to every part of the wedding day now includes adding them as accents to the dress

On a Plunging Back

- When your dress has a deep, plunging open back, the perfect spot for a tuft of flowers is right at the small of the back.

- Avoid the "butt bubble" look by affixing a small cluster of flowers, no more than four to six blooms.

- Greenery and filler are not needed for the back accent, as they would make the floral piece look like a misplaced corsage.

- Choose between white and pastel flowers. Avoid brights, whose contrast can look a bit over-the-top.

On the Train

- Use safety pins to affix one or more floral bunches to the train.

- One floral grouping at the end of the train can present weight issues, making it hard to dance, walk, or turn.

- Place several smaller singles or clusters of flowers in a line down the back of the train, or as accents on the hemline of the train, spaced six to eight inches apart.

- A wider, more dramatic train is ideal for a scattered placement of pinned (never glued) flowers.

as well. We equate the bride with a natural beauty, so what better way to add natural beauty to a wedding gown than with flowers?

The best effects are achieved when a gown is simpler in nature, a sleek satin, charmeuse, silk, or 100 percent cotton gown with minimal detailing. A smooth dress holds as its primary accent that unexpected tuft of flowers, a tiny bouquet of color and texture that sets a gown apart from all the other dresses of the day.

Detailed dresses such as those with crystal-studded bodices may also be adorned with fresh flower pieces, just in smaller and more subtle ways for the best effect.

When adding flowers to your dress, just be sure they match the flowers in your bouquet.

On the Bodice

- A plain or adorned bodice is ideal for placing a flower cluster at the center of the waist in place of a bow.

- Small flowers may be pinned on the shoulder straps of the dress, from front to back, with blooms placed two to four inches apart.

- Avoid placing a floral cluster in the middle of your décolletage, as this effect looks like you're trying to hide a too-low plunging neckline.

- Keep bodice flowers small so they don't restrict your movement.

Pinning Flowers to the Dress

- Buy different sizes of safety pins so that you can see which are best hidden by the size of the floral bunch and which are strong enough to hold the cluster securely.

- Place the flower or bunch on the spot where you want the flower to rest and insert the pin through the underside of the dress to emerge at the spot where the stem meets the flower.

- Angle the pin as you push through so that it comes out of the stem an inch below the insertion point.

- Direct the pin back into the fabric of the dress to secure it in a closed position on the underside of the fabric.

FLORAL WREATHS

Encircle your head with a pretty ring of flowers and greenery for a romantic effect

You might think the floral wreath set upon the head is too much of a callback to Renaissance days, but modern designs have revived this pretty, romantic look to suit the natural floral look desired by brides planning outdoor, casual weddings as well as formal weddings. The personality of a floral wreath is created by the individual flower choices as well as the size of the blooms used in the wreath.

An informal wreath may be lush with wildflowers as well as roses, with plenty of greenery and just-picked-looking heather and dots of baby's breath. A formal wreath might be comprised entirely of perfect baby rosebuds, a thin band of stephanotises, or a dramatic circle of gardenias. As a rule,

Roses and Traditional Blooms

- For formal weddings, and for a more traditional look, top flowers include roses, ranunculus, and stephanotises.

- Flowers may be all white to match an all-white bouquet, or pastels to match a pastel bouquet.

- Bright roses and blooms are not recommended, even with an all-bright bouquet; stick with a tone to match your dress color.

- Smaller filler blooms in a traditional wreath include lilies of the valley and baby's breath.

Daisies

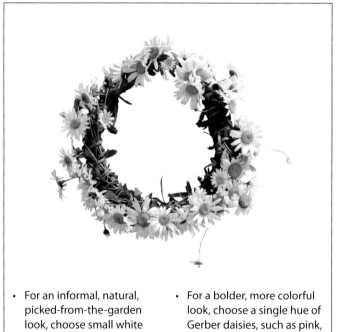

- For an informal, natural, picked-from-the-garden look, choose small white daisies.

- For a touch of color to coordinate with a white and yellow bouquet, yellow daisies are the optimal choice.

- For a bolder, more colorful look, choose a single hue of Gerber daisies, such as pink, red, orange, or yellow.

- As a mix with daisies, or on its own for its resemblance to daisies, check out the chamomile flower.

the simpler the look and the fewer the variety of flowers, the more formal it is.

The ring is the symbol of eternity, so you may want to encircle your head with meaningful, beautiful flowers as a style choice that means more to you than a traditional headpiece and veil would. As another perk, a floral wreath makes such a visual impact that you would be ideally balanced in style with a smaller, posy bouquet made of the same types of flowers in your wreath. Flowers on top, flowers in front of you.

Just Greenery

- Eliminate flowers from your wreath for the ultimate green look.

- The top choice for green wreaths is ivy, for an old-fashioned look with symbolic meaning of fidelity.

- Olive leaves are the top choice in some cultures for bridal wreaths and are often placed on both the bride's and groom's heads to symbolize their union.

- Create a modern greenery look by braiding long strips of grasses for a woven effect.

Affixing Wreath to the Head

- A well-made wreath is measured to fit the crown of the head, with the hairstyle taken into consideration ahead of time.

- Set the wreath on the head at a slight angle to the back.

- Use bobby pins to secure the wreath in two spots by the temples and every three inches across the back of the wreath.

- Pinning the front of the wreath could interfere with the appearance of the flowers, so keep pins to the sides and back.

- Practice moving, including bending over, to be sure the wreath is safely secured.

105

HEADPIECE ACCENTS

Add floral accents to headpieces and headbands for an extra dash of color and style

The average bridal headpiece can cost over $300, especially if it's adorned with Swarovski crystals and intricately hand-applied beading. If you want the bridal look, you can achieve it without the sparkle and shimmer of gemstones, but with the natural beauty of flowers.

When you acquire a very simple headpiece, perhaps a simple satin-covered head covering, a simple silver tiara, or a satin headband at a tenth of the cost of a designer, jewel-encrusted headpiece, you have the foundation for a lovely floral accent headpiece that looks like you spent hundreds of dollars. In reality, the average headpiece affixed with flowers costs under $30.

Single Flowers

- A too-small bloom will look lost on a larger headpiece, and a too-large bloom will look overdone.

- Your best choices for single-bloom headpiece flowers: phalaenopsis orchids and cattleya orchids, which are large and dramatic.

- A small rose, gardenia, camellia, passionflower, or ranunculus can be the perfect single-flower accent to a headpiece that's already accented with rhinestones.

- The single flower needs to be in balance with the width of the headpiece.

Miniature Flowers

- Use miniature flowers to create a detailed look.

- Miniature flowers create the same effect as jewels when used closely together.

- These tiny flowers are ideal for pinning to headpieces, tiaras, and headbands: miniature roses, daphnes, jasmine, stephanotises, but-tercups, candytufts, forget-me-nots, phlox, sweet peas, sedums, snow-in-summer, sweet woodruff, vinca, and viburnums.

Your formality level can always be achieved with the type of flowers you choose, and by now you know that roses, gardenias, calla lilies and orchids spell formal while daisies and wildflowers create an informal look.

The beauty of the floral-accented headpiece is that it can be customized to suit any level of formality, any location, and any season. Springtime brides love to affix tiny, brightly colored spring flowers to their headbands, and winter brides bring touches of evergreen to their hair to coordinate with an evergreen and holly winter bouquet.

YELLOW ● LIGHT

Remember that less is more when it comes to floral accents on headbands, because you want your face to be in the spotlight when you make your first appearance at the ceremony. You don't want a mound of flowers on your head to distract onlookers from the elegant simplicity of your gown. A too-deep hue such as dark purple can be too overwhelming a look, so don't go too dramatic with color.

Sprays and Bunches

- Some flowers grow in bunches, and as such, a small cluster is ideal for headpiece accenting.

- These flowers include alyssums, andromedas, astilbes, azaleas, candytufts, Canterbury bells, Carolina jessamine, celosia, forget-me-nots, forsythias, heather, lavender, lilac, lilies of the valley, mock orange, mountain laurel, phlox, and snapdragons.

- These flowers look best when spaced across the length of the headband or placed in one accent spot just above the ear (as if tucked behind the ear).

Flowers on Headbands

- Fabric-covered headbands are the best choice for floral accenting, as flowers don't adhere well to plastic headbands.

- Consider different widths of headbands, from a modest half inch to a wider three inches.

- Add some visual punch to your headband by selecting one with crystal or embroidered borders, which can frame your flower addition.

- Smaller flowers may be pinned or hot glued onto the fabric of a headband, while larger flowers adhere better with pins.

PERSONAL FLOWERS

107

MOTHERS' CORSAGES

Honor your mother, future mother-in-law, and stepmom with the prettiest corsages possible

The most traditional moms prefer the classic corsage, affixed to either the dress strap or the jacket she wears over the dress.

For the past few years, the collarbone-level corsage has been a mainstay only for traditional-minded moms, as some moms and brides find the look to be too reminiscent of prom corsages from yesteryear. Those who choose to stick with the look say they are of two camps: They either want the most traditional rose-and-gardenia or –orchid corsage, or they want a little something more dramatic, oversize, and artistic.

In this section, you'll explore the different twists you can take with a classic corsage, including adding unexpected

Roses

- A simple, classic corsage may be made with a single, giant Ecuadorian rose in full bloom.

- Triad corsages are created with three roses, plus coordinating flowers such as stephanotises, for a corsage that reaches four to five inches.

- A more dramatic look extends to over six inches, with five to six roses used in a slight S shape.

- The corsage may be monochromatic, such as all white roses, or it may include pastels, seasonal colors, or brights.

Orchids

- Orchids provide dramatic shapes to the moms' corsages.

- Ask moms to show you the size corsage they would like to wear.

- Petite moms look best in smaller corsages, especially

with the shape and drama of orchids.

- Dendrobium or cattleya orchids are top choices for mothers' pieces.

- Cattleya, originating from Costa Rica to tropical South America, are a favorite at cultural weddings.

flowers and greenery for a mom's ultimate personalized flower accent. This too needs to work with the formality of the event, as well as with the style of her dress, so color, shape, and dimension become important factors to share with your floral designer or to keep in mind if you will create the corsage on your own.

Simpler corsages work with both simpler and more detailed dresses and gowns, while oversize and multiflowered corsages do not work with a dress that has a lot of design elements, such as a beaded bodice.

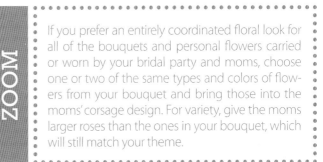
Gardenias

- Make sure moms' gardenia corsages are freshly made so the flowers are in ideal shade and shape to wear.

- Gardenias are so visually stunning that they do not need additional flowers as accenting.

- Gardenias are quite fragrant, so be sure the mothers are aware of the strong aroma.

- For a larger, more dramatic corsage, use two or three gardenias per piece, with or without accenting flowers of other varieties.

Pin-on Primer

- Place the corsage on the mother's jacket or bodice at the exact location she prefers it.

- Stick a straight pin through the underside of the fabric to pierce the flower at an angle through the bottom of the flower head and then right back out again.

- Return the pin through the fabric to secure the corsage in place.

- Tug at the corsage to be sure it's secure.

MOTHERS' FLOWERS

WRISTLETS FOR MOMS
Create fabulous floral pieces for modern moms who don't like corsages

Moms want to look modern, sophisticated, and fashionable at the wedding, and to them, a traditional, pin-on corsage is too old a look, too cliché, and again too promlike.

With so much care put into choosing the perfect gown to wear as the mother of the bride or groom, many moms do not want to puncture the beautiful fabric with a pin-on, nor alter the look of their gowns in any way, such as with a corsage. For these style-conscious moms, the wristlet corsage is the perfect answer. It allows them the honor of a floral piece, identifying them as a mother at the wedding, and it doesn't detract from their fashion statement.

Again, formality is determined by the style of the wristlet,

Roses

- The traditional mom often chooses full rose heads for her wristlet.

- The roses may be of any coordinating color, including all white if she so chooses.

- Be sure the rose heads are bloomed at the time of wearing, since a tightly budded rose does not give the proper textural effect.

- The average wristlet has two or three roses without greenery or filler flowers that can make the piece too large.

Orchids

- A wristlet is best designed as a petite piece, but one dramatic, large orchid may be the ideal balance to the mother's wrist.

- Work with the colors of the orchid, such as including tiny purple filler flowers to work with an orchid's purple streak.

- Be sure the orchid chosen works in balance with the mother's body size, such as a thinner, more elongated wristlet for a more petite mother.

- A plus-size mom can balance her look with a longer wristlet with one or two narrower flowers.

the flowers chosen, and the type of filler or ribbon accent chosen, and a wristlet is acceptable for any formality, style, and location. Moms get to design their own floral looks with the wristlet, deciding if they want a more demure, smaller floral piece in traditional roses, or a larger, more dramatic, artsy statement such as with an orchid or unexpected colors.

This is one area where the moms get to make their own decisions, guided by you, of course.

· · · · · · · · · · YELLOW ● LIGHT · · · · · · · · · ·

The moms' wristlets don't have to match each other, just like the moms themselves do not have to dress alike. The wristlet allows each mom to express her personality and perhaps bring in a meaningful flower from her own wedding day. They don't have to be the same size, the same color, or the same flowers, but they do have to work with the formality of the wedding.

Smaller Wristlets

- Let the beauty of the wristlet be in the beauty of the flower itself, not in a collection of multiple blooms.

- Choose smaller roses, gardenias, orchids, or other flowers to add multiple blooms and still keep a smaller silhouette.

- An alternative to the wrist corsage is a floral bracelet.

- Mothers can determine their best sizes by going to a floral shop to hold different flowers against their wrists.

Larger Wristlets

- A large, dramatic wristlet can add visual punch to a mom's simpler, more conservative and less adorned dress.

- A mom may be able to purchase a less expensive, simpler dress, knowing that her dramatic orchid wristlet is going to impress.

- Larger wristlets are often made of two or three dramatic flowers plus a small amount of greenery or filler, or four to six smaller flowers.

- Larger wristlets are most often longer, extending halfway up the forearm.

TUSSY MUSSIES

Return to a traditional style of hand-carried florals with a silver twist

As an option for you, the tussy mussy is a popular floral option for moms who want to carry something special, yet still fit in with the romantic, traditional look of a formal wedding. The silver cones of a tussy mussy become a keepsake for each mom, often inscribed with her initials and the wedding date, and often put on display with wedding day photos and dried florals from the big day. Traditional or Old World moms say they love the look of the tussy mussy, as it harkens back to the proper wedding practices of yesteryear. The tradition of old meets today's modern designs.

The tussy mussy is an option for a more formal wedding, with the cones made of silver. Mother of pearl is also a creative option for the floral holder. Flowers protruding from the tussy mussy are often a smaller collection, making this a

Metals

- You'll find tussy mussy holders in gold, silver, gilded, plated, enameled porcelain, hand-cut glass, and pewter.

- You can coordinate his and her tussy mussy designs with narrower cones and give the his version to your fathers.

- A smooth metal cone or

laser-cut filigree design has a Victorian look.

- Silver will tarnish over time, so for keepsakes, a less labor-intensive metal would be a better gift for the moms.

- Small tussy mussy cones work as men's boutonniere holders.

Sizes

- Supersmall tussy mussies may be only two inches long and are meant to be worn on the dress.

- Handheld tussy mussies extend from four to six inches, depending on the size of floral bunch to be inserted.

- Choose a tussy mussy size that is no larger than your or the bridesmaids' bouquets.

- If the tussy mussy will contain large-stemmed flowers such as callas or roses, an eight-inch conical holder will provide more stability to your longer blooms.

smart choice for budget weddings. You'll add shine with the silver holder and floral beauty with its contents.

Tussy mussies are also wise choices for grandmothers, godmothers, stepmothers, and other honored women on the wedding day, and many brides are giving the wives of their officiants these same floral pieces as a thank you, a welcome to the wedding day, and a keepsake.

ZOOM

Peruse floral industry wholesale catalogs to find the best array of tussy mussy holders at the lowest prices. Bear in mind that the current financial market for metals will impact the costs of these pieces, as silvers and white golds fluctuate along with the prices of precious metals on the commodities market. Researching and perhaps shopping from floral wholesalers will net you good prices .

Design

- Victorian-era tussy mussies were quite ornate and an indicator of the carrier's wealth and status.

- You'll find filigree tussy mussies with a dotted border around the top, floral scroll designs, intricate Celtic designs, and other detailed designs.

- You can order custom-made metal designs if you would like to match the lace or embroidery in a mother's dress.

- A metal tussy mussy might resemble the opening bud of a trumpet-shaped flower like a daffodil.

Color

- There's no rule that says the tussy mussy needs to be silver or gold.

- While silver and gold were the most common shades back in Victorian days, today's advanced artistry allows for bold colors such as cobalt for a bright blue floral holder.

- Look at colored metals such as those with a blush pink hue for a decorative accent.

- Enamel-based holders can be painted with any design you desire, and the color pattern of the holder may coordinate with the flowers within.

113

MOTHERS' FLOWERS

NOSEGAY BOUQUETS
Choose smaller bouquets to allow the moms to carry their own special floral pieces

In the past, moms had two choices for their personal flowers on wedding day: corsages or wristlets. No one seemed to venture from these traditional forms of floral tribute. Now moms are considered a part of the bridal party, and as such are given their own bouquets to carry.

The key is that moms' bouquets are styled to be smaller than the bride's and bridesmaids' bouquets, tightly packed clusters of gorgeous flowers, often in styles that don't need to match anyone else's. This means the moms get the fun and joy of designing their own small bouquets with the colors that work best for their gowns and the flowers that work best with the formality and season of the wedding.

Formal Nosegays

Nosegays for Outdoor Weddings

- If your wedding will be a formal, traditional one, the mothers' nosegays will often be smaller versions of your own bouquet.

- Keep the formality with the flower choices, such as roses and ranunculus, but add depth and originality with different filler.

- Nosegays made without filler, with just flowers, imparts a more formal look.

- Add something special to the nosegay handle wrap, such as a charm attached to lovely ribbon.

- Incorporate the same types of flowers that will be featured at your outdoor wedding site, such as the apricot-colored roses found en masse in the gardens.

- For an informal outdoor wedding, the mothers' daisies might be yellow while yours are white.

- A tight cluster of tulips makes for a lovely spring nosegay for the moms.

- The moms might carry paler shades of the bridesmaids' richer-tone Gerber daisies or roses.

For the moms' nosegays, you use much of the planning wisdom already shared in this book and add some delightful personalizations that add messages of love and honor to the most important women in your life.

Remember: Nosegays are also the perfect tribute florals for grandmothers, godmothers, stepmothers, favorite aunts, and other special women in your life.

What's to be gained by keeping the moms' bouquets small? It saves money, often costing one third the price of a bride's bouquet, and it still looks elegant and sophisticated.

YELLOW LIGHT

When you let the mothers know they get to design their own nosegays, help them choose the correct size as well as the best flowers to coordinate with the bridal party, your décor, and their own gowns. Scout out Web sites that have galleries of bouquet designs—and don't limit yourself to bridal and florists' Web sites. For example, you'll find a world of possibilities on stock photo agency Web sites.

Subtle Nosegays

- As with your gown, the mothers' gowns may be visual masterpieces, not needing floral accents to make an impact.

- Some moms design very understated nosegays with all one shade of roses, as a concerted effort not to compete with the brides-

maids' or bride's bouquet.

- The key to subtlety is a single shape of nosegay, such as a round with no trailing ribbons.

- Subtle nosegays are most often pastel in tone, including traditional bridal flowers rather than exotics.

Bright Nosegays

- Brights create a visual pop that works perfectly only when the rest of the bridal party carries bright colors too.

- Moms can bring in brights when mixed with pastels or deeper jewel tones, according to the color theme of the wedding.

- Keep bright nosegays on the smaller side as just a touch of color that coordinates with the dress color.

- Never try to match a bright bouquet color to a bright dress color, as it's almost impossible to match tones.

MOMS' FAVORITE FLOWERS

Use the moms' favorite and most symbolic flowers in their bouquets and floral pieces

Add extra sentimentality to mothers' wear-or-carry flowers by choosing blooms that call back to the best times of the moms' lives. There's something very special and indeed spiritual about using the same types of flowers the mothers chose for their own most important moments before your wedding day, or before you even came along!

Since you are personalizing your wedding day in many aspects of the plans, including the menu and song list, the moms get to personalize the symbolism of their bouquets with their favorite flowers. What's more, the act of designing their floral pieces can open beautiful conversations between mother and daughter or future in-laws in which the bride

Flowers from Their Weddings

- Ask the mothers to list the flowers they used in their own wedding bouquets. They can include these in their bouquets at your wedding.

- Don't limit yourself to their bouquets; what did they use in their centerpieces?

- If the mothers wore flowers in their hair at their garden weddings, these flowers can be incorporated into their bouquets.

- Which types of flowers did they choose for their mothers at their weddings? These may be your family's new traditional choice.

Her Birth-Month Flower

- The moms might decide to use their own birth-month flowers in their individual floral pieces.

- Review the list of birth month flowers in the Resource Directory to find which blooms are designated as the moms' birth-month flowers.

- The moms might want to use the birth-month flowers of their own weddings.

- Suggest a personalized mix of your mother's birth-month flower with your birth-month flower for a meaningful piece.

often learns priceless stories about the parents' first date or a flower that brings the moms back to their formative years, even if it's a memory of picking wildflowers as toddlers, walking through fields with a beloved parent (grandparents to the bride and groom).

The moms might want to use the bride's or groom's birth-month flowers as a homage to your presence in their lives.

When you invite the mothers to imbue their floral pieces with blooms that have a history, that history becomes a part of your wedding day as well, and the mothers' own histories are honored as well.

For a mother who has departed, her memory may be honored with the bloom of rosemary, which symbolizes remembrance.

Flowers from Their Childhood

- Ask the mothers to talk about favorite childhood memories associated with flowers.

- Don't limit yourself to flowers; trees are also part of the memory choices. So ask the mothers about cherry blossom trees and willow trees, fruit bushes, and grasses that hold memories for them.

- Ask the mothers: What was the first flower your husbands ever gave you? What flowers were involved in their engagement? What flowers are part of their love story as they grow older together?

Flowers with Symbolism

- Moms can use the language of flowers to add symbolism to their floral pieces.

- Consider the following blooms symbolizing maternal traits: burgundy roses (beauty), cattleya orchids (mature charm), celandines (joys to come), crocuses (cheerfulness), dahlias (elegance), honeysuckles (bonds of love), lotuses (eloquence), magnolias (love of nature), mosses (maternal love), myrtles (vessel or motherhood), oak leaves (strength), olive branches (peace), violets (modesty), white roses (virtue).

GRANDMOTHERS & OTHER MOMS

Honor grandmothers, godmothers, stepmothers, and other moms with their own florals

A wedding is a joining together of two people in love, and the people around the bride and groom also share the spotlight as VIPs of the wedding day. The entire family descended from these people; some play important roles in guiding your lives, and others are responsible for having placed you in the right place at the right time to meet the love of your life. That deserves a corsage or a nosegay, right? Without these women, you might not exist, or you might be living on a different continent, enmeshed in a different world and life altogether.

In any capacity, the special women in your life are partially responsible for how you turned out, and they certainly

Corsages

- Grandmothers and other traditionalists might hold a fondness for the pin-on corsage, so be sure to ask if they'd like this style.

- Create smaller corsages to prevent competing or clashing with the recipient's dress accents such as sequins or bugle beading.

- Stick with white flowers if you are not sure of the recipient's dress color.

- Use the grandmother's, godmother's, or other VIP woman's birth-month flower in her corsage.

Wristlets

- Create identical wristlets for each of these honored women, such as classic white rose wristlets, which will often work with any style or color of dress.

- Keep wristlets on the smaller side, no larger than four inches, to work with every woman's body size.

- Add a meaningful charm to each wristlet and tell the recipient the charm's meaning, such as gratitude, luck, or good health.

- Limit the ribbon bows, which are not very modern looking and may clash with the color the women are wearing.

played a role in creating the warm and welcoming family atmosphere that may have sold your fiancé on wanting you in his life forever. He is marrying into your family, after all. He may love these women, too.

So, given their special place in your life—or in the lives of your fathers, if you're not particularly close to a stepmother—it's time to design special floral pieces for these ladies of your lineage.

Nosegays and Pomanders

- Grandmothers and others will be delighted to resemble the mothers and bridesmaids with their own nosegay bouquets.

- Again, nosegays should be smaller than the bridesmaids' and bride's bouquet.

- Filler and stock allow for budget-friendly nosegays that contain just a few pricier flowers.

- Pomanders, small balls of flowers connected to a wrist-worn ribbon, are a lovely choice for mothers and grandmothers.

Presenting Floral Pieces to Grandmothers and Others

- If these honored women will be present at the site where you will be getting dressed and receiving your own bouquet for pre-wedding photos, take a moment to present each woman with her floral piece.

- As you present the corsage, nosegay, or wristlet, say a few words of thanks and tell each woman what she means to you.

- Prepare a printed love letter to each woman on your VIP list, sharing your sentiments, thanking them for their lifetime of love and support, as the perfect wedding day keepsake.

119

GROOM'S & MEN'S BOUTONNIERES

Select the perfect coordinating designs for the men's and boys' boutonnieres

That little floral accent on the groom's lapel, as well as on the lapels of groomsmen, fathers, grandfathers, godfathers, and ring bearers, often takes a cue from the flowers in your bouquet. You might choose one signature bloom from your collection, such as a rose, and design a stylish boutonniere that all the men wear in a uniform look, or you can follow

the trend of having each man wear a different yet coordinating lapel flower, such as a dendrobium orchid for the groom, a sprig of stephanotis for the best man, a rose for a groomsman, a delphinium for another groomsman, and so on. There's no rule saying all the men have to have matching flowers, and some brides and grooms prefer that their men

Traditional Roses

- The most common boutonniere is a single rose, with or without a sprig of baby's breath and greenery.

- While white is the most popular color, red and sweetheart pink are popular to coordinate with the bridal theme.

- Spray roses allow you to have multiple small roses in one boutonniere.

- Consider the leonidas rose, which is a blend of red and orange, or a peace rose with darker shading at the edges of the petals.

Traditional Dendrobium Orchids

- The dendrobium orchid allows the men to add a bit of unexpected flair to their boutonnieres with an exotic bloom.

- The dendrobium orchid looks best when not accented with baby's breath or other filler flowers.

- Several dendrobiums may be wired together for a slightly larger, more dramatic boutonniere.

- A white dendrobium orchid paired with seeded eucalyptus and eucalyptus leaves provides an unexpected mix of flower and greenery.

have a signature accent all their own. Or, the groomsmen match, but the fathers have different flowers. What matters most, as with all design elements of your wedding, is that the boutonniere works with the formality, season, and style of your wedding and that the flower or flowers you choose are fresh, beautiful, and perfectly crafted to keep their shape while worn all day.

In this section you'll explore the different types of boutonniere options, from traditional to alternative, for all your men (and boys).

········· YELLOW ● LIGHT ·········

The size of the boutonniere is very important, because a tall man wouldn't look right wearing a super-mall boutonniere, while a shorter man would look comical wearing a larger, rounder boutonniere. Be sure to consider your men's heights and relative sizes (lean, stocky, etc.) so that the perfect dimension of boutonniere can be chosen to flatter them all. Lapel width is also a factor for floral dimension.

Traditional Mini–Calla Lilies

- If you have calla lilies in your bouquet, the natural decision may be to create your groom's or the men's boutonnieres with single or triple mini–calla lilies.

- Callas come in white, light green, yellow, even darker cabernet colors.

- Mini–calla lily boutonnieres do not need filler flowers, as their unique shape and curl of the petals provide the perfect amount of visual effect.

- Calla lilies suit formal wedding style requirements just as well as roses and orchids.

The Top Trends in Traditional Men's Flowers

- Most boutonnieres consist of a single, fully bloomed flower, which often costs under $5.

- Use sprays for multiple flowers per pin.

- A new trend to achieve color coordination is to use brights and striped ribbon.

- You'll now find fasteners made with strong magnets that attach the boutonniere from the front to the back of the jacket. Just be aware that anyone wearing a pacemaker will not be able to use magnetic fasteners. Ask all of your men if they're clear for this option.

ALTERNATIVE BOUTONNIERES

Add some artistry and an unexpected flair to your men's boutonnieres with unique florals

For some wedding couples, the traditional rose boutonniere is not what they have in mind. They want something unique, fun, and outside the usual realm of bridal flowers—maybe a floral from their love story, such as the tuberose that was in the engagement bouquet or the lisianthus that graces the garden outside their vacation home.

Besides visual appeal, nontraditional flowers are often less expensive than those bridal roses, orchids, gardenias, and callas that have always been in such demand for weddings and so are priced higher during peak wedding season. Compared to these bridal blooms, nontraditional flowers might cost half as much!

Seasonal Flowers

- For spring weddings, consider a mini-tulip, -daffodil, or -peony.

- For outdoor summer weddings, use a bright Gerber daisy, zinnia, ranunculus, mini–calla lily, or rose.

- For fall weddings, leonidas roses with their orange hue are ideal, as are orange, red, or yellow mums or zinnias.

- For winter, a red rose fits the seasonal theme, and some couples have fun by adding mini–jingle bells to the boutonniere.

Unexpected Flowers

- Lisianthus creates an ideal, colorful boutonniere with or without filler flowers.

- Freesia presents the chance to incorporate a blush color, such as two narrow pink blooms in a single boutonniere.

- Tuberose allows you to include a bridal white flower, but it's not the expected rose or stephanotis.

- Kalanchoes provide the same tiny flower effect as baby's breath, just in colorful star shapes.

When you open your mind to alternative flowers, you find yourself researching and learning about a world of gorgeous flowers that are still masculine enough for the men to wear, and you may also find a bloom to add to your bridal bouquet. Who says the men's flowers have to come from your collection? It could work the other way around! Floral designers say they love it when wedding couples ask to see nonbridal blooms, because they can show off their talents in unique ways and share photos in their portfolios from other types of special events.

Cone of Florals

- A stiff fabric cone can be fashioned to hold a single flower or sprig of flowers.

- A small laser-cut metal cone can also hold florals when pinned to a lapel.

- Most metal cones are made of filigree silver, and they may be solid or of lattice-work construction.

- Small blooms or bunches of filler flowers such as lilies of the valley are ideal for cone boutonnieres.

Nonflorals

- Construct a fabric leaf to take the place of a floral boutonniere. Cut a leaf shape from a swatch of leather, wool, or stiff cotton and decorate as needed.

- For a beach wedding, a starfish-shaped pin can take the place of a floral boutonniere.

- For an autumn wedding, fashion a boutonniere from a small, glued-together arrangement of pinecones with acorn accents.

- If the men are going to wear suits, give them colorful pocket squares to wear, rather than floral boutonnieres.

FLOWER & BERRY BOUTONNIERES

Add a pop of color with tiny berry additions to floral boutonnieres

In any season, and in any formality of wedding, a top trend for boutonnieres is to add a tiny sprig of berries to a single flower or cluster of flowers to add a natural touch to the piece. In light of the trend for "green" weddings, berries are becoming more popular because they bring an organic effect, extra pop of color, and unexpected texture to the men's lapels.

When we say berries, we don't mean blueberries or strawberries of the edible variety. That would just be silly and would obviously wreck a pricy suit or tuxedo. The berries for use in boutonnieres are natural, hard berries that are often used as filler in bouquets and centerpieces.

Grooms who choose berry accents for the guys' boutonnieres like the mix of shapes in their small lapel pieces. Round berries can accent a cone-shaped mini–calla lily or the curl

Stephanotises and Berries

- Tiny white stephanotises provide an ideal basis for an artistic boutonniere, with either white or colored berries accenting the piece.

- The star shape of stephanotises pairs nicely with the round shape of berries, so you can even choose slightly larger berries.

- It can be difficult to match white tones, so be sure to see examples of any white berries to be paired with stephanotises.

- Use faux berries in a boutonniere. This is a subtle look when paired with fresh flowers.

White Flowers, Ivy, and Berries

- A sprig of ivy can add dimension to a traditional white flower boutonniere—whether it be roses, orchids, callas, or stephanotises.

- Ivy symbolizes fidelity in marriage.

- The hand shape of ivy brings the different shapes of the flowers and the dots of berries together as a well-designed floral piece.

- Match the color of the berry to the veins or streaks of color in the ivy, such as a light green or pink, to keep from having more than three colors in a boutonniere.

of rose petals or the dramatic shape of an orchid. The circle effect might also coordinate with the design of the vest and tie, if they haven't chosen a solid color. Think of berry accents paired with flowers as a way to customize the groom's or groomsmen's look, an artistic touch to replace the ho-hum baby's breath.

····················· RED ● LIGHT ················

Make sure that berries are hard and solid before adding them to any boutonniere. Again, hugs are frequent during weddings, as is slow dancing, and you don't want a crushed boutonniere to leave what looks like a bloody stain right over the groom's heart. Ask your floral designer, wholesaler, or supplier to show you the hardest berries in stock, and look at berries in whites and oranges.

Simply Berries

- Use just a sprig of berries— fresh or faux—as the boutonniere.

- A three-inch-wide sprig of berries is the ideal proportion to the standard lapel.

- Stick with one type of berry for this boutonniere. You don't want a grouping of two or more berries to look like a fruit salad!

- A large, dramatic leaf such as coleus, or a single fern, can be a great backing to a sprig of berries.

Berries to Consider

- Each season presents different colors of berries.

- Hypericum berries are popular in all seasons and are the most popular bridal berry due to their range of colors: white, ivory, red, pink, burgundy, peach, yellow, and green.

- For all seasons, look at rosehips, which are tiny red berries, and tallow, which are tiny white berries.

- For a pink wedding theme consider pepperberry, which is a cluster of tiny pink berries that can work just as well as filler in your bouquet.

GREENERY FOR BOUTONNIERES

Make your boutonnieres stand out with well-chosen greenery for added color and texture

While some grooms like the simple look of a single white rose pinned to their lapel, others like a multilayered boutonniere that shows off their chosen flower with a backdrop of natural color. They also like the visual interest of a unique or traditional greenery piece. A backdrop of green coordinates with the greenery and filler in your own bouquet, so this may

be a great way to have him match your florals that will add visual interest in person and in pictures.

As with all personal florals, you'll need to be sure the size of the greenery is well proportioned to both the flower and the lapel. You don't want a tiny flower placed on a large leaf, or it will look dwarfed, and you don't want a gigantic flower and gigantic leaf

Ivy

- Ivy comes in a range of colors, from light green to dark green.

- Ivy might be a solid color such as a deep green, or it might be veined with darker green lines or even light green lines in the center, which opens the opportunity to blend white,

light green, or even pink flowers.

- Mix small and large ivy leaf varieties.

- Make sure the ivy you use matches the ivy in your bouquet.

Fern

- A single fern branch is a popular choice for boutonniere backdrops.

- Choose from maidenhair, leatherleaf, and other varieties found at gardening and floral resources mentioned in Resources.

- A fern branch should

extend only an inch above and below a flower to avoid an amateurish look that dwarfs the bloom.

- Many ferns dry and curl rather quickly in hot weather, so the men should take their floral pieces out of a cooler and pin them on right before the ceremony.

on a narrow lapel worn by a guy who's on the shorter side. Too much greenery can look like a shrub, so avoid overkill.

Overall, greenery in boutonnieres is a top choice for couples who consciously incorporate a very lush, natural look into their entire floral design. If you have chosen lots of greenery in your bouquets and centerpieces, perhaps as a way to save money, your choice of greenery on the lapel ties the entire floral theme together. The groom and other men would look unfinished if their pieces were the only ones without greenery, for instance.

ZOOM

No matter which type of flower you choose for the boutonnieres, but especially if the men are going to wear different types of flowers such as one type for the groomsmen and one type for the fathers, choose a traditional, classic type of greenery such as fern or ivy for their boutonnieres. These readily available types of greenery will cost you less than if you were to go exotic.

Coleus

- Coleus is a type of greenery with lots of color in its smooth, rounded leaves.

- Coleus can be found in the following color patterns: green and white; green and pink; green, pink, and white; and green and yellow.

- Some coleus looks like flowering cabbage plants of the fall, with more of a green and purple or burgundy appearance.

- Be sure that coleus leaves are dry before you use them for boutonnieres.

Evergreen

- For winter weddings, a sprig of evergreen is the greenery of choice for boutonnieres.

- Some varieties of evergreen produce thicker, softer needles, as opposed to spikier ones, so investigate the types at your floral supplier.

- The fresher the cut, the softer the evergreen needles, so this type of greenery should be cut from the tree or branches right before making the boutonniere.

- Think twice about pairing evergreen with a sprig of holly to avoid pinch.

127

SETTING THE GROOM APART

Make the groom's boutonniere extra special with custom flowers, greenery, and accents

In the vast majority of weddings, the groom's boutonniere is designed to stand apart from the groomsmen's, fathers', and ring bearer's boutonnieres. It may be that the groom is the only man to wear a white flower, or that he is the only man to wear a rose, while the rest wear sprigs of stephanotis. Your options are endless, and you'll explore your design choices here.

Again, keep in mind the size that best flatters the groom, as you don't want to go too small or too large for his frame or lapel. Also keep in mind the season of the wedding, since that may inspire a design idea such as his wearing a white tulip and his men wearing orange for a spring wedding.

Your final style consideration is of course the formality

Flower Type

- Choose a flower type from your bouquet, such as a rose, and use that as the only rose in any boutonniere.

- The groom can wear the most formal type of flower from your bouquet, and the groomsmen can wear less formal or filler-type flowers from your or your brides-

maids' bouquets.

- For a beach or destination wedding, the groom can wear an exotic flower such as an hibiscus or bird of paradise. Your groom can wear the same type of flower that was in the bouquet he presented to you when you got engaged.

Flower Color

- If the groom wants to wear a white flower, his men may wear pastels or brights.

- Since many grooms like to add color to their own looks, the new trend is for the groom to wear a bright color, while the other men wear softer shades of the same color.

- If a groom wants to wear pastel, his men can wear brights.

of the wedding, as this will determine if he wears a classic rose or if a tuft of wildflowers to match your casual bouquet would be the perfect fit.

Grooms enjoy having their say in the design of the floral piece they'll wear, so be sure to show your groom the options shown here as well as photos from bridal magazines and Web sites. He needs to know the great many choices he has . . . including that he can add an unexpected accent to his floral piece.

ZOOM

Visit www.fiftyflowers.com as well as the Web sites of both local and distant floral designers to see their galleries of boutonniere styles. With just a few clicks, you may discover the perfect design to help you create the groom's ideal custom boutonniere. The more graphics you can show your groom, the better. Men say they prefer to be exposed to a range of unique designs, whether in print or online.

Flower Size

- The groom can wear a full-size white rose, while the other men wear baby rosebuds.

- If daisies are your theme, the groom can wear a large Gerber daisy, while the other men wear smaller stock daisies in white or yellow.

- Size can be built into a boutonniere by designing a three-flower piece for the groom, while the other men get single flowers.

- Give the groom several flowers, while the grooms-men's pieces consist of just a single flower with ivy.

Top Mistakes in Setting the Groom's Boutonniere Apart

- Designing too large a piece for the groom so that it looks exactly like his mother's corsage or your bouquet.

- Adding crystals and lace in an effort to match your bouquet, but instead creating too feminine an effect.

- Adding too many different flowers to the lapel.

- Adding too many layers to the boutonniere. Always stop at just a floral, a greenery leaf, and one filler, such as berries.

FATHERS' & RING BEARERS' FLOWERS

Choose the right floral accents for the other male VIPs of the wedding party

At most weddings, the fathers and ring bearers also wear boutonnieres, regardless of whether they're wearing a tuxedo or a suit. Some couples also choose to honor their grandfathers, godfathers, stepfathers, and male ceremony participants with boutonnieres of their own.

These men's and boys' boutonnieres are custom-created

to the right size and formality for the wedding, as well as at widths designed to suit each man's or boy's size. To personalize, you might wish to style one type of boutonniere for grandfathers—such as a single white rose— and then have a different type of flower for the godfathers, and so on. Some couples design one type of boutonniere for all of the men,

Boutonnieres in White

- The white flowers of formal or informal boutonnieres can be the same as those in your bouquet.

- The white flowers can also be the same as those used in groomsmen's boutonnieres.

- The most common white flowers for dads and grand-fathers are roses, mini–calla lilies, and stephanotises, with traditional white fillers such as baby's breath or kelanchoe.

- Orchids and gardenias are considered too feminine for men.

Boutonnieres in Pastels

- Dads and others can wear boutonnieres that match the groomsmen's shades in pastels, or they can be a shade darker.

- If the groomsmen are wearing pastel roses, these men can perhaps wear smaller pastel roses or multiples of smaller roses.

- The most popular pastel colors for dads and other men are greens, blues, pinks, oranges, lavenders, and yellows.

- Mix pastels to match the mix of pastel colors in your or the bridesmaids' bouquets, staying within two or three shades of hue.

including the fathers, setting no one apart.

For the boys, boutonnieres are best kept very small, to keep the youngest of ring bearers from becoming annoyed at a bulky boutonniere on the jacket they're already annoyed to be wearing!

Your style choices can be inspired by the season, by your wedding colors, and even by the location, such as an island flower at a destination wedding. The formality also opens the options for informal weddings to include daisies or wildflowers like the ones in your bouquet.

YELLOW LIGHT

Be sure to ask these men about any floral allergies they might have, even if that means ruining your planned surprise in getting them boutonnieres. It would be a shame to impose a runny nose on a grandfather who's allergic to certain flowers, or to waste money when a man has to remove the boutonniere because it's making him sneeze.

Boutonnieres in Brights

- If the groom or groomsmen will have bright boutonnieres, these men can as well.

- The most popular bright colors for men are red, purple, and orange.

- If you're considering bright colors for these men, be sure to let them know ahead of time that you have chosen, say, a red flower so that they can choose an outfit that will not clash, such as a blue striped shirt.

- With bright colors, it's always better to design smaller boutonnieres.

Ring Bearers' Flowers

- The top trend is for the ring bearers' flowers to match the groom's flowers in color and style.

- The ring bearers' boutonnieres can be designed to match the best man's, which can be set apart from the groomsmen in shade and floral type.

- The ring bearers' flowers should be half the size of the men's.

- The ring bearers' boutonnieres can consist of one flower, while the other men's contain several.

- Be sure the boys do not have floral allergies.

FLOWER GIRLS' WREATHS

Designing pretty floral wreaths for your adorable flower girls to wear or carry

While you're certainly the center of attention on your wedding day, a true beauty in every sense of the word, your flower girls receive a different type of attention: Aren't they just adorable?

While a pretty party dress helps to create the adorable flower girl image, it's the flowers that make the impression

all the sweeter. Over the following pages, you'll design your flower girls' wreaths, nosegays, and other floral accents. Your first focus is on wreaths. At first thought, you might think flower girl wreaths are always worn on the head as a delightful crown of flowers, but that is not the only use for this pretty style. Today's flower girls might also carry their wreath

Pastel Wreaths

- Even when flower girls wear white party dresses to match the bride, the most common floral head wreath is made of pastel flowers.

- A pastel floral wreath looks marvelous when coordinated with pastel flower petals in a carried basket or with a colored sash worn around the waist.

- The most common flower girl wreath tones are pinks, yellows, and lavenders.

- Use small flowers, such as baby rosebuds, instead of full, round bloomed roses.

White Wreaths

- Another option is to style the Mini-Me wreath to include the same types of flowers as those in your bouquet, all in white.

- An all-white wreath can be accented with a few pastel or bright flowers.

- If you're on a tight budget, add plenty of white by including just a few white roses and using baby's breath.

- A floral wreath can be made purely of baby's breath—without roses. This keeps it light to wear and inexpensive to make.

hoops in place of petal baskets, and more than one flower girl has held her floral wreath in front of her as if driving a car! The effect, no matter how the girl wears or carries her floral wreath, is always a crowd-pleaser.

Again, your flower and style choices should adhere to the formality and season of your wedding, as well as to the uniformity of your entire bridal look.

One popular trend to consider is to have your flower girls wear floral wreath headpieces if you will wear a floral wreath headpiece or flowers in your hair.

Three-Flower Wreaths

- Rather than have a dozen and a half flowers attached all the way around a wreath, affix just three big roses or flowers to the crown of the wreath and wrap the rest of the circle with ribbon.

- Space these three flowers a few inches apart and separate them with baby's breath or other filler.

- Re-create the look of your three-stone ring by placing one large flower in the center and one smaller flower on each side, then wrapping the rest with satin ribbon.

Tips to Ensure Children's Comfort

- Keep the wreath as smooth as possible, such as with a ribbon wrap around most of the ring, for ultimate comfort.

- Trailing lace should extend just past the girl's shoulders and not down the back where it can itch.

- Place the wreath on your own head first to see if you feel any stems poking your scalp.

- Keep the wreath as light as possible, such as with small flowers rather than full roses.

- Add a small pair of scissors to your emergency bag so that you can easily snip off a flower or leaf that's bothering a child.

FLOWER GIRLS' NOSEGAYS
Design small bouquets for your adorable flower girls to carry

Why choose a nosegay, or a smaller bouquet, for your flower girls to carry? You might like that image of the Mini-Me version of you, or you saw it in a magazine and thought it was sweet, or your site doesn't allow the scattering of flower petals . . . so it would be pointless for your flower girls to carry a basket of petals. Some brides also choose to avoid the cliché look of flower girls carrying petal baskets, and others don't

want to slide on slippery rose petals while walking down the aisle. There are tons of reasons why a flower girl might be given a small bouquet to carry, not the least of which is that the little ones love hearing, "Your bouquet looks just like mine!" from the bride she's looking at in awe on wedding day. Having her own bouquet makes the flower girl feel special.

White Nosegays

Pastel Nosegays

- White nosegays can be designed as a smaller-size match to your all-white bouquet.

- If flower girls are wearing white dresses, an all-white nosegay can get lost in the monochromatic look, so consider pastels or greenery to add dimension.

- Just four or five flowers are all that's needed for a flower girl nosegay.

- At a less formal wedding, the all-white nosegay can be made of baby's breath or your white bouquet filler as a way to save money and still provide a bridal look.

- The flower girls' nosegays can be a smaller-size match to the bridesmaids' bouquets.

- If you've set apart your maid or matron of honor's bouquet as a monochromatic pastel bouquet, with bridesmaids carrying mixes,

flower girls' can match the maid of honor's style.

- Generally, flower girls look best carrying lighter-colored nosegays, because darker hues like burgundies create a more adult effect.

Nosegays are ideal for any formality of wedding, from ultra-formal right down to casual, and your styling of flowers and fillers determines how well they fit into the theme of the day. When it comes to color for the flower girls, you can match these bouquets' hues to the bridesmaids' bouquets, or you can allow the little ones to carry all-white nosegays like your bouquet. The girls' flowers can also match the flowers worn on the men's lapels, such as a nosegay made of all pink roses.

ZOOM

Allow flower girls to help design their own floral head wreaths, but make it far easier by limiting their choices. Show them photos of three to five different nosegays or flowers and ask which of these they prefer. It's courting disaster if you ask a five-year-old, "What kinds of flowers do you like?" because her insistence on daisies could clash with your more formal wedding plans.

Mixed Nosegays

- Choose two or three varieties of flowers from your own bouquet, and then create the coordinating mix from those.

- Choose smaller flowers or sprays for nosegays to add the effect of extra blooms without adding too much size or weight.

- One fun trend is to include the flower girls' birth-month flowers in their nosegay bouquets. See the Resource Directory for a list of birth-month flowers that can be reviewed for your girls.

Wildflowers

- For your outdoor, garden, or informal wedding, the flower girls can carry the same type of wildflower bouquets that your bridesmaids carry.

- You can choose one kind of wildflower in a single color scheme, or you can mix it up with different types in different colors.

- Ask if children have allergies or sensitivities to wildflowers before buying or designing such pieces.

- Choose a wildflower color that matches each flower girl's sash.

FLOWER GIRLS' BASKETS

Bring the traditional flower girl petal basket to life with pretty blooms and accents

It's the traditional accessory of the flower girl— a pretty basket filled with flower petals that she sprinkles ahead of the bride's path. In today's modern times, the petal basket has gotten a makeover. You'll still see the classic white basket, perhaps covered with white satin and tied with little white or pink bows, but you'll also see wooden or bamboo baskets

to reflect a more natural look at "green" or organic weddings. In some ultrachic weddings, the basket is covered with red satin, and the petals are white, carried by a flower girl in a white dress with a red sash.

The basket itself might also have more style, departing from the traditional little round with the hoop handle. Now you'll

Traditional Petal Baskets

Monochromatic Baskets

- The traditional petal basket is a white, round basket with a round or oval handle made from the same material as the basket.

- Baskets may be left in their natural material, such as wood, or covered with material.

- The most common basket material is satin in white, pink, yellow, or other hue that coordinates with the bridal party.

- It's best to fill baskets with petals only halfway, which is just enough for visual effect and saves you money on your petals purchase.

- A new trend in basket décor is to match the fabric color, such as a pink satin, to the petal color, such as all-pink petals.

- Most brides choose a colored petal so that the handfuls the flower girls scatter will show up against a white aisle runner.

- Choosing a monochromatic basket avoids the "too much" effect of having too many colors, which may be the case if your and your bridesmaids' bouquets contain a mix of more than four colors each.

136

see heart-shaped baskets, ovals, squares, butterfly shapes for garden weddings, and fabric braid handles instead of flimsy balsa wood handles seen on the classic woven basket. Not all brides are shopping at a dollar store for their baskets, and many are going the DIY route, if they're not paying over $50 for a basket in a bridal designer's line.

This flower girl accessory has certainly become a stylish carrying piece, and the petals inside— if there are any—serve to play up the natural beauty of the basket itself.

ZOOM

A new trend in flower girls' baskets is to use florals to decorate the baskets and then fill them with something other than rose petals, such as a theme-appropriate collection of seashells for a beach wedding, colorful ornaments at a holiday wedding, or bright oversize confetti that the flower girl tosses into the air as she walks down the aisle.

Perfect Petals for Baskets

- The traditional petal has long been rose petals for their larger size and curl, as well as their coordination with the flowers in bouquets.

- For a romantic, frilly look, other petals with unique shapes and curl include those from ranunculus and peonies.

- As a callback to the "he loves me, he loves me not" romantic notion, your flower girls could scatter daisy petals.

- As a budget choice, your flower girls could scatter carnation petals, which often cost half as much as rose petals.

Basket Accents and Décor

- Customize the décor on the flower girls' baskets.

- A top choice is to spiral wrap a length of ribbon of a coordinating color along the handle.

- The handle and the rim of the basket can be dotted with glued-on daisy heads.

- Glue on inexpensive butterflies or tiny seashells that you can find at craft stores or floral wholesale supply Web sites.

- If you're using ribbon or lace trails on your bouquet, add the same effect to the flower girls' baskets.

- If you're using stick-in décor (such as butterflies or ladybugs on wire) or crystal accents in your bouquet, add the same to the flower girls' baskets.

FLOWER GIRLS' HAIR FLOWERS

Design pretty floral accents for your flower girls to wear in their hair

The beauty of flowers as part of your wedding day décor is that there are so many options for incorporating them into your wedding vision. Here, you'll think about how your flower girls might wear tiny, precious flowers in their hair.

Perhaps you plan to wear fresh flowers pinned into your updo, and your bridesmaids might accessorize with stephanotises pinned into their French twists. Maybe you've decided that your casual outdoor wedding calls for each bridesmaid to tuck a single daisy behind her ear. If you've considered or decided on flowers as your accessory of choice for your crowning glory, the same can be designed for your littlest attendants. You up the cute factor when you bring florals into the flower girls' wedding day look.

Hair florals can be used in any formality of wedding. At a

Hairpin Flowers

- Use either dark or beige-colored bobby pins to affix flowers in girls' hair.

- Jeweled bobby pins, such as those with pink, yellow, green, or another color rhinestones, are available at teen accessory stores for just a few dollars per set.

- Choose hairpins made from colorful enamel theme icons, such as starfish for a beach wedding.

- Check the craft store to find the same type of pearl- or crystal-head hairpins that you are using for your own hairstyle.

Hair Comb Flowers

- For flower girls with ultrafine hair, a hair comb will provide more support and keep the floral piece in place.

- Hair combs are also a better choice when you decide on larger or multiple flowers for the little ones' hair.

- Again, choose a simpler hair comb if you'd like it to be invisible beneath the floral accent, or choose a jeweled or accented hair comb to allow you to use a smaller flower or filler blooms.

formal wedding tiny roses, lisianthuses, or stephanotises can be expertly placed in a child's updo, for instance. At an informal wedding, that daisy tucked behind the ear brings a feeling of innocence and wonderment, and it may even remind you of a time when you were a little girl who would often tuck daisies behind your own ear while playing in the garden.

It's always important to talk to the flower girls' parents about any plans you have for their wedding day look. If, for instance, you envision the little ones with their hair professionally styled in updos with flowers, the parents may worry about the high price of the salon visit. Or they may worry that flowers in the child's hair will attract bees, to which she is highly allergic. You never want to spring this on parents as a wedding day surprise, as it's not your place to make decisions for their children. Always ask first.

Single-Stem Flowers

- The most popular single-stem flowers to tuck behind a flower girl's ear are daisies, either classic or the larger, colorful Gerber varieties.

- Don't trust the tuck on its own. Affix the flower with three or four bobby pins.

- A single-stem flower can also be tucked into the side of a headband worn by a child.

- Forget about greenery or filler flowers when you're considering a single-stem hair flower; the piece shouldn't look like a nose-gay, nor have too much bulk.

Hair Placement Patterns

- Flowers may be placed along the ridge of a French braid that extends down the back of the child's head.

- Flowers may be placed in an arch across the top of the head, resembling a headband.

- Flowers may be used as accents to a full or partial ponytail, either inserted into the gathering of hair or affixed to a hairband.

- A top new trend is a diamond pattern of tiny flowers arranged on the back of loose, flowing hair.

FLOWER GIRLS' SASH FLOWERS
Attach pretty floral accents to the flower girls' dress sashes

A simple fabric sash tied around the flower girl's waist adds a pop of color to her dress. If she's wearing a white dress, the sash can coordinate her with the color of the bridesmaids' dresses—and might even be made from a remnant of a bridesmaid's dress after it's been cut for hemming. If she's wearing a colored or floral dress, the sash can tie her hue to that of the bridal party or the overall floral and color scheme of the wedding.

This accessory has become an essential for color-coordination purposes, and brides love how adorable the little ones look with a big bow tied in the back.

Before you choose sash flowers, you'll need to decide on the color and width of the sash, as these factors directly affect your floral piece design. The width of the sash, for instance, determines the size of the floral piece pinned to it.

Roses

Daisies

- A cluster of three roses is the most popular choice for flower girls' sash accents.

- If the flower girls are wearing white dresses and colored sashes, use white roses.

- If the flower girls are wearing colored dresses with white sashes, use either colored roses or a mix of colored and white roses.

- There's no need to add filler or greenery to this pin-on piece, although a tiny sprig of white flowers like kelanchoe or stephanotis works well with roses.

- Accent the sash with a cluster of daisies measuring three to four inches across.

- The most common floral placement is on the back of the sash, incorporated into the bow.

- Individual daisies can be attached along the entire front of the sash. For example, you can glue or pin daisy heads to the fabric in three- to four-inch intervals.

- A top look is to alternate white and colored (such as yellow) daisies along the front of the sash.

You don't want a floral piece that is small that it looks like an afterthought, and you don't want one that's too large so that it is too cumbersome for the girls.

An important factor is the weight of the floral piece to be attached to the back, front, or side of the sash. Smaller flowers are of course less weighty and may even escape the attention of flower girls over the course of the day, far more so than a big, heavy floral piece.

Design the florals so they are easy to pin onto the sash so that the floral piece can be removed after the ceremony. Kids with flowers on their sashes have complained that they can't sit in their chairs, and some have even reached back and ripped the florals from the dress, ripping the dress as well. So arrange for quick removal.

Pastels

- Daisies, zinnias, and other flat-head flowers work best for flower girls' sashes.

- Even if you're not using the same types of flowers as in your bouquets, you can match the color of flowers.

- For the floral to show up nicely against a fabric sash, choose a brighter color of flower (such as hot pink) to stand against a lighter-hued sash (such as baby pink).

- Pastels work beautifully if all of your girls wear black dresses.

Bright Single Flowers

- A single rose head can be accented with a sprig of tiny flowers and placed anywhere on the sash.

- A single, big Gerber daisy head makes a subtle statement when glued to the front center of a sash.

- The most popular colors of single Gerber daisy heads for sashes are hot pink, orange, red, and yellow.

- Flank a single flower with sprigs of delicate white or pastel flowers such as inexpensive baby's breath, kelanchoes, or lilies of the valley.

141

SINGLE-STEM FLOWERS
Select eye-catching single-stem flowers for children to carry

When you give flower girls single-stem flowers such as Gerber daisies or lilies to carry, you can create a special girls-only look, or tie into the unifying theme of your bridal party. For example, all of the women and girls can carry single-stem flowers, as might you. This has become one of the top budget-saving strategies in today's expensive wedding world, and many brides love the simplicity of the look.

Maybe a single flower is a big part of your love story. Your groom might often bring you a single red rose, rather than a big bunch of daisies, because he knows you love a single, perfect flower rather than a bunch that can wilt in a few days' time. Many brides make their wedding day floral decisions based on what their men's bloom-giving practices are.

First, you'll choose the type of flower, which may be one

Roses

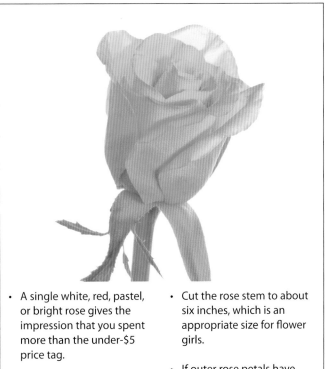

- A single white, red, pastel, or bright rose gives the impression that you spent more than the under-$5 price tag.

- A single rose can be wrapped in ribbon to include a delicate fern or other greenery as color contrast.

- Cut the rose stem to about six inches, which is an appropriate size for flower girls.

- If outer rose petals have started to curl or brown on a hot day, just carefully pluck them off before the flower girls walk down the aisle.

Daisies

- Bright Gerber daisies are a fresh, adorable look for flower girls.

- Order or buy half a dozen daisies even if you need only two or three for your flower girls. This allows you the chance to choose the freshest, strongest flowers.

- Extra daisies are also a good idea in case a flower girl snaps her stem while playing with it.

- Greenery or tiny filler flowers can be wrapped against the daisy for color contrast.

included in your own bouquet. It has to match the formality of your bouquet style, of course, and it can be either white—to coordinate with yours—or one of the colors from the bridesmaids' bouquets. The location and season plays a big part in your design choice here, as a pink tulip would be ideal for a spring wedding, while a stargazer lily would be perfect for a garden wedding in summer.

················ RED ⬤ LIGHT ··············

Remove all thorns or prickly leaves from single-stem flowers, and consider wrapping the stem with a full or two-thirds length of ribbon for more comfortable carrying. Even if you have removed the thorns, the flower girls should still be cautious of their stems' texture. Be sure to instruct flower girls to carry single-stem flowers with the tops leaning back against their stomachs or chests to prevent shaky stems as they walk.

Lilies

- A big, bursting stargazer lily allows you to incorporate soft pastels, such as pinks, to darker tones, such as burgundies.

- Lilies are exotic flowers to most, so ideal if you want an unexpected flower for your girls.

- Stargazer lilies have very strong scents, which may bother small children, so be sure to test this flower out on the children ahead of the big day.

- Look at peace lilies as a smaller, softer version of the stargazer.

Bunches

- Bunches provide more texture and color impact than single-stem flowers.

- Even in bunches, stems should be left long and stems fully or partially wrapped with ribbon.

- Bunches of roses, daisies, lilies, or other blooms do not need greenery or filler flowers to make a visual impact.

- Keep proportion in mind for the littlest girls; if your bridesmaids are carrying six long-stemmed roses along one arm, choose three flowers for the girls.

ALTAR FLOWERS

Make the site of your vow exchange extra special with beautiful altar arrangements

The spot where you will take your vows and officially become husband and wife is a location to pay special attention to when it comes to floral décor. After all, the ceremony is the main attraction of the day! All eyes will be on you as you take your vows and exchange rings, and your ceremony photos will be an everlasting reminder of the big moment . . . that

first kiss as husband and wife. So when you think about it, your altar décor is likely to be seen far more closely than any other wedding site décor you choose. Before the ceremony, when guests are seated and awaiting your arrival, they're looking right at the altar and either admiring the beautiful arrangement or noticing that you've left the altar bare.

Single Altar Arrangements

- Single altar arrangements are designed as a center-piece on the table surface.

- Small arrangements are usually six to eight inches across and work best on small altar tops.

- Make sure to size your altar arrangement to look appropriate on the altar top, neither too large for a small surface nor too small for a big one.

- Single altar arrangements are best planned to be either a wide, low-set grouping or a tall, elevated centerpiece with lots of flowers and greenery.

Dual Altar Arrangements

- On a wide altar, you may want to use a dual floral arrangement of matching pieces.

- Dual altar pieces can symbolize your two lives coming together as one or the joining of your two families.

- The flowers in your altar arrangements do not have to precisely match the flowers in your bouquet.

- Design your altar arrangement with one or two pricey flowers, plus inexpensive filler.

The ceremony site décor you plan—which is the focus of this chapter—sets the stage and tone for your entire wedding. This is the first impression you make on your guests, as well, so think about what you want your altar flowers and ceremony florals to say to them. A formal wedding often calls for elaborate altar floral plans, while a casual wedding might include minimal flowers. You might be the types to want to make a big first impression with oversize, dramatic altar florals, or you might make your statement that you're the simple elegance types with classic, understated florals of more perfection in form than size.

When choosing altar décor, keep in mind that many houses of worship have strict rules about what they do and don't allow for on-site décor, so find out the house rules before you order a lavish altar arrangement. It would be a shame to design and create a floral masterpiece and then find out that you cannot place it on the altar!

Altar Area Arrangements

- Decorate the entire altar area, in addition to your single or dual florals on the altar.

- Set floral arrangements on pedestals on either side of the altar.

- Attach floral garlands to the front and sides of the altar.

- Attach a floral piece that matches the pew florals to the front of the altar.

- Set flower petals on top of the altar, as well as on the floor surrounding the altar.

- Add a floral arch for the backdrop of your altar.

Coordinating Altar Florals with Your Style

- If your wedding style is simple elegance, whether formal or informal, you want to choose smaller, low-set floral pieces with fewer types of flowers.

- If your wedding style is grand and dramatic, whether formal or informal, you want your altar flowers to be taller and more colorful and to contain anywhere from three to eight different types of flowers.

- If you're having an outdoor wedding, incorporate garden-type flowers such as peonies.

- Design an arrangement to match your bouquet.

- Include symbolic flowers (see the Language of Flowers Chapter).

CHUPPAHS & ARCHES

Design the perfect chuppah or floral arch as the location for your vows

When it comes to designing the floral décor for your ceremony, one of the most exciting tasks is designing your chuppah or a floral arch under which you'll take your vows. The deep symbolism of being sheltered and protected as you join your lives, as well as the pure freedom to design your choice of floral structure and the blooms on it, brings both couples and families together to design and often make this sentimental and spectacular décor piece together.

Some families have an heirloom chuppah or arch that all of the siblings use at their weddings, decorating it to their liking, and others have a tradition that a parent or grandparent will make the arch or chuppah out of wood or metal, and

Spring Designs

- Use the brightest mix of whites, pastels, and greenery to take a step beyond bridal white and incorporate the season.

- Besides roses, use spring tulips, peonies, ranunculus, and lilies of the valley.

- Create a natural design

with flowers and greenery attached to the framework of the arch of chuppah, simulating the way flowers grow in nature.

- Set yourself apart from your backdrop or chuppah by carrying brighter colored flowers than those used in its creation.

Summer Designs

- Formal arches and chuppahs are usually crafted with roses, gardenias, ranunculus, and other traditional summer blooms.

- Daisies and wildflowers are ideal for informal weddings.

- Use larger amounts of greenery on all surfaces of

the chuppah or arch, and accent it with lilies of the valley, lisianthuses, or Stars of Bethlehem for a softer bridal effect.

- Informal weddings welcome large, bright flowers, including Gerber daisies and zinnias, especially in summer-friendly tones.

the couple again gets to decorate it as they wish. The metal or wood arch can then be placed in the garden at their new home as a lasting reminder of their big day. This piece has a long life with you, so your design plans are all-important.

The floral design for an arch or chuppah must work with the formality of the wedding and usually contains the same types of flowers as found in the bride's bouquet and thus used in the rest of the site décor. Consider your location and create the same feel for your arch or chuppah. In the photos shown on these pages, you'll see a variety of season-inspired designs, as well as the beauty of both simple and over-the-top floral choices. Again, bringing your bridal style to your chuppah or arch creates a beautiful infusion of your personality and perhaps even your love story when you use the same types of flowers found in bouquets your groom has given you in the past, or your birth-month flowers.

Fall Designs

- Autumn arches and chuppahs include rich, deep colors of fall, including persimmon, burgundy, gold, and hunter green.

- Jewel tones lead the fall and winter trends, so create your arch or chuppah with deep amethyst tones, navy blues, and cranberry.

- To save money in autumn, use seasonal items such as fall greenery, pinecones, and acorns.

- A new autumn décor idea is to drape bunches of dark purple grapes, which give a vineyard effect for an outdoor wedding.

Unique Arch and Chuppah Materials

- Some unique materials for arches and chuppahs are wrought iron, cherrywood, bamboo, birch, and ash.

- Use a wooden trellis that you can find ready-made for painting at home-improvement stores.

- Suspended chuppahs do not have wooden or metal legs, but are instead squares of rich fabric suspended from a tree and then decorated with florals, garlands and hanging flowers, and crystals on wire to catch the sunlight. The effect is a chuppah floating on air.

- Just the same, an arch shape can be created by suspending individual flowers and crystals from a tree using invisible wire at lengths to form the desired effect.

PEW OR ROW FLOWERS

Design eye-catching pew or row flowers to indicate VIP and guest seating

Ceremony seating that consists of just rows of chairs, with no floral or design accents at the ends of the rows, say, "We cut this expense from our budget." It's a big, glaring symptom of cost cutting as well as not paying attention to the kinds of small details that can make a wedding special. These bare chairs attract the wrong kind of attention.

Don't over decorate the ends of your rows or pews, either. Big, puffy tulle bows look like a bad homemade job that you took on to save money.

The key is to choose a simple, classic design. The simple use of a single Gerber daisy on a bright green leaf costs under $5 and is ideal for this décor.

Single-Bloom Designs

- A single, beautiful flower may make all the impression you need, so look for flawless roses or other blooms to use as pew décor.

- Give single blooms a good backdrop with a shiny leaf, a fern, or a satin rib-

bon bow. Pin the flower securely to its center.

- The flower should be at least one half to two thirds the size of the ribbon bow so that it doesn't get overwhelmed by too much fabric.

Bunches

- Hand tie a small bunch of coordinating flowers, such as a grouping of pink tulips for your spring wedding, and affix them to a satin bow.

- Bunches look best when their stems are fully wrapped, rather than tied with a bow in the middle

of cut stems, for a finished look.

- The top trends in bunch flowers for pew décor are roses, daisies, Gerber daisies, and calla lilies for formal weddings, and wildflowers for informal weddings.

Steer clear of puffy tulle bows, since satin bows are the trend of the future, followed closely by 100 percent crisp cotton bows, both of which give you more color options. And if you do wish to add an embellishment to a floral bow, stick with tiny crystal pushpins, pearl-head pushpins, butterfly accents on wire, or tiny seashell accents found at craft stores. These may be within your plans for your centerpieces, so you may be able to use leftover craft supplies if you want to make your own.

ZOOM

You might decide to decorate only the rows or pews where your parents, grandparents, and other VIP guests will sit, rather than decorate forty to fifty rows of chairs. Another option is to make fabric bows for all of the pews or chair rows, but just add florals and accents to the first three rows on each side where parents and grandparents will sit.

Greenery Only

- Just like pew décor made from filler flowers, you can design greenery-only row accents.

- Hand tie a cascade of ivy for a "green" effect, with the added significance of ivy's fidelity symbol.

- Be generous with group-ings of ferns, especially softer ferns with ultradelicate fronds, for a look guests will want to touch.

- Practice greenery origami by curling green or colored leaves such as a pink-hued coleus into the shape of a calla lily. Affix these to satin or lace bows.

Flowers on Seats

- Rather than decorate the ends of the aisles, consider placing a single-stem flower on each guest's seat.

- Single-stem flowers can be left on seats as both décor and as a romantic presentation of your wedding favors.

- Guests in your VIP rows, such as parents, might get white roses, while your other guests get single colorful daisies, tulips, or colored roses.

- Since presentation is everything, wrap the stem with a ribbon bow.

PETAL AISLE MARKERS

Create the perfect pathway to the awaiting groom with lines of flower petals

Extend the floral bounty and the distinctive bridal look along both sides of your path down the aisle by sprinkling flower petals in lines along either side. This pretty and natural look has long been a favorite design choice of brides in all manner of formal, informal, indoor, and outdoor weddings, adding color and a tie-in to your entire floral scheme—all at a low price.

You might think this design style is a simple one, but there are so many options for a personalized aisle path. Choose petals in a single color, such as a line of bright pink flower petals, or mix the hues. You also have design options for the types of petals to use. While the traditional wedding features rose petals, the new trend is to use different types of flower

Color Schemes

- The colors of the petals will set a tone and perhaps coordinate perfectly with the color mix of your bouquet.

- Create your aisle markers with all one shade or color family of petals, such as pale to deeper pinks.

- If you'll have a colored aisle runner, or if the flooring in your indoor site is a hardwood or colored carpet, use white petals.

- If you're carrying a bright bouquet, craft your aisle markers out of the same shade of bright petals.

Pathway Plans

- Most couples choose to have two long, uninterrupted lines of petals along either side of the aisle.

- Create dashes of petals, such as a length of white petals, then a blank space with no petals, then a line of pink petals, and so on.

- Mark your aisles with dots of one-foot-wide circles of petals set every few feet.

- Make your aisle curvy or arched in petal placement.

- Set the petals wide enough apart for your escorted walk down the aisle.

petals for an unexpected and creative effect.

You'll explore some design styles here, and perhaps you'll discover a vision you hadn't thought of before.

Your first concern might be the expense of such a design choice. Aren't rose petals expensive at certain times of the year? Yes, that's true, which is why you might discover a different bloom or a different way to mark your pathway that can cut your budget in half.

Different Types of Petals

- While rose petals are the leading trend in site décor, you can bring in different petal effects by using the softer, rippled edges of peonies or ranunculus.

- Calla lily petals provide larger, curled singles for you to line your path.

- Longer, straighter petals from bright Gerber daisies could give you the artistic look you desire.

- If you'd like to stick with roses, look into rose varieties with some colored edges at the tips of the petals.

Site Consideration for Petal Décor

- Some sites will not allow you to decorate with flower petals because they may pose a slip risk to guests who may in turn sue the establishment, so get permission first.

- At an outdoor site, a breezy day could mean your aisle marker petals will get blown all over the place before your ceremony begins, so think about skipping the aisle markers and using your petal supply elsewhere if you discover the weather won't cooperate.

- Be sure to pick up a few of your aisle petals to preserve as keepsakes of your wedding day.

FLOWERS IN THE TREES

Directing your floral décor upward with flowers in the trees

Weddings and floral décor go hand in hand, and many couples wish to look outside the usual, expected spots for decorating their sites with floral accents. The newest trend is to place floral designs up in the trees, regardless of whether or not the event is an outdoor wedding. While outdoor weddings are the most common site for tree floral décor, more couples wish to decorate their yards and trees with creative florals for an unexpected and special effect, as they may have many visitors over the wedding weekend. If their home is the site of a rehearsal dinner or postwedding party, tree florals create a fantastic floral effect.

If the ceremony will be outdoors, look at your site's tree lines to see where you might place floral pomanders, garlands, and other designs. If the reception involves an outdoor

In Branches

- Attach single flowers to existing branches to create the fanciful look of a "gardenia branch."

- For tree branches that already have flowers in bloom, add a coordinating flower or nosegay to provide one of the colors from your scheme.

- To save your budget, decorate several trees that are close to your ceremony spot or right next to the terrace where the cocktail party takes place.

- Check garden supply stores for small S-shaped hooks that hang on branches to hold florals.

On Trunks

- Ask for the approved method of attaching florals to tree trunks, since your site manager may require ribbon ties without nails.

- Size your floral pieces to fill at least one third of the trunk width, since smaller florals may look lost against a massive trunk.

- Some tree trunks have natural parts where branches split that may be the perfect place to set a floral arrangement.

cocktail party, there too might be the perfect setting for florals in the trees.

Tree florals are ideal for any formality and may be in place just for the walk from the parking lot to the ballroom, welcoming guests with a visual element. They're also suitable for any season and can be designed in any level of grandiosity or subtlety. The idea is to accept that guests love to wander the grounds on their own, even if the reception is taking place indoors.

ZOOM

Ask the site's manager if they regularly decorate their trees with florals and lighting. You might find that they have a design specialist on staff who can put your design into action, or you might find out that the site doesn't allow any florals to be nailed or stapled into trees, so you will have to fashion hooks for hanging them on tree branches.

Suspended Florals

- Use invisible wire, such as fishing wire, to suspend individual flowers such as gardenias, lilies, and daisy heads. This gives the effect of floating or raining flowers.

- For a lush look, suspend flowers at the ends of green garlands, which you can find at floral wholesalers.

- Add some sparkle to your suspended flowers by attaching small crystals to the floral pieces; add larger crystals to their own lengths of wire for a mixed effect.

Lighting

- Ask permission to add lighting elements to any site's trees, as many sites have strict safety rules such as no candles ever.

- Look into creative and colorful LED lights for insertion into tree floral bunches.

- Ask the site manager if they have a supply of hurricane lamps to hang from tree branches and if you can use them to hold florals and LED lights.

- Ask the site manager if they have outdoor spotlights that can be trained on your decorated tree.

FLOWERS IN THE CEREMONY

Bring pretty floral pieces into the symbolism and rituals of your ceremony

Flowers are not just for décor. They can also play an active and meaningful part in your ceremony. Maybe you want to hand flowers to your mothers in recognition and gratitude for a lifetime of love and support. Or you want to enact centuries-old cultural rituals as your ancestors did during their own weddings, exchanging blooms as a symbol of unity. The

living beauty of a flower has long played a part in marriage rites, and today's modern wedding couples who look for ways to pay homage to loved ones often turn to the flower as the perfect offering.

Some religious ceremonies contain a ritual of shaking hands with guests seated near you, wishing them peace. You

Presentation Flowers

- Present single-stem white roses to your mothers to thank them for a lifetime of love.

- Presentation flowers can be incorporated into your bouquet as separately wrapped blooms that you appear to pluck out of your bouquet to present to the mothers.

- Brides are extending the list of presentation flower recipients. Grandmothers, godmothers, and stepmothers are popular choices.

- If you or your groom has a child or children, present flowers to each during a portion of vows that unify your new family.

Exchange Flowers

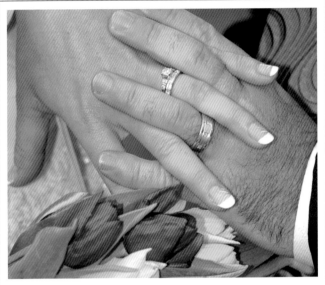

- It's not just the rings that are exchanged today; more couples love the beauty of a flower exchange during the readings, vows, or cultural rituals.

- Incorporate your birth-month flowers, as each of you give the other the

flower from your own birth month.

- Your groom can give you a flower to incorporate into your bouquet or set in front of a religious statue, as a blessing on your marriage.

can turn this ritual in your wedding mass into an opportunity to give single-stem flowers to your mothers as you hug and kiss them.

Flowers may also be offered to religious icons or statues, requesting blessings on the marriage, or handed to children as they participate in your wedding ceremony.

Research any religious lore or symbolism in which flowers play a part, such as lilies being a symbol of Easter and rebirth, as well as additional cultural rites, such as exchanging a certain variety of flower with the groom's family matriarch, or with your own grandmother, or the use of certain flower petals in a unity ritual. Flowers can play a part in religious ceremonies, multifaith ceremonies, and more spiritual marriage rites, all with the universal messages of gift, promise, beauty, and life. You have the freedom to attach your choice of symbolism to any floral element in your ceremony, so work together to write vows or readings that bring the message of flowers into your day. This is one area where the language of flowers comes in particularly handy.

Unity Candle Flowers

- If you'll enact the tradition of the unity candle, choose pretty flowers to encircle the bases of all three candleholders.

- You can also create a floral chain that extends between the candleholders for effect and meaning.

- If your mothers will light the outside candles, they can set their single-stem flowers next to their candles as a blessing on the marriage.

- Design a lush floral arrangement in which your three unity candles stand.

Flowers Handed to Guests

- Start your ceremony early by having your greeters hand each guest a rose upon arrival at the ceremony site.

- Instead of sprinkling rose petals, the flower girls can hand single flowers to each guest seated at the ends of rows.

- Have the child attendants present guests with single-stem flowers upon their exit from the ceremony, along with whatever departure toss-it (birdseed, flower petals) you've chosen to shower you as you dash to the getaway car.

ENTRYWAY FLOWERS

Welcome guests from minute one with attractive entryway floral arrangements

When guests arrive at the cocktail party, you'll welcome them with an immediate impression on the style of your wedding through the florals you set at the entrance. A formation of grand, oversize bridal blooms in crystal vases sets the stage for an elaborate, formal wedding, while bright scattered vases of wildflowers says, "Welcome to our relaxed garden party."

Here is your chance to "paint" the first moments of your guests' experience at your celebration, and you'll do so with the floral arrangements—large and small—awaiting them before they even reach the party setting.

As we've mentioned several times, it's the smallest details that can make the largest impact, and the good news is that

The Doorway

- Set pedestals on either side of the doorway to your cocktail party and place floral arrangements on them.

- Place fully in-bloom, potted flowers, for a less formal look than arrangements in vases, on pedestals on either side of the doorway.

- Set a large floral arrangement on a table just inside the door, surrounded by silver platters of champagne flutes and berries.

- For an understated look, simply hang a color-coordinated floral wreath on the outsides of both entryway doors.

The Guest Book Table

- Attract attention to the guest book table with an oversize, color-coordinated floral arrangement placed behind the guest book.

- This floral piece does not have to match your bouquet design exactly; you could have an all-white entryway floral theme,

while you carry pastel flowers.

- Instead of one large floral arrangement, consider three small, low-set or single flowers in bud vases, alternating with votive candles.

you can choose smaller, more subtle floral arrangements for this section of your wedding floor plan, letting the food at the cocktail party take center stage. Perhaps you want to leave the wow factor for your reception ballroom or tent, so you see this setting as a chance to go a bit smaller with your floral designs and still impress. Then, when the doors open to your reception area, your more dramatic and detailed florals will make an even bigger statement in comparison.

In this section, you will learn how to make a beautiful entryway, which could be a private entrance to a hotel ballroom, the foyer at an estate home or your own house, or the entrance to your tent.

Visit your site in person and take photos of the architectural elements that already exist there, such as a circular table just inside the foyer, a grand staircase to the left, a chandelier, antique tables and chairs, or a fireplace. Then use these photos to guide your floral décor plans.

Restroom Arrangements

- You don't need floral arrangements for both the men's and ladies' rooms; most weddings feature floral arrangements just in the ladies' room.

- A large arrangement is not needed; just a low-set bunch of six to eight flowers in a glass bowl makes a great impression.

- If you're on a budget, this might be the floral item you decide to cut from your plans.

On the Bar

- Keep access in mind, and don't block guests' or bartenders' views or surface areas by setting too large a floral piece right in the center of the bar.

- Just two or three low-set flower bunches in vases, spaced a few feet apart on the bar top, are ideal.

- Set out two to four round glass bowls and float a single flower in each.

- Skip the concept of sprinkling rose petals on the bar top as décor, as petals will stick to guests' glasses.

BUFFET TABLE FLOWERS

Decorate your bountiful buffet table with fresh and fabulous floral designs

Flowers on your buffet table serve a dual purpose: They're there for beauty, and they can work as a budget-saving trick. In the pictures below, you will see floral arrangements and flowers placed on a buffet table fill the space and add lushness and color that make it look like you have a much bigger, fuller buffet table than would appear if you had only half a dozen chafing dishes and a few platters set on a big, long table.

Adding the elements of color and texture to a buffet table makes the food look more appetizing as well, since it's received a royal treatment of décor. This is not the same spread of dishes that everyone has seen at every family picnic and

Florals between Platters

Florals as Table Centerpieces

- Floral arrangements and vases between food platters create a more lush-looking buffet table.

- Greenery in the floral arrangements coordinates with the greenery of salads and platter garnishes.

- Place platters and chafing dishes at least two feet apart so that items are well spread out.

- With floral arrangements placed around a buffet table, you might need one half to two thirds the amount of food to make your buffet look plentiful.

- Design one large centerpiece for each buffet table, aiming for a two- to three-foot width as an eye-catching design accent that still takes up lots of space and requires fewer dishes.

- Each centerpiece on each buffet table should match in color and style.

- If you're planning a "green" wedding or just like the look of all-natural greenery, design your table centerpieces to include just greenery and perhaps some rounded river stones for effect.

158

birthday party even if you have the exact same menu items. By virtue of dressing up your buffet table with florals, you turn even a budget buffet into a smashing smorgasbord.

In the photos here, you'll learn which types of floral arrangements and placement plans best accent your buffet dishes, and you'll also learn how to tie the florals in with your cocktail party theme.

Architectural Floral Designs

- Add plenty of height to your buffet table arrangements to give the impression of a grander floral presence.

- Use flowering branches that stand up to three feet high, arising out of a larger floral arrangement.

- Use decorative branches and twigs such as white birch to use the bridal white color scheme in a more architectural way.

- Add height through the use of tall (twenty-four- to thirty-six-inch) glass vases, which you'll fill with water and submerged flowers.

Safely Using Florals with Food

- Because guests will be very interactive with the food items on your buffet table, be sure that a reaching guest cannot knock florals or leaves into platters of food.

- Glass vases containing florals do a great job of keeping flowers and greenery out of reach and out of serving platters.

- Do not use any flowers, greenery, or flowering branches with berries on them, as most berries are extremely toxic.

- Talk to your floral designer about the safest types of greenery to use near food.

PLATTER FLOWERS

Enhance the wow factor of your cocktail party platters with well-designed floral accents

Just as floral arrangements on a buffet table make the spread seem more lavish, small floral accents on each food platter can make each dish seem more gourmet. Here is where you focus on the individual serving platters that will be used throughout your cocktail party, including the platters that will be carried by waiters for hand-passed hors

d'oeuvres, those set on a buffet table, and those at food stations. Today's catering and banquet staff have added a flair of presentation style by using decorative and unusual platters, not limiting themselves to plain silver platters. Now you might see cobalt blue oval platters, bamboo rectangular platters with a glass top on which sushi is served,

Platter Décor

- A single flower is often the best accent to a platter.

- Establish your floral accent theme for all hand-passed platters, such as a rose head and two pansies in your wedding color theme, so that all platters match.

- Or, match the flower type to the type of food on each platter, such as a pink pansy to coordinate with a platter of pink shrimp cocktail.

Asian-Themed Décor

- For any Asian-themed platters such as sushi or yakitori, accent the platter or serving bowl with either fresh flowers or vegetables cut into the shapes of flowers.

- Red and gold are popular Asian symbols of good luck,

- so pair a red flower with a gold tassel as your unifying platter décor theme.

- Line the outside edges of each rectangular platter with lengths of bamboo.

160

and even platters made of ice to keep seafood cold and fresh.

As you think about how you'll accent your platters, you must first ask to see the caterer's planned supply of platters and serving bowls. By viewing the selection of crystal, glass, silver, and decorative platters—whether in person or in pictures of the caterer's prior events—you can plan your accent florals to work with the foundation of each platter. Tying the two together makes any featured food item look perfectly styled.

Latin-Themed Décor

- Bring in lots of reds for your Latin-themed cocktail party or for Latin-themed stations or platters.

- A new trend in theme décor pairs flowers with colorful, whole habanero peppers.

- Artistic display encourages caterers to work their magic, such as surrounding a sweet flower with cut rounds of jalapenos.

- Plan your platter flowers to bring in no more than two colors from your wedding color scheme, such as red and orange.

Just Greenery

- Make use of inexpensive greenery, including various types of lettuces and herbs such as rosemary, chives, flat-leaf and curled-leaf parsley, and other greens as your garnish for each platter.

- Ferns and other bouquet-type greenery may look unappetizing to your guests.

- Look into vegetable leaves such as squash leaves and flowers as your green décor.

- Seaweed is a great accent for Asian-themed and seafood platters.

BISTRO TABLE CENTERPIECES

Center your cocktail party tables with the perfect, subtle floral arrangements

The tables and chairs in your cocktail party space offer cozy, intimate seating for natural gatherings of guests who are enjoying the pre-reception fare. These tables offer a great opportunity for small and subtle floral décor.

You don't want oversize floral arrangements on these tables, as the nature of these tables is to allow guests to see and talk to each other and they need plenty of table space to hold their drinks and plates. There's just not enough room for big floral pieces. So here you have an opportunity to make an impact without spending a lot of money, and you also get to use a color theme that might not have made your final cut for the reception. For instance, if you chose all-white

Low Bunches

- Low-set bunches work best for cocktail party tables, as too much height obstructs views.

- With smaller bistro tables, often seating four to six people, you'll only need three to six flowers for each centerpiece.

- Peonies, roses, and ranunculus are the top choices for cocktail party table flowers in formal settings.

- Informal wedding bistro centerpieces might be created with bunches of daisies, tulips, or wildflowers.

Single Blooms

- Use a low or mid-height vase to hold a single rose at each table.

- Bud vases might hold a single bright Gerber daisy.

- If you'll have calla lilies in your bouquet or décor, a

- single calla lily in a bud vase works extremely well with your formal theme.

- For island, beach, or destination weddings, an exotic bird of paradise provides color and ties in with your theme.

centerpieces for the reception tables, here is where you can use the summer brights you originally considered when you first started planning. By using your second choice in color and theme, you get the best of both worlds.

Cocktail party tables might be set indoors, outdoors, or both, giving your guests their choice of where they'd like to sit during the hour or hour and a half of your cocktail party, so keep sunlight and hot or cool outdoor temperatures in mind when you make your floral choices for these pieces.

Flower Heads

- Instead of using stemmed flowers, create a stylish look by filling small glass vases with water and submerging flower heads.

- The top choices in flower heads for vase contents are white, red, and bright orange roses.

- Flower heads can be accented by strips of grasses or long, thin leaves submerged in water.

- If you don't like the submerged look, fill a small platter or short glass vase with rose, daisy, or other floral heads.

Flower Petals

- As the ultimate budget saver, skip the flowers and flower heads and sprinkle color-coordinated rose petals on each table.

- Alternate the color pattern of petals on each table, with some tables bearing all white flowers and others bearing all pastel flowers.

- Rather than sprinkle petals all over the tabletop, place a small pile in the center of the table.

- For a simple look, fill a small to medium glass vase with flower petals.

FLOWERS ON THE PIANO

Make that baby grand piano look even more spectacular with a lovely floral topper

When you first discovered your ideal reception site, you may have fallen in love with the baby grand piano on display in the cocktail party room. Or, your hired musicians or band will bring in their own piano for the instrumental pieces you desire during your classy and elegant cocktail party. However the piano's existence is determined, it presents you with a great opportunity for a floral accent.

It might seem that a gleaming piano needs no extra décor, but a simple floral piece on top of it shows that you paid attention to every detail in the room and know how to perfectly style the tiny bridal touches that bring life to your setting and more of your personality into the day.

Low-Set Arrangements

- Since a piano is large, create a medium-size floral arrangement such as a bunch of eight to twelve flowers in a vase.

- There's no rule saying you can have only one floral piece on the piano, so look into three or four small vases with two to three flowers in each, set out with votive candles.

- If you'll display a photo of yourselves, all you'll need is one low-set floral containing three to four flowers.

Large Arrangements

- Make a grand impression on that baby grand with an oversize floral that contains stand-up flowering branches for height.

- Orchids are ideal for heightened piano pieces, so consider just one multi-bloom orchid plant to place on the piano.

- You might prefer width over height, so look at two-foot-wide rectangular glass or silver vases to spread out the lushness.

- Tall branches extending outward give width to an arrangement, so explore flowering branches and grasses as inserts.

The choices of size and formality are up to you. Some couples prefer grand, arching florals set in candelabras, and others use the same type of low-set bunch that decorates their cocktail party bistro tables to tie the look of the room together.

The piano has become more than just a focal point for a musician in a tuxedo. Now, in addition to floral arrangements, some couples place a photo of themselves on the piano, or they choose this location to display photos of other family weddings. When guests visit the piano to see the pictures, the pianist gets to ask for requests.

Remember that pianos are not always black; some are white, which may inspire a different color scheme and floral choices for your optimal décor. And a piano top may be set with an oval or round fabric or long runner on which to place décor.

Departing from Color Schemes

- If your bistro tables have pink flowers, your bar top has bright pink flowers, and the flowers in your reception ballroom are all pastel, you might wish to make this piece your all-white bridal arrangement.

- If all of your flowers are bridal white, use a dra-

matic burst of red roses as contrast.

- If you're having a fall wedding, coordinate this floral piece to match the colors in the trees outside.

- Use all greenery and branches.

Important Planning Tips

- If your band is bringing in their own musical instruments, be sure to specify that a piano will be among them. Most bands achieve a piano sound with a keyboard that is too small for a floral piece.

- Ask the musician if he or she is allergic to flowers, which might prevent you from placing your arrangements right near the sensitive artist.

- Ask the site manager if they allow florals and other décor to be placed on their piano; some sites protect their baby grands and don't allow accenting.

FLOWERS IN ROOM DÉCOR

Turn plain mantels and windowsills into additional spotlight décor areas

Look around the room where your cocktail party will take place. Do you see other details that can be accented with florals on your wedding day? The best and most talented floral designers and wedding coordinators have an eye for finding that one decorative detail, such as a chandelier or windowsill that is the perfect place for a beautiful floral accent, and placing even the smallest, most unassuming flower or bunch there brings an entire corner of the room to life.

On these pages you'll think about some of the room elements that you can bring to life with just one tiny floral embellishment.

Flowers on the Mantel

Flowers on Tables

- Many sites feature fireplaces, whether working or decorative, with mantels perfect for floral accents.

- Design an elongated mantelpiece that stretches across one-third the length of the mantel for the best dimensions.

- A long mantel welcomes three or four smaller floral accents, such as clusters of white roses in low-set vases, interspersed with candles.

- Mantels are natural showcases, so drape a lush green garland along the length of it, with the ends trailing toward the floor.

- Your site may have an array of tables throughout the building, on which you can set floral pieces.

- Tour your site to scout out the presence of any coffee tables or end tables next to couches and seating areas.

- All you need for these table areas are small bunches in plain glass vases, or a single flower floating in water in a small vase.

- Pillar candles and votives fill out your look, so tables are ideal for flower petal additions.

Is there a spiral staircase with a banister that can be adorned with garlands and flowers? Is there a marble staircase leading down from the terrace to the grassy grounds? Each step can feature potted florals on either side, or you can place a pure floral garland on the handrail.

Pull aside the curtains and look at the detail of the big picture windows and the decorative wooden windowsills. You'll find out below how to turn this, the number one room detail for décor, into a showstopper that extends far beyond the boundaries of the room.

Plan a visit to your site so that you can take photos, take notes, and make plans to bring floral loveliness into the ideal nooks and crannies of your room. Take lots of digital photographs so that you can later "explore" the room for additional floral accenting and other décor, and don't forget to take photos of hallways for their décor opportunities as well.

Again, be sure to check with your site manager to be sure your floral and décor plans will be allowed and to find out what the site typically creates for existing floral décor in each season.

Flowers on Windowsills

- Set a small, low-set floral such as a single ranunculus, peony, or gardenia in a tiny vase on each windowsill in the room.

- Match the color of your windowsill florals to a color seen through the window.

- Mix flowers with seasonal items such as holly leaves and berries for winter weddings, gourds and pinecones for fall weddings, seashells and starfish for summer weddings, or items for your theme.

- Keep lit candles far away from windowsills.

Flowers on Stairs

- Set a small potted flower on each step of stairways either inside or outside for an added dash of color.

- If budget is an issue, place potted flowers on every other step.

- Use ceramic vases to hold bunches of coordinating flowers to tie into your décor.

- Use larger potted flowers or vases on the bottom step and smaller versions on each step above.

SWEETHEART TABLE

Set your bride and groom table apart with the perfect floral arrangement

When you forgo the big, long table that has traditionally served as the seating for the bride, groom, and entire bridal party and instead have just one small table for you and your groom alone, this is called the "sweetheart table." This seating arrangement has become a trend for several reasons: A small, round table for two is easily set up right at the front of the dance floor, and room for a schematic-busting long table for sixteen people is no longer needed. What's more, a sweetheart table gives the bride and groom a few minutes alone to eat in peace and share some undisturbed conversation time. When the bride and groom are seated at their table, guests don't usually approach.

Low-Set Centerpieces

- Design a smaller version of the guest table centerpieces, such as four low-set roses instead of twelve.

- Set out three to four small glass vases in a row across the front edge of the table and fill them with single flowers, such as gardenias, peonies, roses, ranunculus, or other wide blooms.

- Use small, round vases, fill them with water, and set a single floating flower in each.

- Add some sparkle to low-set centerpieces by adding crystal-studded wire stick-ins or theme adornments.

Your Bouquet

- Save over $100 by simply placing your bridal bouquet front and center on the table as your centerpiece.

- Using your own bouquet on the sweetheart table can set your tabletop décor apart from guest tables' pastel or bright décor.

- Lay the centerpiece flat on the table for a natural look; with a ribbon-wrapped handle, you won't be able to stand it upright in a vase full of water.

168

This means you have a spotlight table all to yourselves, and it invites your choice of special floral décor. After all, your table at the front of the dance floor is in full view of all of your guests. Often, the wedding cake is placed right next to or behind it, which means lots of pictures will capture the beauty of your table décor.

On these pages you'll get ideas for either using the same centerpiece design you're using at each guest table or for doing something a little different and special to set your table apart.

The sweetheart table is functional as well as fashionable. Your guests must be able to see you, and you must be able to see what's going on in the room. It's silly to hide behind a gigantic table centerpiece when you're the only ones at the table. So think low set and design floral accents for the front of your table, since that is in guests' eye line as well.

All of the Bouquets

- Give your bridesmaids a place to put their bouquets by having them set them in a line on top of your sweetheart table.

- Six to eight bouquets usually form a complete, uninterrupted line across most sweetheart tables.

- Flower girls' and moms' nosegays can be placed at both ends of your bouquet lineup centerpiece for the perfect height and color blend.

- If you have a small table, set your bouquet on top and surround it with a bridesmaid bouquet on each side.

Color Schemes

- You can match your sweetheart table florals to your bouquet colors.

- If you chose to carry a colored bouquet, and have color in your guest table centerpieces, choose all-white florals for this table.

- If you have an all-pastel color scheme, set your table apart by using florals a few shades brighter than the centerpiece and décor flowers.

- Use all-white table florals, plus your monogram spelled out in pastel or bright flowers on the front of your table.

CAKE TABLE
Surround or decorate your wedding cake with style-coordinated florals

You would think a grand, elaborate wedding cake wouldn't need any extra accenting to make an impression, but even the most majestic cake masterpiece can be made all the more impressive with the right placement of florals on the table surrounding it.

Think about the cake design you plan to request or have already ordered. Depending on your personal style, and the formality and theme of your wedding, it might be a highly detailed cake of five tiers that costs more than your wedding gown, or it might be a simple, elegant cake of three tiers with the most subtle icing decoration. No sugar-paste humming-birds or flowers for you.

Bouquets

- Instead of using your bouquet and bridesmaids' bouquets on your sweetheart table, place them around the base of the wedding cake.

- Use only the bridesmaids' bouquets to encircle the base of the wedding cake, as you may wish to take additional photos with your bouquet throughout the reception.

- Have your floral designer create nosegays to match the bridesmaids' bouquets, and use these expressly to encircle the cake base.

Roses

- Instead of bouquets, set single roses in low-set vases around the base of the cake.

- Vases can be set one foot apart in good, natural spacing to allow the cake base décor icing to show.

- Surround your cake base with roses that have been stem cut to three to four inches in length.

- Match roses to the cake's color scheme, such as white frosting and pink roses.

Whatever your style and size of cake, well-placed florals placed all around it can enhance the look of any décor your baker plans to create for your cake. So that elaborate cake with pink floral icing pops with the addition of fresh pink florals around the bottom layer of the cake. Or a small cake looks larger with a ring of matching white florals around the base.

The color scheme of your cake table florals is up to you. You can match the color of the frosting, such as white or off-white, but keep in mind that some buttercream frostings do appear off-white, so ask to see a sample before you order pure white flowers. Or, you can use your florals to bring out the hues of the colored icing details, such as piped-on roses, dots, swirls, or other embellishments.

There is a formula to figure out what size cake table flowers to use: They should be no taller than one third the height of the bottom layer. Any more and it obscures the bottom layer from view, actually making your cake look smaller.

Daisies

- If daisies are included in your bouquet and wedding décor, it's a brilliant tie-in to bring daisies onto your cake table.

- Set out low vases and fill them with three to six white or yellow informal daisies or two to three larger Gerber daisies.

- For a more informal look, place wide, colorful Gerber daisy heads on the table around the base of the cake.

- Your baker can create sugar-paste Gerber daisies or ice colorful Gerber designs on the cake.

Flowers on the Cake

- One of the lasting top trends in cake design is the cascade of fresh flowers starting at the top layer of the cake and extending down to the bottom layers.

- Your cascade design could be lush and full, with dozens and dozens of flowers, or you might choose to go more subtle with just a few flowers arranged on each cake layer.

- Check the list of edible flowers in the Resource Directory to select blooms that are safe to embed in your frosting.

171

GIFT TABLE

Bring a touch of floral elegance or a pop of color to your gift table

In some families, wedding guests bring envelopes containing checks for the bride and groom. In other families, guests bring wrapped gifts. And at most weddings these days—since we live in a global society with guests jetting in from all corners of the world, with their own gift preferences—the gift table contains a mix of envelopes and wrapped gifts. Some couples set out a decorated birdcage or mailbox in which guests insert their gift envelopes as a way to keep the gifts safe and in one place. They then collect pretty wrapped gifts alongside the decorated envelope receptacle. No matter how the gifts are collected, the gift table presents a floral décor opportunity!

First, you have the gift envelope receptacle, that birdcage or mailbox that's often the item affixed with fresh flowers,

Tabletop Ideas

- If it works with your color scheme, plan your florals to coordinate with the expected whites, pinks, and silvers seen on most wedding wrapping paper.

- Use pink or silver gift-wrap ribbon as an accent in these floral arrangements.

- Keep all florals and décor to the front edge of the table, as gifts will perhaps cover the entire surface, which means you won't need décor for the sides or corners of the table.

Birdcages and Mailboxes

- Affix three to four roses or flowers to match your floral theme to the top peak of a birdcage.

- Entwine ivy lengths along the top and side bars of the birdcage, dotted with white flowers.

- Use two to three varieties of flowers to give a more planned effect to your birdcage or mailbox décor.

- Encircle the base of the receptacle with greenery or garlands for a lush look, and add spaced dots of white or colored florals.

garlands, and greenery. Then there is the gift table itself, which may be decorated with garlands and florals to match those on the other special tables in the room, such as the guest book table and the cake table. One mismatched, undecorated table in the room would look odd, right?

It's always best to create one unified look for these special, functional tables, such as low-set pink and white roses in matching square glass vases and tiny square votives, or green garlands extended along the front edges of the tables, with tiny white flowers embedded along the lengths. Choosing different styles and different flowers will not convey a sense of different purpose for each table, but will instead make it look like you threw together different looks with leftover flowers—or that you tried too hard to save money. Look back at the previous two spreads to help you design a coordinated table look, and consider the following ideas for your gift-specific items. If you expect many wrapped gifts, many large boxes, or gift bags containing wedding presents, decorate the front skirt of the tablecloth instead.

Behind the Table

- The wall space behind the gift table is a terrific place to decorate with theme florals.
- Ask for permission to string green garlands, studded with color-coordinated flowers, on the wall in an arch shape behind the gift table.
- Purchase an inexpensive wooden trellis (five to six feet tall is ideal) and set it against the wall behind the table for decorating with garlands and flowers.
- Lean an oversize photo of the two of you against the wall, resting on the back edge of the table.

Additional Décor Options for the Gift Table

- If you'd like to use white flowers as your table décor, ask if you can use a colored tablecloth—such as a pink or yellow that coordinates with your theme—to provide color contrast for florals and petals.
- If you're using solid-colored tablecloths throughout the room, set this table apart with its own floral-patterned linens, accented by votive candles and individual flower heads or single-stem flowers set on the table.
- Be prepared for some guests to place their large or heavy gifts on the floor in front of or under the gift table. Decorate pretty oversize baskets with handle flowers and place one on either side of the front of the table for overflow or oversize gifts.

173

TENT FLORAL DÉCOR
Turn a basic rented tent into a wonderland of florals, garlands, and lights

If your wedding plans include a tent set up in a garden, on the grounds of an estate or country club, or even in your own backyard, you don't have to stick with just a plain, unadorned tent. Consider your tent to be a blank slate, ready for your floral design genius and transformation into a beautiful wonderland of greenery, flowers, and lights that looks even better

than the most expensive ballroom in town.

The key to decorating a tent is to look at both the outside and the inside for your floral plans. Guests, after all, will likely wander the grounds on a beautiful afternoon or evening, seeing the tent from all angles. When you focus on décor for all views, you show that you have put a great amount of

The Tent Entrance

- Drape thick floral garlands around the top and sides of the entrance to the tent.

- Affix a large floral arrangement, such as an arch of flowers and greenery, above the entrance.

- Set grand pedestals, either rented marble or painted

wood, on either side of the tent entrance, and place color-coordinated, oversize floral arrangements on each.

- Sprinkle rose petals along the pathway to the entrance so that guests can walk on florals just like the bride.

The Tent Ceiling

- When a tent is erected, the support system of steel or metal beams inside the ceiling of the tent should be obscured with garland wrap or draping.

- Add some extra light to these obscuring garlands by entwining strings of white fairy lights.

- Use decorated ceiling beams or the fabric ceiling swaths as points where you can affix lengths of clear wire holding individual flowers, crystals, or both for a suspended "'rainfall" effect.

thought into the three-dimensional showcase of your wedding scene. You'll turn that tent into more than a simple setting or shelter from the sun or rain. On these pages, you'll consider new angles and views of the tent so that you can style your perfect coordinated floral accents for a setting that sets an unforgettable tone.

On the Walls

- The walls of a tent—both inside and outside—are the perfect blank surfaces for affixing small or medium-size floral bunches directly to the tent surface.

- Use birdfeeder or floral hanging poles, inserted into the ground, to hold up potted plants and florals.

- These top metal frame structures are sites where you can attach lengths of floral or greenery garlands to drape along each wall for an arched effect.

- Lean decorated wooden trellises against the outside walls of a tent.

Tent Support Poles

- Most tents require support poles at various points within the tent. You can hide them with your choice of spiral-wrapped garlands studded with flowers.

- You can also wrap these poles with inexpensive fabric or tulle and affix florals to the fabric either in one spot or in a succession all the way down the poles.

- Ivy and greenery are perfect for obscuring poles if you are on a tight budget.

- Entwine poles with fairy- or twinkle-light strings.

FLOWERS FOR WATER FEATURES

Add floral décor to existing fountains, ponds, and pools at your reception site

Some of the loveliest reception settings include water features such as spouting fountains, garden ponds filled with colorful koi swimming among the rocks, babbling brooks that flow across the grounds, and even beautiful swimming pools that are lit up in the evening to glow in Caribbean ocean tones of blue.

These water features are gorgeous on their own, and they may have played a part in your choice to book the site as the setting for your glorious reception. You just love the look of the fountain, or you always dreamed of having your cocktail party poolside just like you've seen in celebrity wedding coverage.

Floating Florals

- In a pond, set one floating wreath, no larger than a foot wide, containing flowers that coordinate with blooms that already exist in the pond landscaping, rather than your floral scheme.

- Use Styrofoam circles covered with pinned-in florals and greenery to float in a pool, and use your wedding color scheme florals to tie in your décor.

- Place small floating florals inside the pool of a large fountain.

Around the Edges

- If the site manager forbids floating flowers in a fountain or pond, place small floral pieces around the outside edges of the structure.

- Rather than plan vase-set flowers, set small to medium potted flowering plants around the edges of

ponds or fountains.

- For a circular fountain, you'll only need four floral arrangements for the front, back, and sides of the fountain.

- Plan to take potted trees and flowering plants home with you after the wedding.

176

They are, though, great opportunities for you to extend your floral plans and make them even more beautiful—especially when the sun sets during your celebration and these water features are lit up to show off your floral designs, such as a spotlight on a fountain or floating florals in the pool lit from underneath in an eye-catching glow.

With all on-site water features, you'll have to get permission from the manager of the location to be sure you're allowed to decorate the feature. Some site managers don't want the delicate ecosystem of a koi-filled pond damaged by the presence of flowers or greenery that's toxic to the fish, and some don't want setup and cleanup workers jumping into fountains to affix garlands to a valuable statue. It would be a shame to plan and invest in water feature décor that you soon find you can't use.

On the Rocks

- For existing fountains, set single flowers such as gardenias or lotuses on one to three levels of the rocks that lead downward to the pool portion.

- If a pool has a rock formation leading into a waterfall that drains into the pool, set larger floral arrangements on this feature.

- Alternate floral groupings with safe LED lights to give each water feature extra visual interest.

- If tiki torches are allowed on the grounds, spiral wrap the torch bases with garlands and flowers.

Important Considerations about Water Feature Florals

- Some florals can be toxic to fish in ponds.

- Some site managers do not want florals in their pools for fear of clogging the filters.

- Your site might already have floating floral pieces of their own that you can arrange to be set out for your wedding. Be sure to ask how they decorate their water features for weddings.

- Ask which kinds of flowers and plants will be in bloom on the grounds and surrounding water features at the time of your wedding.

DOOR DÉCOR

Make each doorway extra special with a floral touch that coordinates with your décor

Your site may have one main entrance doorway, or, as in the case of an estate home or your own home, it may have many doors. Each door presents an opportunity for a floral décor touch. For under $5 each you can create an accent for each door, welcoming guests as they move throughout the location and again showing that you paid mind to the tiniest of

details and took advantage of every stylish opportunity to add multifaceted floral effects to your reception location.

Doors have long been a symbolic part of wedding lore and tradition. The groom carries the bride over the threshold. The bride and groom are introduced for the first time as husband and wife when they walk through a door into their reception

Wreaths

- A simple wreath hanging on the door works for every season and every formality of wedding.

- Create spring wreaths containing pastel-colored tulips and hydrangeas.

- Create informal summer wreaths made of Gerber

daisies, wildflowers, or bright roses.

- Use plenty of florals and berries to give wreaths more texture.

- Match the fabric of wreath bows to the color and type of fabric your bridesmaids are wearing.

Doorknob Décor

- Hang a floral pomander on each doorknob. Use these tiny, four- to five-inch rounds of tiny flower balls to add a dash of color to doorknobs.

- Choose color-coordinated ribbon to affix pomanders to doorknobs.

- Another attachment option is to use a fabric braid, such as a pink silk braid, that you can buy ready-made at a craft or fabric store.

- For luck, use the feng shui rule of a red or gold cord to attach the pomander to the doorknob.

room. Culturally, doors also hold symbolism, such as the Dutch practice of painting the doorway of the bride's house green so that she may enter into a prosperous marriage.

At your reception location, you can add symbolism to floral door décor by using birth-month flowers or referring to the language of flowers for bloom meanings. But the larger concern for most brides and grooms is purely decorative. This is where you get to design an added floral touch like a master painter's final flourishes on a portrait.

ZOOM

Count the doors of your reception site, including restroom doors, and see how large your floral project or order will be. If there are too many doors to consider decorating, keep your décor plans only to the doors on the first floor of the estate or home, or only to doors that lead to the outside areas of your reception location, such as terraces or exits.

Over-Door Arches

- You've seen those beautiful half-circle windows shown in *Architectural Digest* and other home-décor magazines, so create the same arched effect with flowers above every door.

- Ask the site manager how arches may be affixed to on-site doorways.

- Arches can be made purely from garland and greenery.

- If arches are not possible on your doors, take the next best step by lining the top of each door frame with a length of floral garland.

Doorway Accents

- Set potted flowers on either side of a doorway entrance.

- If a mailbox sits next to a doorway, use that as a makeshift planter and fill it with color-coordinated blooms and greenery.

- At a home wedding, get rid of any deck or lawn décor such as flamingos or garden gnomes to make way for floral décor.

- If you think wind chimes bring good luck, hang a floral-themed wind chime near a door.

LOW-SET CENTERPIECES

Design centerpieces that don't block your guests' view but still make an impression

When you're considering centerpiece styles for guests' reception tables, you'll probably think about the centerpieces you've seen (and maybe even won) at other weddings you've attended. Some may have been breathtaking with their oversize cascade of soft blooms, and some may have been subtle and romantic. Some may have been a very obvious step

taken to save money, such as a single flower in a bud vase looking lonely and forlorn at the center of an enormous table for twelve guests. You know when a centerpiece just doesn't fit with the table style, so here's where you'll begin designing your own traditional floral pieces for guests' tables.

We'll start with small, low-set centerpieces. These are the

All-White Arrangements

- The traditional bridal arrangement of low-set flower centerpieces often includes the most traditional blooms: roses, stephanotises, calla lilies, ranunculus, and gardenias.

- If you'd like to step away from traditional, expected white blooms, consider

white tuberoses, coneflowers, and lisianthus.

- When you design an all-white centerpiece, you usually have to use a greater number of flowers to make a visual impression.

Pastel Arrangements

- The most common low-set arrangements contain pastel mixes of roses, lilies, callas, and filler flowers such as stephanotises or lilies of the valley.

- Blending two or three shades of pastels in a low-set centerpiece allows you

to make an impact with fewer individual flowers.

- For a traditional look that's halfway between all-bridal and seasonal stylish, choose one pastel color from your theme and mix it with white florals and greenery.

classic choice, both friendly to the budget by virtue of needing almost 50 percent fewer flowers than elevated styles and functional for guests whose views of you and each other are not blocked by eye-level florals. Low-set centerpieces rise no more than one foot off the tabletop, with some styles preferred at no more than six inches above the tabletop.

Formality is conveyed, again, in color and the individual floral choices you make. When you're designing a small, low-set centerpiece, each flower carries a significantly larger amount of "style stamp," meaning that every wide-open rose connotes

an elegance and exorbitance, more so than if grouped in clusters of dozens of roses.

Don't forget that a set table has color, style and formality accents in the form of decorative china (perhaps with a floral flair in the pattern design), stemware, flatware, colorful plate chargers, and the linens on the tables themselves. It could be that your best choice is a simple, low-set floral meant to bring out the beauty in the place settings, not stand alone as the sole focus on the table.

Seasonal Arrangements

- For a springtime wedding, create centerpieces from low-cut, tightly wrapped bunches of tulips, such as three-inch stem height pinks, yellows, whites, and reds.

- In summer use bright roses and daisies.

- In autumn choose low-set (three-inch stems, tops) clusters of mums in rich fall shades of burgundy, gold, persimmon, and merlot.

- In winter choose low-cut red roses for a festive holiday look, as well as deeper jewel colors of purple and emerald green.

Multiple Low-Set Pieces

- There's no rule that says you have to stick with just one circular centerpiece for each guest table.

- Choose two to four pretty low-set vases (two to four inches high) and add two to four flowers in each for a gathering of centerpieces.

- For oval or rectangular tables, line up three to six (or more) small vases that contain two to four flowers in each as a linear group centerpiece.

- Add visual dimension by using vases in different sizes.

ELEVATED CENTERPIECES

Raise your centerpieces above the tables for an elevated style for all formalities

The placement of your centerpieces could make all the difference, and elevating them above the table extends your floral design upward to create a grander, more visually stunning effect when guests first walk into the room. It's a misconception that elevated centerpieces have to be enormous, containing dozens and dozens of flowers each.

Today's candelabras and wrought iron centerpiece holders allow you to elevate more moderately sized centerpieces, as the holders themselves are so beautifully decorated in their own entwined or Tuscan-inspired designs or even offer several levels for the placement of two to four nosegay-size floral pieces. The advent of decorative centerpiece holders allows

Formal Elevated Centerpieces

- Design these as larger, more elaborate versions of your bridesmaids' bouquets, with 30 to 50 percent more of the same types and colors of flowers.

- Use the top bridal flowers such as roses, gardenias, and calla lilies.

- Include just two or three gardenias or other pricy blooms in these centerpieces and fill liberally with stock to add volume.

- For formal weddings, elevated centerpieces usually come in the same color scheme as your or your bridesmaids' bouquets.

Informal Elevated Centerpieces

- At less formal weddings, either indoors or outdoors, you do not have to design elaborate, enormous bridal-flower-filled centerpieces.

- Not all elevated centerpiece holders require round bouquet-type florals; consider tall, thinner candelabras and their vase-type tops

- designed to hold a bunch or nosegay.

- Use informal, inexpensive flowers such as tulips, Shasta daisies, begonias, peonies, and zinnias.

- Use more greenery in informal centerpieces, such as masses of ivy.

you to create the impression of a more elaborate centerpiece just by virtue of lifting them up with décor below.

There is one big factor to keep in mind when considering elevated centerpieces: the existing décor of the reception room. When a room has color-contrast moldings, elaborate cathedral ceilings, fireplaces, and other room accents, elevated centerpieces are often used to "point" to the architectural elements above, creating a more unified look and thereby often requiring more modest floral arrangements. If the room is basic, elevated pieces add acents.

Adding More Height

- Bring the eye upward with flowers with sturdier stems to stand tall above the centerpiece, such as sunflowers, birds of paradise, and roses.

- Consider flowering branches such as apple blossoms, cherry blossoms, and dogwoods that can stand more than a foot above the holder.

- Use nonflowering branches such as white birch to give height and dimension.

- Use straight or curly topped bamboo for any style or formality of wedding. Bamboo is a symbol of good luck.

Multitiered Elevated Centerpieces

- The new brand of centerpiece holders features unique ways to lift florals upward, including tri-tiered designs for multiple floral groupings and pillar candles.

- Use a vase on each level to hold small groupings of flowers and cascading greenery.

- Lay nosegay bouquets, which you have measured to fit the diameters of each layer, on each tier.

- Alternate nosegays or vase-set bunches with pillar candles so that you need only one half to two thirds the floral pieces.

183

ROUND CENTERPIECES

Master the art of the traditional, round centerpiece for your guests' tables

Considered the most traditional of bridal centerpieces, the round design is what most people immediately think of when considering centerpieces. It's also the style that most floral designers feature on their Web sites or show you during consultations. Most couples don't even know that they have additional options, such as elongated centerpieces to suit an oval or rectangular table. Since we are looking at traditional centerpieces on these pages, we'll start with the classic round centerpiece and then explore additional shapes and sizes so that you can design your dream floral accents for all your festive and elegantly appointed tables.

Right now you might be questioning whether or not your

All-White Round Centerpieces

- Create the effect of multitype white floral centerpieces by packing each with both large and small rose heads as well as rose sprays.

- Use one to three pricy blooms, such as gardenias, and fill the rest of the centerpiece with less expensive white florals such as stock and lilies of the valley.

- Fill a round, white centerpiece just with stock, lilies of the valley, lisianthus, Bells of Ireland, Queen Anne's lace, and other small blooms.

Colored Round Centerpieces

- The concept of color ranges from all pastel, to a mix of pastel and brights, to all brights.

- The most common trend for colored round centerpieces is to combine the two brightest colors in your or your bridesmaids' bouquets.

- Dual-toned centerpieces look more styled and elegant than mixes of four to six different colors.

- Pastels mix better than brights when paired with white flowers, as a bright and white arrangement can be too stark.

planned round centerpieces will work for oval-shaped tables, and the answer is yes. Rounds will work for any shape table, but it's nice to know that you can style centerpieces in different shapes if you want to.

The hallmark of the round centerpiece is its fullness, whether you pack it densely with all blooms and few greenery pieces or flip the proportion to include more greenery than flowers. The choice is yours, but what you're after is a full, round shape and the perfect vase or holder as its foundation.

ZOOM

Check craft stores for inexpensive tin centerpiece bowls, which look much like their pricier silver counterparts. Don't worry if you can't find thirty of the same exact bowl style. Floral designers often select centerpiece bowls that have slight variations for visual appeal. Glass centerpiece bowls and square shapes are also available at craft stores for a fraction of bridal Web site prices.

Round Centerpiece Containers

- The following creative holders, vases, and bowls make great settings for your centerpieces: glass round cylinder vases, low-set round vases, tin-footed pedestal bowls, and mint julep cups.

- For a really creative twist, use top hats with waterproof bowls set inside.

- Set waterproof bowls inside garden baskets.

- Centerpiece containers make great take-home gifts for guests.

Under Round Centerpieces

- Make round centerpieces look even larger by placing round mirrors beneath them, and add votive candles on top for the reflection of the flames.

- Set the centerpieces atop round sprinklings of flower petals.

- Create pedestals for the centerpieces by painting craft-store-bought rounds of one-inch-high wood platters in a color that coordinates with your wedding hues.

- Set a silver platter beneath a glass or silver centerpiece holder.

ELONGATED CENTERPIECES

Stretch your floral centerpiece look with rectangular and oval designs

When your reception tables are oval or rectangular, designed to seat over ten guests apiece, you can style your centerpieces to complement the shape of the table. Since the table is elongated, so too is the centerpiece. This means you may have an oval-shaped centerpiece for an oval table, or a rectangular centerpiece to fully center a longer rectangular table.

Many couples are choosing to have their reception site set with tables of different sizes and shapes .The mix of table styles allows couples to suit their guest list groups more effectively than awkwardly dividing natural circles of family or friends into the prescribed eight to ten slots at a standard round table. That family of twelve can sit together

Oval Centerpieces

- Find oval silver or glass centerpiece bowls at a craft store.

- Use a good mix of different-size flowers so that a single-bloom design doesn't come out looking like a big pink football.

- Go for height at the center of the oval and taper down with smaller flowers at the edges.

- Oval centerpieces may mean you have more space to fill, so do it with more greenery rather than pricy flowers.

Rectangular Centerpieces

- Visit a craft store to purchase rectangular glass vases or wood containers to paint in a color that matches your theme.

- Create painted rectangular box centerpieces and fill them with colorful fruits and flowers.

- For long tables, create multiple rectangular centerpieces and set two to three of them along the length of the table.

- Measure the width of the tables to be sure you're not creating centerpieces that are too large for guests' dining space.

at one long table, while a group of fourteen colleagues get their own oval table, and that group of six friends gets a spacious round table nearby. The freedom to choose tables in all shapes gives you the freedom to custom design centerpieces that complement each table style.

Elongated centerpieces work with all formality levels and seasons—it's always up to the types of flowers you choose, your color scheme, and the smallest details within the floral arrangements.

ZOOM

Ask your site manager for the tabletop dimensions for each of their tables in stock, and then create a table placement chart when your guest response cards are in. You can then create your seating chart, knowing how many guests you'll place at each large and small table, and work with your floral designer or volunteers to design well-size elongated centerpieces to suit each table.

Narrow Centerpieces

- For long, narrow tables, design thin, narrow centerpieces.

- Design long, narrow flowerboxes and set two to three to a table.

- Give the impression of long, narrow centerpieces by placing small square glass

vases with single flowers in them in a line down the center of the table.

- Use an S-shaped flowerbox; fill it with flowers and greens.

- Check gardening Web sites and catalogs for unique flowerboxes to use for centerpieces.

Nonfloral Centerpieces

- A traditional centerpiece for a beach wedding is a round or elongated container filled with sand and seashells.

- Place starfish and seahorses, found at a craft store, in each sand-filled centerpiece.

- While fruits are used in some nonfloral center-

pieces, so too are vegetables with great color, such as red bell peppers or gourds and pumpkins at fall weddings.

- For a winter wedding, create a centerpiece made from glass ornaments dotted with tiny white or colored flowers.

187

FLOATING FLOWER CENTERPIECES

Floating floral centerpieces are one of the least expensive and loveliest design trends

Water is an essential element in all of nature, the essence of life, and a must for vitality, which is why water has quickly become one of the most popular, symbolic décor choices for weddings.

A single flower floating in a beautiful water-filled glass or crystal bowl is the picture of traditional elegance, a look that fits all wedding styles and formality levels. There are more creative decisions than you might expect with this style of centerpiece, which makes it a natural choice for the wedding couple who wants a gorgeous look regardless of the fact that this is one of the most budget-friendly décor choices possible. One flower. One bowl. One generous helping of water.

Single Floating Flowers

- In a standard glass bowl or vase, at least six inches across, float a single flower for a classic, elegant effect.

- The flower should take up no less than a quarter of the space in the bowl.

- To give the flower more flotation, allow it to sit on two to three of its own leaves.

- Add colored glass stones to the bottom of the vase or bowl to add a complementary hue.

Dual Floating Flowers

- In a larger bowl or vase, float two matching flowers to symbolize the union of your two lives.

- Again to symbolize your union, float a flower matching those in your bouquet with the same type of flower the groom wears in his lapel.

- Large flowers such as gardenias look terrific nestled together in a medium-size bowl.

- For best effect, choose the same color for both flowers.

This can cost less than one-tenth of the average bountiful centerpiece expense, but it makes twice the impression.

For formal weddings the most popular floating flower is the gardenia, even though its weight might mean that it's not actually floating. It could be resting on the bottom of the bowl with the water level reaching just the start of the petals.

For informal weddings daisies and lilies are the top floating-flower choices, and floating flower petals work for all wedding formality levels, styles, and locations.

ZOOM

Prearrange with your site manager for you to deliver the bowls and blooms, and then have site staff fill and place these floating flower center-pieces on each of the guests' tables. You have to specify that you will not be coming in to do this task.

Flowers En Masse

- Use enough flowers to fill the entire surface of the bowl, with blooms floating on top of the water and colored stones at the bottom.

- Fill the vase with enough flowers to submerge all or many of them. This effect is now most commonly done with rose heads.

- Fill your vase two thirds full with flower heads and then fill the rest with water for a floating and surface effect.

Floating Flower Petals

- For the ultimate budget choice that still provides a festive and pretty look, float rose petals in the bowl or vase.

- For a larger, more formal petal, use calla lily petals.

- For petals with color, consider tiger lilies, peace roses with darker pinks on the edges of the petals, or striped petals.

- Just a few flower petals are needed for best effect for a medium-size vase or bowl.

ARCHITECTURAL CENTERPIECES
Bring texture and height to traditional centerpiece design plans

In this section you'll discover a world of flowering branches and reeds that have taken over the architectural style of floral arrangements, with more brides and grooms welcoming the natural look of "green" elements to their centerpieces. Adding height and drama in the form of unique branches that reach upward to the ceiling, tent, and sky, couples with any style or formality of wedding bring a big dose of wow factor to their traditional centerpieces—or they make these architectural items the sole items in their centerpieces.

In most cases, branches are supremely inexpensive. When branches are in season, such as in spring when there is a wealth of cherry and apple blossoms, you'll pay a fraction of what the usual flower-filled centerpiece would cost. And outside of spring, you can have flowering and exotic branches

Flowering Branches

- Consider the following flowering branches for your centerpieces: cherry, peach, prune, quince, North Star cherry, forsythia, pear, apple, magnolia, and Malus or crab apple.

- Crab apple trees of this variety produce branches with pretty white flowers (snowdrift crabapple) or pretty pink flowers (Madonna crabapples).

Nonfloral Branches

- Consider the following uniquely shaped branches: curly willow, birch, manzanita, twig coral, natural coco bunch, and kiwi vines.

- Also consider the following straight-line branches: natural reed, natural river cane, and bamboo.

imported at prices that are still friendly to the wallet. Your floral designer or an in-the-know gardener friend may have to force the blooms on these branches by following a series of steps including putting the stems in hot water, cutting them repeatedly, and placing them in a cooler. But the efforts are worth it when you produce height, texture, and pretty florals for your architectural centerpieces.

ZOOM

Visit www.save-on-crafts.com to see examples of the branches and blooms mentioned in this section.

Berry Branches

- There's a tremendous variety of berry-bearing branches, particularly in fall when hypericum berries provide rich orange, burgundy, and red tones.

- In winter, holly berry branches bring a festive tone.

- Bittersweet branches come in two varieties: one with red and orange berries for summer and another with a mix of red, orange, and brown berries for fall.

- Some couples choose high-quality faux berry branches in their centerpieces to avoid toxic berries.

Other Unique Accents

- The following decorative branches are commonly used in architectural centerpieces: orange queen silk blossoms; lunaria, or silver dollar branches, also known as a money tree; royal blue prunus; and pampas grass plumes.

- Each branch of a money tree has quarter- to half-dollar-size circular white leaves, inspiring this tree's name.

- While most floral centerpiece stems extend twelve to thirty-six inches, the usual lengths range between thirty and forty inches.

191

ASIAN CENTERPIECES

Create East-Meets-West centerpieces to accent an Asian-themed wedding

For an Asian or East-meets-West-themed reception, the most common way to infuse the cultural theme is in the catering. The second most popular is in table décor. This means designing centerpieces that carry a distinctive Asian flair.

The basis of your Asian centerpieces will be in the blooms and branches you choose—which you'll learn more about below—and you can accent your centerpieces with various good-luck charms as found in Asian cultures and in the practices of Eastern feng shui. Some couples work the color red into their arrangements, and others select lucky numbers of flowers or branches, such as five or nine items in each arrangement. They may also bring gold cord into the ribbon

Symbolism

- Asian floral décor often holds great symbolism, and in the Japanese tradition particularly, the following items are highly symbolic: bamboo (prosperity), plum tree elements (constancy), pine sprigs (longevity), and gold and red cord (love and luck).

- Look to the Eastern philosophy of feng shui to mix elements of earth, water, fire, and air by using glass, water, florals, and colors that correspond to these elements.

- Avoid overdoing it, as Asian décor often focuses on one floral piece with meaning.

Containers

- Consider using traditional Asian soup bowls, found online or at Asian gourmet markets, for themed patterns, colors, and the ideal decorative base for your florals.

- Set out pretty bamboo or reed baskets in which you've set water-safe bowls for the centerpieces, and then fill the outer bowl with black stones or pebbles to cover the inside base.

- For larger tables, use shiny new woks or ikebana flower basket bases as the holders for centerpieces.

designs or cascading accents as another good-luck ritual, and some even insert gold coins into their arrangements for prosperity. You might choose to place gold coins at the bottoms of your glass vases for effect, or tie them into the floral arrangement as a whole.

The entire table setting works as an extension of your Asian-themed centerpieces, so consider choosing plates, chargers, or table platters that bear good-luck insignias or Eastern design patterns around the edges of plates, with floral colors matching the designs in the plates.

ZOOM

If your wedding will take place in the month of January, prepare traditional kadomatsu arrangements, which are placed at the entrances of homes and businesses to bring good luck, health, happiness, and prosperity for the coming year. Kadomatsu baskets contain good-luck elements, such as bamboo and flowers attached to a wooden or ceramic vase, and make wonderful centerpieces.

Florals

- One commonly used Asian-themed floral is the tall orchid plant, which you'll find in white, shades of pink, orange, yellow, and red.

- Cherry blossoms are a traditional Japanese décor motif, used both as fresh flowers and painted on centerpiece bowls and vases.

- Lucky bamboo and Oriental lilies bring an Asian theme to centerpieces.

- For floating or water-based centerpieces, use a single lotus flower.

- Bonsai trees make perfect centerpieces; check nurseries for inexpensive plants.

Bases

- Color match a silver or gold circular base to sit beneath your choice of container, vase, or bowl to extend the good luck "shine."

- Design or buy circular wood bases on which your centerpiece vases or bowls can sit.

- Use soba trays, bamboo or reed eight-inch squares, as an accent to your centerpiece bases.

- Choose or rent plates or chargers that are painted with Asian icons, cherry blossoms, or lucky koi.

CULTURAL CENTERPIECES

Bring a bit of your culture into the design of your day with stylized centerpieces

A top trend in personalizing weddings is to use the colors, themes, symbols, and foods from your heritage in your centerpieces and décor. Since you are blending your lives together, you might be in a position to creatively mix and match his and hers heritage items.

Traditional bridal flowers may be used to accent any cultural

items you plan for your pieces, and you'll use your floral choices to set the formality of your theme. For instance, a cascade of roses and gardenias gracing a Tuscan-inspired centerpiece of bread, wine bottles, and grapes turns that collection into a high-formality design. Dots of bright daisies turn that same centerpiece into a less formal, garden-appropriate centerpiece.

Tropical

Not all island heritages are alike, so don't assume that one Caribbean island's native flower would work for all backgrounds.

Some islands' national flowers include the following:

- Bahamas: yellow elder
- Bermuda: blue-eyed grass
- Cayman Islands: wild banana orchid

- Hawaii: hibiscus, bird of paradise, and rhododendron
- Tahiti: Tahitian gardenia
- Virgin Islands: yellow trumpet or yellow elder

Complete the island theme by setting your florals in a vase or container of sand and adding in beach grasses, sea glass, and seashells.

Latin

Use the following national flowers from these Latin countries:

- Argentina: ceibo
- Belize: black orchid
- Brazil: cattleya orchid
- Chile: Chilean bellflower
- Costa Rica: purple orchid
- Cuba: butterfly jasmine (mariposa)

- Mexico: dahlias, zinnia, calendula, and gladiolus
- Paraguay: jasmine-of-Paraguay
- Portugal: lavender
- Spain: red carnation, daisies, bougainvillea, poppies, and sunflowers due to their long seasons of full sun

Start by researching your own culture. You can check with family members, elders, and even cultural associations, which you can find online. These associations offer masterful articles, brochures, and in-the-know members who can advise you on the symbolism of many cultural décor items, and you may even find big discounts by ordering through the association itself. Many of these associations have Web sites where you can buy or rent party décor items, and find lists of local, national, and international resources.

While you're online, research the flowers and greenery native to the land of your ancestors, such as edelweiss from Switzerland and other lesser known varieties. You can then find some of these locally or have a floral designer import them for use in your centerpieces and other décor.

When you discover a particular flower native to your culture's homeland, continue your online research to see if there is an association dedicated to that particular flower. You'll find that the gardening community runs various clubs and groups devoted to lilies, tulips, orchids, and other blooms.

European

Use the national flowers of these European nations:

- Austria: edelweiss
- Belgium: red poppy
- Denmark: marguerite daisy
- France: iris
- Finland: lily of the valley
- Germany: knapweed (traditionally a flower that unmarried people wear)
- Greece: wildflowers
- Italy: lily
- The Netherlands: tulip
- United Kingdom: tudor rose
- Wales: daffodil

Additional Theme Ideas

- For additional nations' flowers, visit www.theflowerexpert.com.
- Combine your two heritages by using both your cultural flowers in your centerpieces if they blend together well, or just as small accents to your traditional centerpiece design.
- Add a note on guests' tables, or print it in your program, that explains the significance of the national or cultural flowers in your arrangements.
- Use cultural flowers to decorate the buffet or platters on which you serve culturally inspired dishes.

OUTDOOR GARDEN CENTERPIECES

Create garden-themed centerpieces that are perfect for outdoor locations

When you set your reception in an outdoor garden location, whether at a botanical garden, estate home, or even your own backyard where your years of gardening and landscaping investments have transformed your own land into a wonderland of blooms, you can tie your centerpieces into your garden theme.

Some sites are so well bloomed and magnificently planted that you might think you have very little to do when it comes to décor. But your one vital task is to design centerpieces that tie into both your surroundings and the colors of your bridesmaids' dresses, bouquets, and other accessories—the finishing paint strokes on a 90 percent completed floral masterpiece.

Roses and Brights

- The most common floral arrangements for garden weddings bring in the staples of bridal florals: roses, lilies, peonies, and other soft-curling petal flowers.

- Pastels are the number one choice for garden weddings unless the location is planted with vivid brights such as purples or reds.

- Bring plenty of greenery into your centerpieces to mimic the greenery of the garden around you—and thereby use fewer expensive flowers.

Spring Flowers

- The springtime months of March, April. and the beginning of May often produce warm-weather days that allow ceremonies, cocktail parties, and entire receptions to be held outdoors.

- One of the most popular springtime floral centerpieces contain tulips, either solo or mixed with other springtime blooms such as hyacinths and hydrangeas.

- Another springtime flower that works well alone in any size container is the peony, with its wide, fluffy petals and range of pastel colors.

The beauty of a garden wedding is in being surrounded by the hundreds of different florals and trees, in all their glory and stages of bloom, with Mother Nature serving as your site decorator. From sprawling green lawns to trellises filled with bright roses, to hydrangea bushes and trees in peak bloom, your site gives you the gift of life added to your scenery. Now it's time for you to set your tables.

Tour your site grounds during the season of your wedding, such as the summer prior to your June wedding, to see what will be in bloom. Visit the borders of lilacs, walk beneath the umbrella of willow branches, take photos of the colors you see all around you, and then bring several of these existing blooms into your centerpiece plans.

Matching to Trees

- The best way to coordinate your garden wedding centerpieces is to match them to the elements of the surrounding trees.

- Magnolia trees can be a lovely backdrop to magnolia-based centerpieces.

- Flowering bushes work in the same category as trees.

- Incorporate flowering branches as well as other items you see in the garden, such as rocks, strips of moss laid over the inner parts of the vases, and wheatgrass or Bermuda grass.

Other Sources of Inspiration

- Tour botanical gardens to see the various types of garden flowers and greenery that are in bloom at the time of your wedding.

- Go to flower shows held in convention centers. The largest of these shows often include displays of party tables set with floral accents and centerpieces designed with a garden theme.

- Look at floral designers' Web sites to see what they designed as centerpieces for garden weddings; print out images you love.

- Look at caterers' Web sites to see their promotional photos, often including well-set, garden-themed tables.

AUTUMN CENTERPIECES

Bring the feel of fall color and texture into your autumn wedding centerpieces

You're not limited to pumpkins and mums for your autumn wedding. While you may see such expected images on the covers of magazines at the grocery store, be uplifted by the many ways you can turn fall floral design into a colorful, texture-filled masterpiece for your tabletop design.

The autumn wedding season runs from September to November, and much depends upon where you live in the country. After all, the leaves on the trees start to transform from bright summer greens into autumn reds, oranges, and golds at many different times of the season, depending upon the weather conditions in each region. Weather Web sites offer tracking tools so that you can see where the autumn

Fall Colors

- Design a centerpiece that reflects the mix of autumn colors in the trees: rich shades of cranberry, persimmon, and gold.

- A monochromatic centerpiece, such as all cranberry, can still include lighter and darker shades of the same color family to add depth.

- Brown is a top neutral for weddings, often called "the new black," and plays a big part in autumn floral décor.

- Browns, tans, and oranges rule the autumn wedding color scheme trends.

Seasonal Fruits and Berries

- Seasonal fruits have long been added to floral centerpieces, with pomegranates adding rich red color.

- Flip the proportions of the floral and fruit centerpieces to contain 90 percent fruit and 10 percent accent flowers, such as piles of pomegranates dotted with

- white or pink flowers.

- With apple orchards and family farms in their prime season, stock up on bright red or green apples for centerpiece accents.

- Consider fall pears for a softer, pastel centerpiece accent.

foliage is in peak season, and while Mother Nature doesn't adhere to our calendars of when leaves must be bright orange to match our wedding plans, you can certainly plan your centerpieces and wedding décor to capture hues within the range of the season. And even if the tree leaves pass their peak before your wedding, you get to revive those vibrant colors with your masterful centerpieces.

On these pages, you'll design your autumn centerpieces by looking at the different layers of a fall floral look.

ZOOM

While you won't shop from there, your local craft store will show you a world of autumn silk flowers and branches in a range of fall colors, which can serve as design inspiration. If you fall in love with the look of a vibrant cranberry-colored leaf garland, snap a photo of it with your cell phone and vow to create the real version of it with fresh cranberry-colored leaves and matching fall florals.

Seasonal Produce

- Long considered a great budget-saving trick, using fall produce as centerpieces adds fun and festive seasonal accent to your décor.

- Set a large, uncarved pumpkin at the center of each table; surround it with seasonal flowers and votives.

- Fill a platter or wide vase with gourds of different sizes in unique shapes and colors.

- Autumn corn contains yellow, gold, brown, and orange, so build these colors into architectural centerpieces, along with color-coordinated flowers.

Fall Centerpiece Accents

- Consider using the wealth of fall centerpiece accents found in nature or at craft stores.

- These items include fresh colorful leaves, faux autumn leaves in high-quality silks, acorns, pinecones, stones, natural reed bundles, and fall flowering branches such as hypericum.

- Visit a home-improvement store to find bulk bags of river stones and mulched wood to use in centerpiece planters, vases, and pots. One bag should suffice for thirty or so centerpieces.

WINTER CENTERPIECES

Design festive centerpieces to suit your winter wedding theme

The winter months are attracting more wedding couples who want a different look and feel for their big day. They want a winter wonderland effect rather than a summer or spring, warm-weather fairy-tale wedding.

The fairy-tale image of winter weddings takes on a new dimension with lots of icicles and twinkle lights; silvers, blues, and reds; snowy scenery; and rich, celebratory winter holiday meals. The holidays, for many people, hold deep memories of family celebrations, cultural celebrations, or get-togethers with family and friends (perhaps for the only time each year), so this is a perfect season for a wedding!

Beyond the style and sentiment of the winter holidays, it's common knowledge that the winter season is the least expensive time of year for weddings. In the wedding industry,

Flowers in Bloom

- Don't fear that you're limited to poinsettia and evergreens, since a wide range of flowers are in bloom in winter.

- When it's winter in your location, it may be hot and steamy season elsewhere globally, so consider choosing several imported flow-

ers for use in your winter wedding theme.

- If your wedding takes place in the January, February, or March, shop the post-holiday winter sales to take advantage of 60 to 80 percent off décor, including plants, vases, and holiday-color accent décor.

Color Schemes

- White and silver are a top winter wedding color theme, combining well with glass or crystal vases or holders for an ice-and-snow look.

- Holiday reds create a vivid, festive impression, so mix reds in colors from brights to deep reds to give center-

pieces more depth than just one shade of red.

- White, silver, and blue also tie into the winter theme.

- Jewel tones of emerald, sapphire, deep purples, hunter green, and navies are top color schemes for winter.

sites and vendors often charge one third their regular fees, so couples find that they can have their dream wedding on an affordable budget. And some vendors are known to throw in lots of freebies to attract business during the slowest months of the year. With that seasonal perk in mind, you might find yourself free to plan larger, more elaborate florals, or add additional floral pieces to your décor plan.

Winter has different meanings in different parts of the country. On the West Coast, it might mean temperatures of sixty degrees. On the East Coast, it might mean snowfall and temperatures in the twenties and thirties. In the Midwest, with lake effect snowfall, you could be looking at single digit days. You'll have to take into account the frigid depth of the winter week you're looking at and how practical it will be to host a wedding in your area at all. If all signs are go for a winter wedding, then here are your planning tips for centerpieces.

Decorating with Ice

- While water is a top décor element for spring, summer, and fall weddings, ice comes into play for winter wedding centerpieces and décor.

- Order or make circular, square, or uniquely shaped ice blocks and set your floral arrangements or vases on top of them; set them in stylish bowls or vases to catch ice melt.

- A flat ice platter can be the setting on which you set floral vases and votive candles.

- Commission small ice sculptures for each table.

Nonfloral Accents

- Use plenty of evergreen in your centerpieces for color and that great scent.

- Fill tall vases with evergreens and other greenery, with candles surrounding them.

- Fill crystal bowls with clear or white ornaments, with candles and flower petals on the tables surrounding them.

- For architectural centerpieces, insert long sticks of candy cane in your centerpieces, after first locating the different colors of striped and solid candy canes in the confections markets.

COLOR-BASED CENTERPIECES

Work within the boundaries of a single color theme to create outstanding centerpieces

Your centerpiece dream might not have anything to do with the season, your culture, a theme, or a shape, but rather with the specific colors you want. Perhaps you chose a bridesmaid look of sage green dresses and pink flowers, and that's the signature color scheme for your wedding. You might even have chosen foods, cake décor, or favors that work in that color scheme.

It might seem too limiting to keep everything to a pairing of two colors, but with the right planning, you can create an ultracoordinated look throughout the settings of your wedding day events, giving the impression of a very intentional color-coordinated design. Bringing that to your centerpieces keeps you in two color families, but it still gives you a range of

Red and Pink

- Bright, vivid red centerpieces are softened by the addition of same-size-flowers in pink dotted throughout.

- Larger red flowers are balanced by smaller pink flowers or tiny pink filler blooms.

- Add height to an all-red centerpiece with sprays of pink flowers standing tall in the arrangement.

- Graduate the colors from red to lighter red to darker pink to lighter pink, capturing a range of hues that can be reflected in your bridesmaids' wardrobe as well.

Blue and Purple

- Jewel tones for winter work well as centerpieces when you blend the deepest shades of both blue and purple for rich depth.

- Consider flowers such as tulips and coneflowers for your blue tones, and tulips and lavenders for your purple tones.

- Collections of lilacs or lavenders get bright pops of color with the addition of small blue flowers for contrast.

- In pastel tones, light blue and soft purple create a romantic look for summer-time garden and backyard weddings.

hues. For instance, that sage green can be paired with greens just a touch lighter or darker to give depth and dimension to floral pieces.

Why choose only two colors? Some couples don't like the busy look of multiple colors. Some brides say they get a headache looking at bouquets or centerpieces that have a lot going on. So for them, and perhaps for you, a dual-tone color scheme is the way to go.

You might even take this two-tone-only plan so seriously that you'll eliminate any greenery or tiny white filler flowers from your centerpieces to keep the arrangement purely in the colors you're blending.

Visit the paint department of home-improvement stores, or specialty paint stores near you, to look at paint chips that show five to seven colors in the same family as your chosen hue. Your wish for yellow can range from a barely there blush yellow, to bright sunny yellow, to a deeper gold. You can use these sample strips to choose your flowers.

Yellow and Orange

- Yellow and orange hues work in spring, summer, and fall.

- The top orange flowers are roses, alstroemerias, spray roses, bronze calla lilies, orange Mokara orchids, Asiatic lilies, Gerber daisies, birds of paradise, pincushion proteas, and hyperi-

cums with orange berries.

- The top yellow flowers are roses, Asiatic lilies, alstroemerias, yellow spray roses, Gerber daisies, button stray chrysanthemums, oregonia, yellow oncidium orchids, sunflowers, lily grass, solidaster (tiny yellow filler), and yellow hypericums.

Black and White

- The black-and-white motif is created with white flowers and filler set in black vases.

- The top white flowers are roses, spray roses, calla lilies, tulips, daisies, Gerber daisies, hydrangeas, ranunculus, peonies, stocks, lilies of the valley, stars of Bethle-

hem, and baby's breath.

- Carry the black-and-white theme into your vases. For example, use pearlized white vases on black bases.

- Carry the black-and-white motif to the tabletop design, with china patterns of black-and-white design.

PEDESTAL FLOWERS

Put your tribute florals on a pedestal in memory of departed loved ones

If you're missing beloved relatives or friends as you plan your wedding day—whether they are parents, grandparents, siblings, or other valued and missed loved ones—you might want to create a tribute to them on your big day. While some couples simply write a message in their wedding programs, saying that all floral arrangements stand in memory of departed loved ones, others choose to create a special dedicated floral piece to mark the presence of those dear ones—in spirit—with a breathtaking display of florals. These arrangements often get a place of honor at the ceremony, perhaps placed next to the altar, and are also displayed at the reception, perhaps next to the table display of family wedding photos.

Tribute Pedestals

- Rent or borrow a pedestal at least three feet in height; set a large, cascading floral arrangement on top of it.

- The most popular color of tribute pedestal flowers is white, except in some Asian cultures for which white is the color of death and therefore bad luck for living guests.

- Make sure your pedestal is wide enough at the base, over one and a half feet, to give it a sturdiness to prevent its being knocked over by guests or children.

Pedestal Shapes

- Stone pedestals commonly used for garden décor come in decorative styles with curled Roman edges at the top and bottom.

- New styles of circular pedestal columns can be ringed at the bottom with fresh flowers that match those in the floral arrangements.

- An alternative to the heavy pedestal is the stand candelabra, which has a thick metal post and one to three holders for nosegay-size floral pieces. This item allows you to pay homage to multiple loved ones or branches of the family.

These tribute flowers can be large or small, always in keeping with the grand scheme of your floral décor plans, and you can also personalize the piece to carry even more symbolism and significance toward the departed loved ones you're honoring. Perhaps you'll use a loved one's favorite, signature flowers, such as the peace roses your grandmother once grew in her own garden. Or, you might choose to give your tribute arrangement deeper meaning by selecting flowers with symbolism from the language of flowers (see below). The flowers might be ones from your heritage, allowing you to honor ancestors from many generations in your lineage.

On these pages you'll explore options for designing tribute florals that would make your there-in-spirit loved ones proud and your present guests smile in remembrance of them. If relatives believe it's too soon for such a tribute, make your decision based on good timing.

The Language of Flowers

The language of flowers can be used to share sentimental messages dedicated to your departed loved ones.

Some of the most popular flowers used for their symbolism on pedestal floral arrangements are:

- Baby's breath (everlasting love)

- Anemones (unfading love)

- Pink carnations (I'll never forget you)

- White roses (eternal love)

- Tea roses (I'll always remember)

- Rosemary (remembrance)

- Yellow zinnias (daily remembrance)

Formality Levels

- At a formal wedding you'll create large, draping tribute flowers filled with the same types of formal bridal flowers as in your bouquet— roses, orchids, gardenias, callas, lilies of the valley—in a grand display.

- Use a big collection of one type of formal flower. Most

choose several dozen white calla lilies.

- Another formal tribute pedestal plan: Set out a single plant containing a dramatic, tall draping orchid plant in white or colored flowers.

VASE FLOWERS

Design sentimental, vase-presentation floral arrangements in memory of loved ones

If a pedestal seems a little much for your wedding style, or if you have no realistic sources for renting or making a pretty pedestal to join your ceremony décor, you can still include a tribute in the form of a beautiful vase arrangement.

For this larger arrangement you'll need a much larger vase, such as a six- to twelve-inch-wide glass rectangle for an elongated arrangement that owns the table on which it sits. You're not limited to clear glass, though. Depending on the style and location of your wedding, you can also choose a decorative ceramic vase, a terra-cotta, earthy vase for an informal setting, a decorative Asian vase to suit your theme wedding and heritage, or an oversize silver pedestal-foot

Vase Flowers with a Photo

- A common display for vase-set tribute flowers is to set the vase next to an eight-by-ten-inch framed photo of your departed loved one.

- The photo may be hung on a wall behind the vase to prevent guests from handling the valued photo frames.

- Create a printed note, also set in a small frame (three-by-five-inch is fine), so that guests know who the departed relative is and also perhaps why you chose the flowers you did.

Vase Flowers with Candles

- With or without a photo of the deceased, add a grouping of small white votive candles to surround the tribute florals.

- Match candles to a color in the tribute vase for coordinated effect.

- Stick with small votive

candles in protective glass holders to keep your guests safe and fire risk to a minimum.

- Choose a pillar candle or votive candles in a scent that always reminds you of the departed relatives, such as roses or clean cotton or lavender.

vase, among many other options. This vase will become a keepsake after the wedding, as a meaningful addition to your home décor.

Once you have the foundation set for your tribute arrangement, it's time to think about the florals you'll display in it. Your choices are many, of course. You may choose one type of flower such as long-stem roses in masses of several dozen. Or you might go with elaborations on your guests' table centerpieces, such as doubling or tripling the size of that exact same floral design. Or you might go architectural, with long-stemmed callas or birds of paradise to incorporate your wedding formality and location.

Make sure you match the size and sturdiness of the vase to the florals you insert in it, since a heavy collection of many flowers and branches could put a tall or narrow vase at risk of being knocked over, which would be a very upsetting occurrence at your wedding.

Smaller Vase Tribute Flowers

- If your budget does not allow for a large, arching floral arrangement, you can achieve the same effect with smaller vase florals.

- Four-inch mint julep cups hold a trio of roses or a single fully bloomed peony as an elegant floral.

- Float one gardenia, peony, or rose in a vase filled with water as a simple, yet effective tribute vase display.

- A clear or colored glass bud vase, such as the cobalt blue you've set your guest tables with, can hold a single white rose in remembrance.

Honoring Multiple Loved Ones

- Choose one unifying remembrance flower such as a rose bouquet to honor all.

- Count up the number of departed relatives and friends in your circle; and use that same number of flowers in your arrangement.

- Frame a beautifully printed list of the names in your departed tribute list.

- Choose one type of flower for relatives on your side of the family and another type for the groom's side.

- If you'll display framed photos of all your ancestors, accent each frame with its own small vase containing a single flower or floating flower; add a few votive candles to the display table.

PERSONALIZED FLOWERS

Use your departed loved one's favorite flower in special tribute floral arrangements

If you've put a lot of thought and energy into infusing your day with floral elements that are not just pretty or theme appropriate, but actually mean something to you, you may want to use the same mind-set when planning tribute flowers for your departed friends and relatives.

To get you started, as you search for the perfect blooms

that your loved ones would have named as their own favorites, here are some questions to ask yourself:

What were the flowers this person wore or carried at his or her own wedding?

What were the flowers this person often displayed in his or her home?

Single-Type Floral Arrangements

- If you're honoring one parent or loved one, create a tribute containing a group of that person's one favorite flower, such as all gardenias.

- For a smaller tribute vase, use just one flower that was the departed's favorite.

- Add color by mixing different hues of the departed's one favorite flower, such as daisies.

- Display the departed's birth-month flower in a cluster or as a single bloom in a small vase, bud vase, or floating-flower display.

Multiple-Flower Tributes

- Your departed loved one may have adored several different types of flowers, so create an arrangement containing all of them.

- Reproduce the flowers used in your departed mother's or grandmother's bridal bouquet, which you can

discover through family wedding photos.

- Use the types of flowers that were prevalent in your loved one's own love story, such as the roses she received at engagement, the calla lilies from her wedding, and the orchids her husband always gave her.

When you or your family sent this person flowers for a birthday or a get-well gift, which types of flowers did you send?

Did this person have a stated favorite flower?

Did this person collect anything that contained images of flowers, such as teapots or books?

What is this person's birth-month flower?

What are your favorite floral-inclusive memories of holidays and visits with this person, such as helping him or her tend a garden, pick daisies, or plant tulip borders?

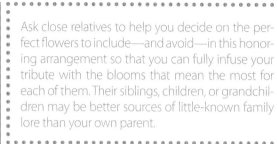

ZOOM

Ask close relatives to help you decide on the perfect flowers to include—and avoid—in this honoring arrangement so that you can fully infuse your tribute with the blooms that mean the most for each of them. Their siblings, children, or grandchildren may be better sources of little-known family lore than your own parent.

What They Grew

- It's especially meaningful for garden-loving loved ones' tribute flowers to include blooms from their own gardens, so pick and choose with love.

- Use the same types of flowers that your loved one grew in his or her prized garden, sharing the story of his or her green thumb with guests in a printed, framed narrative.

- Set out a basket containing flower seeds as a take-home tribute, inviting guests to plant, say, daisies in the departed's honor.

Other Ways to Include Tribute Flowers

- Add your mother's favorite flower to your bouquet, such as a single gardenia to match the ones she carried in her own wedding bouquet.

- Set a single flower on the table in front of each photograph of your departed loved ones.

- Set out small potted mini-roses at each departed loved one's photograph; then take these home to plant them in your own garden.

- Give each mini-potted flowering plant to that honored person's closest relatives to take home and plant in their own gardens.

TRIBUTE FLOWERS

SINGLE-STEM FLOWERS
Keep your tribute simple by displaying single-stem flowers

On these pages we'll expand on the idea of using just one flower instead of an arrangement in honor of departed loved ones. You just read about that cobalt vase with a single white rose as an accent on family photo tables, and we'll now explore the idea of longer-stem single flowers placed or presented in your loved one's honor.

A single flower can make more of an impact than an arrangement that looks like a centerpiece reproduction, especially when you select a pristine bloom in perfect budding stage, with the stem tied with a ribbon or bow. First you'll begin thinking about the ideal flower choice, and then you'll decide how you will use each flower to properly honor your much-missed loved ones.

The only functional issue you need to keep in mind is how

On-Chair Placement

- Place the tribute floral on a chair in the front row, signifying where your departed parent would have been sitting.

- If your father has departed, place his boutonniere on a chair left unoccupied in his honor.

- If it's not too difficult for a surviving parent, he or she can place the flower on the departed's chair after that parent escorts you down the aisle (as in, "The rose made the walk in your place").

Photo Placement

- Lay a single rose in front of a photo displayed on a pedestal at the ceremony.

- Lay a single flower in front of the photograph of your departed loved one on the family photo table, with this photo being the only one to get the floral tribute.

- If multiple relatives are departed, lay several flowers in front of a group family tribute photo.

- If a photo is hung on the wall, lay the flower on top of the frame.

to keep these single flowers protected, fresh, and cool until the moment during the ceremony or reception when they will be presented. A common mistake is exposing these important single blooms to the elements, carrying it on a hot day from the ceremony site to the reception site, for instance. By far, the best course of action is keeping single-stem flowers in a carry-along cooler, or asking your site manager to place your later-use flowers in a cooler of their own.

Guest Book Placement

- Set your single-stem memory flower in a vase on the same table as the guest book.

- Share the significance of this single-stem flower with guests by setting out a framed statement that this flower is in memory of departed loved ones.

- Choose a beautiful vase for this single-stem flower, either matching the color scheme of the wedding or selecting an ornate silver or simple glass vase.

- Use a family heirloom vase to hold the tribute flower to add more significance to the display.

Ceremony and Reception Presentations

- During the ceremony, present your surviving parent with a single-stem flower as a token of thanks for the marriage example he or she set for you.

- Have the officiant say a few words about all of your departed loved ones, at which point you will take a single-stem flower blessed by the officiant and insert it into your bouquet.

- At the reception, if your father is not present for a father-daughter dance, you can dance with your brother while holding a single-stem flower representing your dad.

211

WREATHS

Design and display tribute wreaths in the symbolic shape of eternity

A twist on the traditional tribute floral arrangement is the floral wreath, designed in a circle to symbolize eternity—just like those wedding bands. When you lose a loved one, he or she stays with you in memory for eternity, and on your wedding day you may find the circle to be your ideal style for a tribute floral.

On these pages you'll explore the different designs for creating tribute wreaths, as well as several plans for how to display them or use them in a remembrance ritual that becomes a part of your ceremony or a meaningful post-ceremony private moment for just your immediate family members.

Some couples create their remembrance wreaths before their big day and begin their wedding weekend with a visit

Wreath Florals

- Remembrance wreaths are most often displayed on artist easels at weddings.

- Most tribute wreaths are designed with only one type of flower, such as white roses, to symbolize a purity of meaning.

- Some small wreaths include one to two different types of flowers, while large wreaths include three to six different types of flowers.

- The most commonly used flowers for wreaths are roses, lilies, carnations, Stars of Bethlehem, lilies of the valley, and Bells of Ireland.

Wreath Colors

- Most remembrance wreaths are pure white, containing one or more different types of flowers in a white hue.

- You do not have to match this wreath to your bouquet or centerpiece colors if you will display it at the ceremony or cocktail party.

- One trend in remembrance flower color schemes is to use the color pairings of the sports team that the relative was known to love.

to their loved ones' gravesites or mausoleums, where they place the floral wreath, say a prayer, and share a moment in spirit with their departed loved ones. The couple may go alone, or they may go with their entire families as a way to acknowledge the departeds' influence on the family and get out some of their emotions over those loved ones not being physically present at the wedding itself. This visit is a way to process their feelings and also to feel freer to get outwardly emotional as they place the wreath in private. If your loss is still fresh, or if you wouldn't want your guests to focus on their own lasting grief on your wedding day, this pre-visit could be the ideal plan for you.

On these pages you'll start designing your remembrance wreath or wreaths, incorporating flowers that were their favorites, or ones with symbolic messages you love.

Wreath Display Tips

- Remembrance wreaths are most often displayed on artist easels at weddings.

- Don't stand a wreath upright on a plain table, as the weight of it will make it slide down repeatedly.

- Check a craft store for decorative plate tabletop stands, which hold onto the bottom edges of the wreath for a secure upright display.

- A wreath may be suspended from a wall hook using a pretty, color-coordinated ribbon or length of lace.

Floating Wreaths

- If your site features a swimming pool, pond, or fountain, your remembrance wreath or wreaths can be set atop the water's surface as a floating tribute.

- Test a sample wreath out before your wedding day by ordering or making an exact replica of your tribute wreath and trying it out on a water surface.

- Floating wreaths cost less to make, since florals only need to decorate one side of the round.

- Include safe, votive-set candles in floating floral pieces.

BEACH & OCEAN FLOWERS

Design tribute flower pieces and wreaths for casting out onto the waters

If your wedding will take place on the beach— either lakeside or oceanside—or on a yacht, you have the perfect opportunity to cast tribute flowers into the water as you remember your departed loved ones.

Tossing flowers into the ocean has long been a ritual in many cultures, with some bearing the interpretation that

you are offering flowers out to the souls of the departed that now exist as part of nature out in the horizon. Other cultures practice water-based floral rituals as an offering to the gods and mythic characters who are said to transport the souls of the departed to the hereafter. And still others hold fast to the concept of water being the main element of life, and by

Single Flowers

- Give each guest a single short-stemmed flower to toss into the water.

- Decide if you wish to cast all white flowers, or if you wish to create a colorful bloom tribute with multiple hues of flowers.

- If stems are too unwieldy, hand out flower heads such as daisies, which are better floaters than rose heads.

- If you prefer, keep this ritual to yourselves; be the only ones to toss your single white, red, or other-colored flowers out to sea.

Wreaths

- Fashion smaller wreaths, almost the size of bracelets, for your guests to throw into the water.

- Toss two wreaths into the water, one for relatives and friends on each side of the family.

- A third wreath might be thrown in memory of departed friends you share in your own relationship.

- Wreaths may be made purely of greenery, without roses or other blooms, as a way to save on your floral budget.

offering gifts to the sea, you support the "lives" of those who have passed to another realm. And some couples just like the practice of throwing flowers into the sea and watching them float gently on the waves. No deep spiritual meanings for them.

On these pages you'll learn how to design the floral pieces that you can use in your on-the-water remembrance rituals, again looking back at previous pages to decide on your loved one's favorite flowers, colors, and other personalized choices.

·········· RED ● LIGHT ··········

Be sure to call the tourism department of the beach site where you plan to cast your floral pieces, as many townships and municipalities have strict laws about what is considered littering. Another factor is the environmental hazard to sea life, which coastal authorities frown upon. You wouldn't want this lovely tribute moment to be interrupted by an officer in uniform handing you a ticket or stopping you from casting your wreath.

Petals

- Rather than throw stemmed flowers, wreaths, or bouquets into the water, toss handfuls of pretty petals.

- The most popular petal color is white for these watery tributes, with bright colors coming in a surprising second place.

- Again, the two of you may be the only ones to sprinkle your flower petals into the surf or over the railing of the yacht to decorate the water surrounding your floating ceremony.

Trends in Water-Based Tribute Florals

- When flowers are tossed out to sea, written messages of love may be attached to the wreath for extra meaning. Just be sure that the paper you use is biodegradable. Don't laminate it.

- You don't need ribbons or bows on floating wreaths, especially those that are sent out to sea. Again, these may not biodegrade, and they can harm sea life.

TRIBUTE FLOWERS

TOOLS & SUPPLIES
Arm yourself with the best tools for your DIY wedding floral projects

We've entered the do-it-yourself (DIY) age in weddings, with more couples wanting to craft and create many of the most special elements of their wedding day. The primary reason is, of course, that you can save a large amount of money by making your own floral pieces. Professional floral designers, after all, must make a profit over their costs of buying flowers wholesale, and then they tack on high prices for their labor and the

overhead expenses to keep their storefronts functional and their employees employed. While their mastery with florals is unquestioned, the pure issue of money reigns as a top reason why more couples seek instruction on how to make their own bouquets, centerpieces, and other floral décor items.

Another reason for DIY floral projects is that couples want to infuse their weddings with a meaningful sense of "We did

Cutting Tools

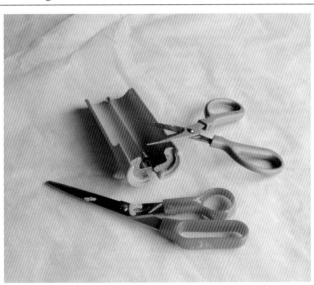

- Floral scissors come in several different sizes, and you can find these at craft stores and floral supply wholesalers.

- You'll need two separate types of cutting tools—all-purpose or floral scissors for cutting stems, and a leaf and thorn stripper that

easily slides down the stem to remove every trace of growth.

- Invest in a floral knife, such as an X-acto Knife that you'll use to cut Styrofoam and thick materials.

- Sharpening cutting tools often for best effect.

Floral Wire

- Invest in specialty floral wire, in twenty-two gauge, since you may be wrapping stems and sometimes replacing stems with this sturdier material.

- Some floral designers have mastered the art of inserting thin wire into the stems of Gerber daisies, roses and

other flowers, to give them invisible added support in bouquets and centerpieces.

- You can find floral wire in craft stores or floral supply wholesale shops, as well as at regular florist shops, in different colors to work with your design.

this!" When guests stand in awe of a gorgeous floral arch or a breathtaking bouquet, the beaming bride and groom (and/or parents, friends, and other helpers) enjoy the pride of knowing their handiwork is professional quality—not to mention that a bouquet made by a mother or grandmother means all the more to the bride carrying it down the aisle.

In this chapter, you'll learn the basics and some advanced tips on making your own floral pieces, but first we have to make sure you have all the tools you'll need to ensure your projects turn out with expert flair.

Inside the Vase

- Floral foam, also called "oasis," is the green-colored block of foam that sits inside a vase, soaked with water, to provide support and a water source.

- Wrap oasis with thick green leaves if it's placed inside a glass vase.

- Floral clay is commonly placed inside vases and containers for floral support.

- If you'll use silk flowers or only branches, use floral foam without water.

Additional Tools and Supplies

- Floral tape is a top floral tool, available in green, light green, brown, and white in various widths with which to wrap your stems. Floral tape has an elasticity to it, which makes it perfect for holding your bouquets, boutonnieres, and corsages tightly in a bunch before you wrap it with ribbon.

- Pliers are useful for bending stems that you have wired together. Choose needle-nose pliers to access areas inside your bouquets or arrangements or to provide that end-of-stem curl on a boutonniere.

- Spray adhesive allows you to affix items such as moss, stones, small florals, and greenery to floral foam.

DIY FLOWERS

HAND-TIED BOUQUETS

You can easily assemble hand-tied bouquets for yourself, your bridesmaids, moms, and flower girls

Hand-tied bouquets are the traditional style bouquets you see in magazines and carried by most brides, because they fulfill the traditional bridal look and are among the easiest to create. Floral designers say they charge less for these types of bouquets, since they are so easy to create and take so little time to complete, which is great news for your DIY plans.

Your first step in creating your own hand-tied bouquet is to decide on the types of flowers you'd like to use, and you'll match your choices to the formality and color scheme of the wedding. In previous chapters, you've explored all these styles, so you probably have a clear picture of the hues and tones you want in your bouquet.

Assembling Your Flowers

- On a large work surface, lay out a large amount of flower stems, and remove all the leaves and thorns.

- Wrap each stem with floral tape from top to bottom in a spiral design.

- Gather individual flowers in your hand, alternating bloom types, until you achieve the desired size and effect.

- Tilt the bouquet toward you and evaluate it. Where is it lacking in blooms and which blooms need to be moved or removed? Wrap floral tape around the stems.

Adding Greenery and Filler

- Select your greenery stems such as ferns, grape leaves, or other greens.

- Using a floral knife or stem stripper, remove the leaves from all but the top of the stems.

- Pick up your floral cluster and begin adding just a few stems of greenery around the outside edge, using floral tape to secure in arrangement.

- Use floral scissors to cut all the stem bottoms to a uniform level.

Next you'll determine the size of your bouquet, taking into consideration your height and body frame, knowing that a small round bouquet may be more flattering to your figure than an oversize cluster. A smaller bouquet also will not hide the details of your dress as you carry it down the aisle. There are many details to keep in mind before you get started on making your bouquet!

Next determine how many bouquets you need to make. When you know the scope of the work ahead, you might wish to invite a few friends to help you assemble all the bouquets you need for your big day.

Stock up on more flowers and supplies than you think you'll need; you're apt to make mistakes, or your first try might look flimsy or sparse. You can use extra flowers in other décor projects. The average bride's bouquet contains thirty to fifty flowers, while bridesmaids' bouquets contain twenty to thirty, so have an extra 20 percent supply of flowers on hand.

Wrapping the Handle

- Hold one end of the ribbon against the stems right under the flower heads.

- Begin wrapping the ribbon length in a flat spiral all the way down the length of the stem handle until you reach the bottom and pin or tuck the end.

- If you'd like trailing ribbon extending from the handle, use fresh lengths of ribbon, tie to the top of the ribbon wrap, and cut the length desired.

- Finish the ribbon ends with an angular or V-shaped cut for finished effect.

Accenting the Handle

- Tie the extended ribbon lengths into a large decorative bow at the top of the stems.

- Affix crystal- or pearl-headed pins of the same style and color in a straight line down the front, side, or back of your ribbon-tied stem handle.

- Pin any silver charm, saint medallion, or other meaningful accent to your bouquet handle.

- Trim the ends of the bow ribbons, again angling the ends or creating a V- or S-shape.

SINGLE-STEM & BUNCH BOUQUETS

Keep it simple with single-stem and bunch styles for your easy DIY bouquet projects

A quick, simple, and inexpensive DIY project for your or your bridesmaids' florals is to create single-stem flowers to use in place of bouquets, or fashioning a simple ribbon wrap to cluster informal bunches of flowers for a more casual wedding.

Single-stem and bunch bouquets, by virtue of being easy to create, are also great budget-friendly choices, as there is very little labor involved. Compare the description below to the ultradetailed Biedermeier bouquet, which can take hours and hundreds of tiny flowers to affix in painstaking concentric circles, using both glue and pins. With this style of bouquet, you have just three easy steps.

Your bouquet choice, as you explored earlier in this book,

Single-Stem Roses

- Choose a rose with a head that's just about to bloom for best appearance on your wedding day.

- Choose a rose with a straight stem, strip it of leaves and thorns, and cut the stem to a length of twelve to fourteen inches.

- Ribbon wrap either the entire stem or simply tie a bow. Store your ribbon-bow-only single-stem flowers in a vase of water until it's time to walk down the aisle.

Single-Stem Callas

- Gather the stems, perhaps moving the green leaves to the top of the collection, nearest the blooms.

- Wrap the stem and leaves in place with floral tape all the way down the stem.

- Wrap the entire stem with satin ribbon to give the flower enough sturdiness, or skip the tape and ribbon wrap and just tie a satin bow around the top third of the stem for decoration.

always coordinates with the formality of your wedding and the design of your wedding dress, so these styles offer the simplest class of effort for both formal and informal weddings. For instance, a single-stemmed calla lily works for a formal wedding, while a single-stemmed Gerber daisy suits an informal wedding. Your choice of ribbon must also work with the style and formality of your day, so look at lovely satin ribbon—some containing tiny pearl edges—for your more formal event, lace ribbon for your romantic Victorian garden wedding, or bright satin ribbon to match the color of

that daisy for your casual backyard wedding. In the informal realm, brides are choosing striped ribbon, plaids, and even ribbons with funky circles or color blocks to add a punch of creativity to their self-made designs.

The type of ribbon you use to create your single-stem or bunch bows and ties can also be used as coordinating décor for other parts of your wedding day, such as the fabric placeholder in your guest book or the ribbon you use in your DIY favors, and even the ribbon you use in your flower girls' hair.

Single-Stem Daisies

- Carefully remove the plastic brace set just below the flower's head for support during shipping just before it's time to walk down the aisle, but leave it on as you wrap the stem.

- Daisy stems should be wrapped tightly with

floral tape to give it extra strength, then covered with a ribbon wrap and tied with a ribbon bow.

- If you cut the stems to a six- to eight-inch length, you can wrap them with lace instead of ribbon.

Bunches

- Gather your chosen wild-flowers, tulips, peonies, daisies, or other flowers and begin assembling your chosen arrangement of blooms.

- Begin with larger flowers in the center; then build in circles around the outside.

- Wrap the entire collection of stems with floral tape, cut across the bottom for a uniform cut level, and then wrap the entire stem collection with ribbon or lace in spiral fashion, going once down and then once up to tie in a bow at the top.

221

CENTERPIECE ARRANGEMENTS

Perfect the art of DIY floral centerpiece arrangements in four easy steps

Making your own centerpieces is one of the easiest jobs possible for a wedding, since you're assessing how it looks as you go along. Need more pink over there? Just stick in a rose. There is a method that will guide you, and you'll learn it on these pages.

You'll first need to collect the flowers you want to include

in your centerpieces. Depending on the size of your centerpieces, prepare yourself with more than enough flowers to give you plenty of choice in flower-head size, type, and color. Small centerpieces typically contain twenty flowers, medium contain thirty to forty flowers, and large contain forty to sixty flowers. Each one also needs filler and greenery to fill in the

Prepare the Flowers

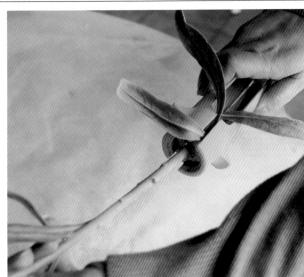

- Different flowers need different preparation depending on their fragility.

- "Force" flowers that have not yet bloomed by setting them stem-side down in a bucket of warm water for a few minutes and then in cooler water.

- Use floral scissors or strippers to remove leaves and thorns.

- Using a wide container, set the stems in the arrangement you're considering, then choose each stem from that collection.

Prepare the Vase

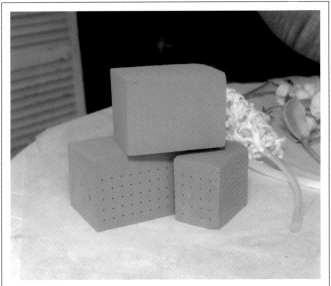

- Make sure the vase is clean before you begin.

- To help you balance the initial stems you set in, run four pieces of Scotch tape in a wide grid pattern across the opening of the vase so that you can set your first few flowers in each "square."

- Place your vase on top of a lazy Susan so that you can easily spin it for easier access to all sides of the container.

- If you're using a wide vase or planter, set two foam blocks inside the container to hold stems in place.

spaces between the blooms until it looks right to you. So don't skimp on your floral order, or you'll end up with wimpy-looking centerpieces that give away your DIY secret. You can use any extra flowers in your other décor.

Set yourself up at a big table so that you have plenty of room to spread out your piles of flowers by type. You can lay them flat or set them in individual vases or buckets, which is actually a better idea for protecting delicate flower heads from getting crushed by the weight of other flowers or nicked by thorns that haven't yet been removed.

Centerpieces are the most popular group craft, with plenty of volunteers willing to help. So make a light lunch, pour some iced tea, and make it a flower-arranging party. Be sure to give yourself plenty of time to assemble your centerpieces, which need to be done on the day of the wedding. You need two hours for ten centerpieces, and three hours if you're making more than fifteen.

Assembling the Centerpiece

- Place your larger, dramatic flowers in the center, inserting stems into the foam inside the vase. Start placing additional stems around those flowers, removing the placement tape as you go.

- Alternate colors so that you have all three hues evenly spaced, for instance, and add ferns and greenery as you go to give the piece dimension.

- Step back, see if the round of flowers is symmetrical, and then pull out and trim any stems that stand out badly.

Finishing Touches

- Add taller flowering branches or architectural pieces at this point.

- Add filler flowers such as lilies of the valley or baby's breath throughout the arrangement, making sure you're not adding too much or too little.

- Add a few inches of water so that the arrangement has plenty to drink throughout the day.

- Fill the planter with decorative stones to cover the interior items, and lay pieces of moss on top of the stones.

CENTERPIECE FLOATING FLOWERS

Design the perfect floating-flower centerpieces in one short craft session

These centerpieces are best assembled on-site, since it's way too hard to transport water-filled containers without spillage. So gain access to your cocktail party or reception rooms an hour before the wedding and set out your vases on each table.

Keep in mind that tables of ten or more usually require two to three smaller vases of floating flowers, so factor your vase

purchase based on the number of guests that will be seated at each round, oval, or rectangular table. Again, load up on extra vases in case you have any breakage when you transport your vases to the reception site, or as you assemble the floating florals. A good 10 percent more vases than your original count is usually a fine overstock, and you can give extra

Preparing Your Vases

- Be sure your vases are ultraclean, with a fresh pass through a dishwasher if vases are dishwasher safe, to avoid watermarks.

- Don't be tempted to use vases right out of the box when you buy them in bulk; vases accumulate

the dust of any wrapping paper or materials used in packaging.

- Remove price tags from the bottoms and sides of the vases before you fill them.

Preparing the Flowers

- Cut flower heads at the tops of the stems so that little to no stem shows under the flower.

- Cut flower heads as you go so you don't create a table filled with flower heads crushing each other.

- Have a volunteer follow you

around with a trash bag so you can discard cut stems and leaves.

- When you're placing flower heads onto the water surface, keep other handfuls of flowers and greenery away from the tablecloth to avoid water splashes and greenery smears.

224

vases to volunteers or your officiant as gifts or keep them for décor in your own home.

As you stock up on supplies, go to the craft store to buy multiple bags of colored or clear stones to place in the bottoms of each of your vases. An empty vase looks fine enough, but it's always a great idea to take that extra step and place a handful (one cup) of decorative stones in the bottom of each vase. Some whimsical couples like to play up a beach theme by adding tiny items such as treasure chests and mermaids found in the pet supply store where aquarium supplies are sold. Others create ceramic or glass placards bearing the table number written in waterproof ink and submerge them in the bowl as functional décor.

Don't overdo it with décor items meant for the bottoms of these vases. Since floating flowers tend to bloom more while in water, they often spread out dramatically and can obscure any trinkets you've stashed in the bottom of the vase.

Assembling the Centerpieces

- With your vases filled with the desired level of water, go table by table to place a single flower in each, laying it flat so that it floats.

- If flower heads start to sink, try laying one of their own leaves from your cut stems underneath for buoyancy.

- Add loose flower petals in quarter-cup amounts to each side of the flower, or add the petals before the main bloom so that it has something to rest on.

Accenting the Centerpieces

- Waterproof LED lights can be placed inside these vases to give your centerpieces an extra glow.

- Floating candles are best used in place of floating florals, rather than with them, since blooms with drying leaves can catch on fire.

- Place color-coordinated votives all around your floating centerpiece vases.

- Place flower petals (matching the flower in the vase) on the tablecloths surrounding the centerpieces to give the impression that the colors extend outward for drama.

DÉCOR FLOWERS
Dream up additional décor projects for your DIY wedding projects

Your DIY list might also include projects you believe will be ultrasimple to do, such as placing flowers on your wedding cake. But be aware that some flowers are toxic when they come in contact with food. A smart DIY plan is necessary.

Speaking of a smart DIY plan, you can use the extra flowers you ordered for your centerpieces, bouquets, and other décor for the accent pieces shown below, costing nothing

and saving you from the disappointment of waste. Bruised outer petals can be pulled off of roses and ranunculus, and voilá, you have a beautiful single rose to use elsewhere. If you've truly ordered too many flowers, leaving you with fifty extra roses or tulips, cut the stems to a four-inch length and slip each clean, perfect flower into guests' napkin rings for an extra dash of style.

Cake Flowers

- Acquire organic flowers, even though they may cost more, since they have not been treated with pesticides.

- Choose flower heads for their beauty and color; rinse them well with water, laying them on paper towels to dry naturally for an hour.

- Cut stems to one- to two-inch lengths and insert each flower into the cake.

- If you want toxic blooms on your cake, have a baker make them from sugar paste.

Seat Flowers

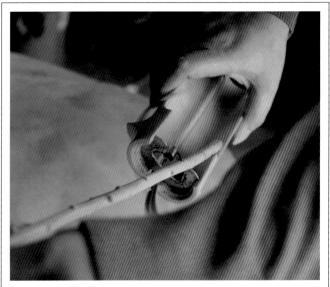

- Choose flawless single flowers for placement on guests' ceremony seats.

- Take each stem and strip it of thorns using floral scissors or a stem stripper.

- It's best to remove leaves from each stem.

- Place dry single flowers on each seat at a uniform angle.

- Do not use stargazer lilies or other flowers that have visible yellow or orange pollen on the blooms, since these pollen spores can stain the seats and thus guests' clothing.

226

Have extra ivy? Keep it away from food, since it's toxic, but use it to spruce up or make garlands or lay lengths on windowsills, mantels, or on a platter on an end table. These DIY touches make it look like you hired a celebrity wedding coordinator to add floral embellishments all around your site.

That's the beauty of a good DIY floral project: No one can tell you made it yourself!

Garlands

- On a large, flat surface, lay lengths of evergreen, olive branches, ivy, or other fresh greenery on top of each other, covering each branch two thirds of the way as you go, forming a long line of overlapping lengths.

- Use green floral wire or tape to wrap the branches together tightly.

- Use floral tape to attach single floral blooms, pinecones, or other accents where desired.

- If wire is used, cover it with a floral tape wrap.

Wreaths

- Collect a large amount of greenery and blooms for each wreath.

- Use a Styrofoam wreath or lightweight wire wreath round as the basis for your wreaths.

- Using floral wire, spiral wrap lengths of greenery to form the initial round, and twist the ends of the wire back into the arrangement.

- Pierce each flower through the head with wire to make a U shape; then use the two ends of wire to affix each flower to the wreath.

DIY FLOWERS

227

FLOWERS BY SEASON

Choose flowers that are in season to give you the most plentiful, inexpensive varieties

You've read a lot about using in-season flowers for your bouquets, centerpieces, and other décor, since their availability means fresher delivery of locally cut blooms, a wider variety of color variegations, and much lower prices than if the same types of flowers needed to be shipped in from Ecuador, Asia, or another far-off land. While any flower can be found at any time of year, imported from some corner of the globe, it's always best to focus on in-season flowers to ensure your odds of getting the best and most beautiful selection and avoiding any global weather fiascos that could potentially ruin a crop and prevent your shipment (or make it triple the price!).

In this chapter you'll receive a starter list of the types of flowers that are considered in season at certain times of the year. Keep in mind that this list is considered a national average. The weather may be milder in November where you live, so you might have access to additional summer flowers in addition to your locally grown florals and greenery.

Use this list as a guide, research further, ask your floral designer for additional ideas on what the always-evolving floral industry has discovered in the various reaches of the global community, and use the floral associations listed in this chapter to find out more about each type of flower. You might find that lilies come in different colors than you expected or that lilacs would be your perfect filler flowers.

As you explore these lists, you may be inspired by mention of a flower you never thought to bring into your décor plans, and your groom too may discover a flower type that would be perfect for his own boutonniere or as a gift for honored women on his side of the family.

Spring Wedding Flowers

- Anemone
- Bells of Ireland
- Casa Blanca lily
- Crocus
- Daffodil
- Delphinium
- Hyacinth
- Lilac
- Narcissus
- Peony
- Ranunculus
- Stargazer Lily
- Sweet pea
- Tulip

Summer Wedding Flowers

- Alstroemeria
- Bells of Ireland
- Chrysanthemum
- English lavender
- Forget-me-not
- Freesia
- Gerber daisy
- Hydrangea
- Iris
- Larkspur
- Lily
- Lisianthus
- Queen Anne's lace
- Snapdragon
- Stephanotis
- Stock
- Sunflower
- Tuberose
- Yarrow
- Zinnia

Fall Wedding Flowers

- Allium
- Aster
- Alstroemeria
- Amaranthus
- Anemone
- Chrysanthemum
- Cosmos
- Dahlia
- Freesia
- Gerber daisy
- Gladiolus
- Hypericum berry
- Iris
- Juniper
- Kalanchoe
- Lily
- Marigold
- Orchid
- Rose
- Salvia
- Star of Bethlehem
- Sunflower
- Yarrow
- Zinnia

Winter Wedding Flowers

- Acacia
- Amaryllis
- Anemone
- Asiatic lilies
- Bells of Ireland
- Camellia
- Carnation
- Casa Blanca lily
- Chrysanthemum

- Cosmos
- Cyclamen
- Daffodil
- Evergreen
- Forget-me-not
- Gerber daisy
- Helleborus
- Holly
- Jasmine
- Narcissus
- Orchid
- Pansy
- Phlox
- Poinsettia
- Ranunculus
- Stargazer lily
- Star of Bethlehem
- Sweet pea
- Tulip

Wedding Flowers Available Year-Round

- Baby's breath
- Bachelor's button
- Calla lily
- Carnations
- Delphinium
- Eucalyptus
- Gardenia
- Gladiolus
- Heather
- Lily of the valley
- Orchid
- Rose
- Scabiosa

BIRTH-MONTH FLOWERS

Personalize your flower choices according to your birth month's symbolic blooms

For many years the floral industry has promoted a symbolic tradition of each month having a special flower known as a birth-month flower. Brides and grooms have long incorporated their birth-month flowers into their wedding designs as a way to bring a personal touch and deeper significance into their floral pieces, and they also use birth-month flowers to honor their parents, departed relatives, their own children, and, yes, even their pets.

Another popular way that couples use the birth-month flower is to embrace the birth month of their wedding, which marks the start of their new life together and gives their big day an actual birthday. At the wedding and on anniversaries, they'll incorporate the birth-month blooms of their union.

Taking this personalization a step further, they'll share the story of their wedding birth month—or the inclusion of their own or parents' birth-month flowers—in their wedding day floral pieces and tribute arrangements so that guests can appreciate the special, thoughtful steps that went into designing each element of the day.

Your birth-month flowers can be combined in your bouquet, including both his and hers blooms, and you can also bring in the birth-month flowers of your children to give your bouquet a truly family-oriented symbolism—provided that each flower complements the collection as a whole. Tulips and holly would be a strange combination, for instance. We've provided two flowers for each month, giving you more of a selection for combinations and the blending of special family blooms.

Want to add even more meaning? Look at your birth-month gemstones, such as emerald for May, and bring those colors into your bouquet and décor. This just makes the symbolism even deeper, giving you a fresh combination of the two major birth-month specialties with plenty of color to work with.

If your birth-month flowers don't work with your desired bouquet or centerpiece plans, such as daisies not fitting in with your formal wedding sea of roses and calla lilies, then use those daisies as a theme at another of your pre- or postwedding events.

Spring Birthdays

- March: daffodil or jonquil
- April: daisy or sweet pea
- May: lily of the valley or hawthorn

Mix these with non–birth-month spring flowers such as peonies and hydrangeas for extra floral effect and texture.

Summer Birthdays

- June: rose or honeysuckle
- July: larkspur or water lily
- August: gladiolas or poppy

Fall Birthdays

- September: aster or morning glory
- October: calendula or cosmos
- November: chrysanthemum

The key is in the autumn color base; use plenty of reds, oranges, golds, and browns.

Winter Birthdays

- December: narcissus or holly
- January: carnation or snowdrop
- February: violet or primrose violet

MAGAZINES & WEB SITES

Stock up on the newest and best wedding flower books and Web site resources

Knowledge is power, and there's no better way to collect knowledge on different types and formalities of flowers and greenery than doing your homework through books, magazines, and Web sites. Here we've collected some of the top print resources for you to review as you begin your floral design season with the best education possible. You want to be familiar with a wide range of different types of flowers and plants and see a wide world of visuals to inspire you.

Within these suggestions you'll find titles from some of the wedding industry's top designers who create wedding florals for celebrities, and you just might decide to copy the bouquet of your favorite star. You may find the perfect image of your dream centerpiece, and with it, all you'll have to do is gather the same types of flowers and floral tools to complete an identical design for one fiftieth of the cost.

These floral experts have spent years taking classes, working weddings, and fulfilling the wishes of thousands of brides and grooms before you. So, take advantage of their experiences and you just may become a new creative genius, figuring out ways to improve upon that celebrity coordinator's or big-name floral designer's masterpiece of cake florals.

Find these books and resources online and look at the bookshelves in gift shops and card stores, where they always seem to have the most visual wedding books in stock. Even your floral designer likely has these books for sale and is probably using them daily!

Best Floral Magazines

- *Better Homes and Gardens* (special issues): www.bhg.com
- *BloominNews:* www.bloominnews.com
- *Fleur Creatif:* www.fleurcreatif.com
- *Floral Design:* www.floraldesignmagazine.com
- *The Flower Arranger:* www.theflowerarrangermagazine.co.uk
- *Flower Essence:* www.flowersociety.org
- *Flower magazine:* www.flowermag.com
- *Fusion Flowers:* www.fusionflowers.com
- *Horticultural magazine:* www.hortmag.com
- *Master Florist:* www.masterflorist.com

Best Floral Web Sites

- *Better Homes and Gardens:* www.bhg.com
- Bridal Guide: www.bridalguide.com
- *Brides:* www.brides.com
- The Flower Expert: www.theflowerexpert.com
- HGTV: www.hgtv.com
- Home Depot Garden Club: www.homedepotgardenclub.com
- The Knot: www.theknot.com
- Martha Stewart: www.marthastewart.com
- *Modern Bride:* www.modernbride.com

Best Craft and DIY Web Sites

- About.com: www.about.com
- All Crafts: www.allcrafts.net
- Craft and Hobby Association: www.hobby.org
- DIY Life: www.diylife.com
- DIY Network: www.diynetwork.com
- Downtown Crafts: www.downtowncrafts.com
- eHow: www.ehow.com
- Love to Know: www.lovetoknow.com
- *Martha Stewart Weddings:* www.marthastewart.com
- Pash Weddings: www.pashweddings.com
- Pioneer Thinking: www.pioneerthinking.com
- Save on Crafts: www.save-on-crafts.com

FLORAL ASSOCIATIONS

Check with the country's top floral associations for new flower ideas

Floral associations are a premier source of information for you as you build your floral design scheme, consider the right types of greenery to include in your designs, match your plans to your locations, choose local or organic flowers, find qualified floral designers, and look for resources to allow you to create any of your own floral projects. These organizations offer a wealth of the latest information, since they make it their business to know exactly what's going on in the floral industry. For instance, you might learn here that the rose crop in Ecuador took a bit of a hit from an insect infestation, so your best source of roses might be from another southern country.

National associations provide valuable information on the floral business as a whole, while links to your state or regional floral associations deliver a gold mine of listings of several important resources. One is a collection of all their member floral designers who have passed stringent tests and met high levels of expectations, professionalism, and additional training. Another benefit of checking out local floral associations is that they will list the area botanical gardens and nurseries where you can go to get free or nearly free access to in-season plantings and displays where you can learn the difference between Shasta and Gerber daisies.

Last but not least are the listings of seasonal sales, where you may be able to buy all the roses you need for your wedding décor plans, at half the price you'd find anywhere else.

ZOOM

Find your local floral association by visiting www .localflowershop.com/florists/florist-associations .cfm. Most have their own Web sites where you can find out about nearby suppliers, shows, and events where you can see floral designers' work and read articles about the florals you have in mind for the location of your wedding.

Gardening Associations

- American Horticultural Society: www.ahs.org

- Garden Club: www.gardenclub.net

- Garden Club of America: www.gcamerica.org

- Gardeners of America: www.tgoa-mgca.org

- Gardeners.com: www.gardeners.com

- Garden Conservancy: www.gardenconservancy.org

- National Gardening Association (to find flowers by color and season) www.garden.org/plantfinder/

- National Garden Clubs: www.gardenclub.org

- Sierra Club: www.sierraclub.org

Flower Associations

- African Violet Society of America: www.avsa.org

- American Bamboo Society: www.americanbamboo.org

- American Camellia Society: www.camellias-acs.com

- American Fern Society: www.amerfernsoc.org

- American Floral Industry Association: www.afia.net

- American Rhododendron Society: www.rhododendron.org

- American Rose Society: www.ars.org

- Association of Specialty Cut Flower Growers: http://www.ascfg.org/

- Azalea Society: www.azaleas.org

- Garden Conservancy: www.gardenconservancy.org

- Herb Society of America: www.herbsoc.org

- International Floral Distributors: www.ifd-inc.org

- New England Wild Flower Society: www.newfs.org

- U.S. National Arboretum (shows what's blooming in which hardiness zones across the country): www.usna.usda.gov

These are just a few of the many flower associations out there, so use the links on the national association pages to help you find clubs and groups dedicated to the types of flowers you have in mind.

Professional Florist Associations

- Independent Florist's Association: www.myifa.org

- Master Florists Association: www.masterfloristsassn.org

- Retail Florist Association: www.etfa.org

- Society of American Florists: www.safnow.org

- Wholesale Florist and Florist Supplier Association: www.wffsa.org

- World Flower Council: www.worldflowercouncil.org

Other Associations Important to the Floral Industry

- The Food and Drug Administration has terrific information on the safety of imported florals and greenery, plus details on conflict regions that could influence your importing decisions: www.fda.gov.
- Check out www.organicgardening.com for links and articles on "green" gardening.
- Check out www.hgtv.com for articles on backyard gardening tips that could translate into the same types of pairings that would work perfectly for your centerpieces and site décor.

ADDITIONAL INSPIRATION

Find additional sources of inspiration for your own wedding floral styles and projects

- Wedding Flower Shop: www.weddingflowershop.com/blog/

- Wedding Paper Divas blog: www.blog.weddingpaperdivas.com

Other Circles of the Wedding Industry

Check out the Web sites of wedding industry experts such as wedding coordinators, florists, bakers, caterers and others at:

- The Association of Bridal Consultants: www.bridalassn.com

- The International Special Event Industry: www.ises.com

- *Special Events* magazine: www.specialevents.com

- Elegant Bridal Productions: www.elegantbridal.com

- Great Bridal Expo: www.greatbridalexpo.com

Visit bridal showcases found at nearly every hotel on nearly every weekend of the year:

- 4PM Events: www.4pmevents.com

Entrepreneurs

Look at the many e-businesses and entrepreneurial enterprises of crafters and businesspeople listed at the following sites:

- eBay: www.ebay.com

- Etsy: www.etsy.com

- Ladies Who Launch: www.ladieswholaunch.com

- LinkedIn: www.linkedin.com

Wedding Floral Blogs

- Bizarre Wedding Flowers blog: www.bizarreweddingflowers.blogspot.com/2008/01/green-wild-collar.html

- BloomeryWeddings.com: www.bloomeryweddings.com/blog/

- BridesClub.com blog: www.bridesclub.typepad.com

- Fall Wedding Flowers blog: www.fallweddingflowersblog.com

- Find Cheap Flowers blog: www.findcheapflowers.com

- Wedding Flowers blog: www.weddingflowersblog.blogspot.com

Floral Design Courses

- You'll find terrific floral design courses offered at your local craft shop, so ask for their upcoming class schedules and when they'll be doing wedding crafts.

- Community education centers often provide spring and fall classes on different floral design projects.

- Check with your local florist, who may offer nighttime courses as a way to make a little bit of extra money.

- Check with your local floral school or a community college for floral design courses.

- Some garden centers and family farms invite local crafters to give floral design classes as a way to promote their businesses. Check your community events calendars, arboretum course schedules, and the events handouts at nearby nurseries and farms.

PROJECT MATERIALS

Collect the most useful DIY materials for all your wedding flower projects

If you'll create part or all of your many wedding floral creations, you're going to need fantastic supplies—and you're probably going to want to find them on the inexpensive side. So we've collected some of our favorite resources for you here, hoping to lead you to the ideal source for your floral bouquet holders, cones, frogs, vases, bowls, ribbons, tulle, stick-ins, charms, and anything else you could possibly want as you design and make anything from your bouquet to your chuppah décor, centerpieces, and flower girls' baskets, and more.

There are two schools of people who craft their own wedding floral pieces: those who love the process because they've found great materials, and those who trudge through each step becau[se] they're dealing with inferior materials that make the job very d[if]ficult. We'd like you to be in the first school, since we know th[at] having the best tools and materials puts you on par with profe[s]sional floral designers and the pieces they create. Yours can co[me] out just as well!

Take your time while searching for the ideal materials, since yo[u] never want to rush into a purchase just to get it done. And alwa[ys] be a smart consumer by making sure that sites are secure, have [a] street mailing address, have a good return policy, and offer detail[ed] information on their products. And here's a money-saving tip: if yo[u] know any other brides-to-be who are also searching for tulle, flo[ral] supplies, or crystals to add to their bouquets or other items, see [if] you can combine your orders to split the shipping costs, or save ev[en] more money by ordering an agreed-upon style of product in bu[lk] that you can split.

Let friends and relatives know that you're searching for great D[IY] materials. Don't be embarrassed to let them know you're maki[ng] some of your own items. DIY weddings are all the rage right no[w] and your trusted crafter friends may be able to point you to their ow[n] favorite sites, stores, and suppliers.

Floral Supplies

- BJ's Wholesale: www.bjswholesale.com
- Costco: www.costco.com
- Floral Arranger: www.floralarranger.com
- Floral Craft Resource: www.floralcraftresource.com
- Flower and Craft: www.flowerandcraft.com
- Martha Stewart: www.marthastewart.com
- M&M (supplies Spanish moss): www.mossdistributors.com
- Sam's Club: www.samsclub.com
- Wedding Flowers and More: www.weddingflowersandmore.com

Craft Supplies

- All Crafts: www.allcrafts.net
- Art Cove: www.artcove.com
- BJ Craft Supplies: www.bjcraftsupplies.com
- Craft Site Directory: www.craftsitedirectory.com
- Factory Direct Crafts: www.factorydirectcrafts.com
- Floral Trims: www.floraltrims.com
- GelStuff: www.gelstuff.com
- JKM Ribbon: www.jkmribbon.com
- Michaels Crafts: www.michaels.com
- Save-on-Crafts: www.save-on-crafts.com

- Target: www.target.com
- WalMart: www.walmart.com

Vases, Bowls, and Centerpieces

- Bride's: www.brides.com
- Floral Supplies and More: www.floralsuppliesandmore.com
- The Knot: www.theknot.com
- Martha Stewart: www.marthastewart.com
- Michaels Crafts: www.michaels.com
- Save on Crafts: www.save-on-crafts.com
- Target: www.target.com

Fabric and Tulle

Check the aforementioned craft sites for fabric bolts and samples.

Additional sources include:

- Bridal Fabric: www.bridalfabric.com
- eBay: www.ebay.com
- eHow: www.ehow.com
- Fabric Warehouse: www.fabricwarehouse.com
- House Fabric: www.housefabric.com
- Joann: www.joann.com
- Michaels Crafts: www.michaels.com
- Textile Fabric Store: www.textilefabricstore.com

DELIVERY CHART

Use this chart to organize your floral deliveries by location and time, with special instructions noted

Site #1:

Address: _____
Items to Be Delivered: _____
Delivery Time: _____
Delivery Details: _____
Contact Phone #: _____

Site #2:

Address: _____
Items to Be Delivered: _____
Delivery Time: _____
Delivery Details: _____
Contact Phone #: _____

Site #3:

Address: _____
Items to Be Delivered: _____
Delivery Time: _____
Delivery Details: _____
Contact Phone #: _____

Site #4:

Address: _____
Items to Be Delivered: _____
Delivery Time: _____
Delivery Details: _____
Contact Phone #: _____

Notes

Flowers We Want to Use:

_____
_____
_____
_____
_____

Flowers We Don't Want to Use:

_____
_____
_____
_____

Others' Favorite Flowers:
[ ] Bride's Mother: _____
[ ] Groom's Mother: _____
[ ] Bride's Stepmother: _____
[ ] Groom's Stepmother: _____
[ ] Bride's Grandmother: _____
[ ] Bride's Grandmother: _____
[ ] Groom's Grandmother: _____
[ ] Groom's Grandmother: _____
[ ] Bride's Godmother: _____
[ ] Groom's Godmother: _____
[ ] Child: _____
[ ] Child: _____
[ ] Other: _____
[ ] Other: _____
[ ] Other: _____
[ ] Other: _____

PHOTO CREDITS

INDEX

INDEX